EAT WELL LIVE WELL

with The Sensitive Foodie

EAT WELL LIVE WELL

with The Sensitive Foodie

An **accessible, practical guide** to eating a **whole-food plant-based diet** with over **100 delicious recipes**

KAREN LEE

Edited and produced by:
Deborah Taylor, Book-Launch Your Business,
www.booklaunchyourbusiness.com

Designed by:
Joanne Lloyd, www.joannelloyd.net

Page layout by:
Catherine Williams, www.chapter-one-book-production.co.uk

Cover and diagrams by:
Andy Prior, www.andypriordesign.co.uk

ISBN: 978-1-9160261-0-0

Disclaimer

This publication contains the opinions and ideas of the author and is designed to provide useful information in regard to the subject matter covered. It should not be regarded as a substitute for competent, relevant advice from a registered health professional. If you have or suspect a health problem, it is recommended you consult with a health professional before starting any programme. The author and publisher disclaim any liability, loss or risk, personal or otherwise, that may occur directly or indirectly from the use of this book.

DEDICATION

Dedicated to my wonderful family with my love,
eternal gratitude – and cake!

FOREWORD

Having practised as a doctor for 38 years, I'm seeing patients get sicker than ever before and at younger ages than ever before. Despite all the progress in medicine, we are not healthier. We all know that fruits and vegetables are healthy. Yet our supermarkets have only one isle of the healthy stuff. How can there be such a big disconnect? Is the food industry, the pharmaceutical industry, and the medical industry really hand in glove or is it just a coincidence?

It doesn't really matter. What matters is that we take charge of our health and stop outsourcing it to someone else. And that's a pretty simple thing to do. Children easily connect the dots and Karen's young daughter was her initial inspiration. In this beautiful book, Karen describes her journey to a healthier lifestyle in a way that anyone can relate to. Most of us have grown up with the myth that we are omnivores, we believe that eating animals or their products is normal, natural and necessary. Our conditioning allows us to treat fellow earthlings as commodities rather than sensitive beings much like ourselves.

Growth requires change, and disease reversal requires a shift in consciousness. By following Karen's passionate journey and personal stories through the insightful chapters, anyone can connect the dots to a higher consciousness and a healthier lifestyle.

What I particularly love in Karen's work is the large number of recipes that are tried and tested. If we can marry health with taste, what more do we need? Karen has also loaded the book with tips to help you with your health journey, recognising that it's not easy to change habits but once the habits are changed, they become a way of life. And as she takes you through her narrative, she stays real without becoming dogmatic.

It's a matter of personal pride that I was a part of Karen's journey. I believe that the only person that we can change is ourselves, and each of us can be a catalyst in someone else's growth. Having had my own personal journey to a healthier lifestyle, I know that I would never go back. I am healthier, happier and more connected than ever before.

I wish you, the reader, the very same. May *Eat Well, Live Well with the Sensitive Foodie* be a turning point in your life, a catalyst for you to connect the dots. I wish you perfect health and abundant happiness and I know this is possible through change. We are all connected and our personal health is interconnected to the health and happiness of all other beings on the planet. We are all in this together.

Dr Nandita Shah
Founder and Director of SHARAN-India

CONTENTS

PART TWO: THE RECIPES

PROLOGUE

I love food and everything about it – the flavour, the textures, the eye-catching visuals; the pleasurable satisfaction of just eating. I love meals with family and friends, the excitement of going out and trying new food, discovering new flavours or just the soothing comfort of a home-cooked meal packed with childhood memories.

I've always been amazed at people who are not interested in what's on their plate or get little enjoyment from it. People who pay little thought to what, when or even why they're going to eat.

In contrast, much of my day is spent focused on food. I wouldn't describe it as an obsession, but it's become an essential and enjoyable part of my life. Creating, planning and then eating gives me great pleasure – at least it does now that I understand the full impact of the food I eat on my body. It's been a long journey of discovering how 'good' can be so bad and, fortunately, how to make it good again – both literally and metaphorically!

Discovering that certain foods were making me ill and deciding to make changes is definitely on the list of 'Best decisions I've ever made'. Being a bit of a foodie, I decided that if I was going to have to do without my favourite foods, I would find out how to create equally delicious 'Karen friendly' alternatives. Because as far as I'm concerned, eating 'free-from' food should never mean eating food free from flavour. After all, who wants to eat dull rabbit food? Not even rabbits in my experience!

How Did I Get Here?

Hindsight, as they say, is a wonderful thing. Looking back, it's easy to identify a clear thread that runs throughout my life. Well, it's obvious, when you know what to look for. But back then, it wasn't clear at all.

My mum tells me I was an easy baby – apart from the vomiting. At the age of six months, I couldn't keep my milk or food down and I'd become a skilled vomiter. I lost weight and lacked energy. At the time, the doctor was perplexed; nowadays they would call it 'failure to thrive'.

Mum was worried and frustrated, so the doctor prescribed 'some drops' which eventually did the trick. Recently, I asked her if they'd ever considered that it might be milk I was reacting to. No. It was the end of the sixties and milk intolerances were pretty much unknown in those days.

When I look back on my childhood, I have many marvellous memories. But in between all the fun and frolics runs a persistent pattern of nausea, vomiting and headaches – all soothed by my patient mum with dispersible aspirin and milk of magnesia. These two simple medicines became a staple in my life. In fact, I can still picture the blue milk of magnesia bottle sitting on the kitchen worktop, the lid and edge stained white from repeated use. I still feel queasy just thinking about it.

Recognising Normal is Abnormal

When something has always been a certain way, it's hard to recognise what is normal and what is not. My cycle of headaches and vomiting were just part of my life. The headaches would increase in intensity over a period of time, peaking with a migraine, completed with a good puke. Then things would settle down for a while until the cycle started again. Over-excitement, stress or a change in my routine could send me rushing to the toilet to vomit too, so I was a bit of nightmare when it came to holidays.

Because I'd always been that way, it just became normal to me. Even though I'd worked as a nurse and looked after many different people, it never occurred to me that this might be abnormal – until I had my own children. I noticed that they hardly ever threw up or had headaches, and that was when I realised my 'normal' was 'abnormal'.

Growing up in the seventies and eighties was an exciting time in the realm of convenience meals and fast food. These new and exciting products were the face of a burgeoning convenience food industry, designed to save time and effort in the kitchen. Full of refined sugars and oils, added flavours and colourings but low in essential nutrients, these new products appealed to the body's love of sugar and fat. They hit the pleasure spots, which assured repeat purchases. As kids we loved it, and pestered Mum to buy it. Looking back, it was a recipe for disaster for my sensitive body and signalled the start of a downward spiral for my health.

By the time I reached adulthood, headaches and migraines were a fully established part of my 'normal'. I had a deep love of cake, bread and all things dairy. I also had a weight problem. I was always on a diet, yo-yoing from a size 12 to 16. I loved experimenting in the kitchen, cooking up new recipes and flavour combinations. I thought I knew all about healthy food and nutrition – although I was regularly led astray by my love of cake.

This time in my life was also accompanied by stress – and lots of it. There was the art of juggling children and work, family responsibilities and emotional challenges. Life was of full of activity, dilemmas, challenges and loss, and there was plenty of all of them. Women are experts at caring for others but not so much when it comes to themselves. Lack of time, relaxation and exercise all added to my pot of metabolic stress.

And one day, that pot started to overflow.

2008 – The Year of Change

Some years are more difficult than others. For me, 2008 was the worst of years. I was working in a neurosurgical Intensive Care Unit (one of the most challenging environments possible) and also studying for my degree. My husband worked long hours and often travelled away, so I had to manage the children and their activities as well. I also had some deeply emotional issues going on in my personal life. My health was blighted by major difficulties with my periods and a minor heart problem, both of which were being investigated. It was a lot to deal with.

As a family we ate pretty healthily, or so I thought. Then my 11-year-old daughter suddenly declared that she was a vegetarian. A marshmallow toasting session at Guides had led to a discussion about gelatine. She decided that using animal bones in food was disgusting and declared she would never eat anything from a dead animal ever again.

I thought this would be a short-lived phase but wanted to support her choices. I started to replace the meat in our meals with some of the processed meat-substitute products on the market at the time. Although that meant I didn't have to cook different meals for everyone, in some ways it meant we were eating more junk food than before. This had a bad effect on my already over-wrought body. My metabolic bucket of tolerance was already full and it started to overflow.

Every day, I woke up with a stiff neck and by the end of the day it developed into a headache, sometimes mild but often a migraine. Some days I woke with a headache which only got worse. My eyes ached, I had no energy and I felt awful. Looking back, this was probably the first sign of my autoimmune disease, but as I've already said, hindsight is a wonderful thing.

Only ibuprofen and codeine tablets seemed to help, but I couldn't carry on taking those long term, so I decided something had to change. I needed to lose weight again and around that time, Carol Vorderman's *Detox Diet* was the latest craze, so I decided to give it a go.

The programme involved cutting out anything that might be 'bad' for you, including dairy, refined sugar, fat, meat, processed foods, tea and alcohol. It was a struggle, but the idea was that you would rest your body for 28 days, kick-start your metabolism and have rapid weight loss before going on to eat a more modified version of the plan to keep losing weight.

While I don't think I ever managed to finish the full 28-day programme, once the first few days of caffeine and sugar withdrawal had passed, I felt much better. My horrid headaches eased and I felt more energised. But of course, I wanted to have my cake (and cheese and bread) and eat it too, so I soon fell back into my old ways – and so the old symptoms returned as well.

Even though changing my diet had helped, I didn't want to believe that food was the issue, so I focused on looking for other potential causes. First, I went to the opticians, in case it was my eyes causing the problem. Nothing untoward showed up and all I left with was a lighter purse and a lovely new pair of glasses.

Next was my GP. But my complaints were received with little sympathy. Knowing where I worked, my doctor thought I had self-diagnosed a brain tumour. After a cursory neurological examination, she declared there was nothing wrong and told me to keep taking the anti-inflammatory pain killers. I mentioned to her that I felt better when I changed my diet but all she gave in response was a snort of derision followed by 'Well, if it works for you then do it.' There is a certain irony that a few years later it was my eyes and a severe case of optic neuritis, which was serious enough to cause temporary sight loss, that led to a diagnosis of multiple sclerosis, an incurable neurological autoimmune disease.

But it was my GP's irksome medical response that motivated me to deal with the underlying problem and not paper over the cracks. I was taking full responsibility for my own health. In a society in which it's normal to look for solutions through medication and quick fixes, this can be hard to do. Having the right motivation makes it easier, but it would be so much better not to have reached that point in the first place. Fortunately, there is a growing awareness today about the food/health connection; huge progress in a very short period of time.

That's how I came to return to the detox plan, but this time making more detailed notes about how different food made me feel. It was hard work to do it. Sometimes I ended up cooking three meals to suit everyone's needs – not something I'd recommend! Learning to adapt recipes helped, but I resented everything the others ate because I couldn't. I sulked big time, although this passed as my metabolism calmed and I started to feel better.

Saying no to certain foods suddenly became far more positive for me. My mind-set switched from seeking pleasure to focusing on self-protection and self-healing. I reminded myself that eating this way was my choice and so it was up to me to reap the benefits.

Inevitably, there were lots of judgements from other people about what I was doing. Everyone seemed to have an opinion. It was hard for those around me to understand. Thankfully, their concern came from love (well, mostly). But the results were so profound that I had no doubt it was working and I felt empowered to continue on my own path no matter what the dissenters said.

I decided to have a food-intolerance test. This identified dairy and yeast as two major problems for me. This made sense as they appeared in all my favourite foods; most pre-prepared products contain one or both of them. Even the most 'natural' food colourings and preservatives are grown on yeast. That meant I also had to steer clear of fermented products, so items like vinegar or meat substitutes like Quorn were also off the list.

It soon became clear that if I wanted to clear my system, cooking from scratch was my only option. At this point, I started to eat meat again, just because it could be simple and unadorned. It was only a couple of years later when we were living in India that I understood that this wasn't the best solution.

Indian Adventures

A year or so after starting my journey into overcoming my food intolerances, our life as a family was turned upside-down by an unusual opportunity. We were settled in our comfortable life in a small countryside town, the kids embedded in the education system and all our family and friends nearby. Suddenly, my husband was offered the opportunity to move to India for a work assignment. Of course, any sane person would say no … wouldn't they? I surprised even myself by unhesitatingly saying 'yes'.

After six months of uncertainty, negotiations (and tantrums) with the children and the expenditure of a lot nervous energy, we found ourselves in Bangalore: two adults, two pre-teens aged 11 and 12, four suitcases, a guitar and a whole new life to begin.

Talk about a culture shock! The noise, smells and sheer number of people was overwhelming. Fortunately, the children took to their new school and extraordinary adventures amazingly well, and life started to fall into some form of routine, even if it was a haphazard and crazy one. Suddenly I had time on my hands and decided to study nutritional medicine. I wanted to understand more about the food/health connection so I could use it to help me overcome my dairy and yeast intolerances. And I wanted to drink wine again.

One day I received an invitation to a dairy-free workshop. Here, I met a wonderful woman called Dr Nandita Shah and my world began to shift on its axis once more. A homeopath from Pondicherry on the East coast of India, Dr Shah heads an organisation called SHARAN-India (Sanctuary for Health and Reconnection to Animals and Nature). She has dedicated her life to promoting a healthy, sustainable and compassionate lifestyle and has a vision for a diabetes-free India. Quite a task!

Dr Shah talked about why we as humans don't need to consume any dairy or dairy products and gave a small demonstration on how to make dairy-free dishes. Both the information and the food was fascinating. But what was most convincing for me was Dr Shah herself. She oozed authenticity, passion and an amazing energy. She was so healthy she glowed! I wanted to feel like she looked.

I decided to learn more and later attended her 'Peas versus Pills' course. Here I learnt the real cost of a Western processed diet and the amazing healing properties of a whole-food, plant-based diet. My entire understanding of 'healthy food' was turned on its head and my way of eating changed for ever. In fact, this experience was so profound I realised I had to share the message, and The Sensitive Foodie Kitchen was born.

Welcome to My World

Time is a great healer. So is effort and knowledge. Taking the time to start from the beginning, to learn how to cook from scratch in a different way and explore how real nutrition from a whole-food, plant-based diet helps the body has been worth the effort. Fortunately, these days I'm not alone in this quest and there are many other voices out there with a similar message. Having experienced the profound effect of eating for health and learning how to create food that makes everyone happy, it's time to share that passion with you.

Social media might make you think the world of whole-food and health is full of beautiful young things whipping up exotic dishes in just moments then sharing them with their equally beautiful young friends. This is not the reality for most people, though. Family life and feeding bourgeoning young minds is challenging at the best of times. Workplace commitments, after-school activities and financial constraints are every-day difficulties for most people. A raw spirulina and spinach creation is just not going to hit the spot!

Eat Well Live Well with The Sensitive Foodie is my blueprint for eating great food that everyone will love. And it just so happens to be good for the body, the mind and the environment too.

The first half of this book explores three main themes:

1. The connection between the food we eat and our health.
2. The amazing human body and its constant battle to keep us working well.
3. That everything in our world is connected and how a whole-food, plant-based diet can make a difference to the world around us.

The second half of the book is made up of a collection of over 100 recipes, taken straight from The Sensitive Foodie Kitchen. Each one has been tried and tested for both taste and ease of cooking. You'll also find top tips and sound, practical information around how to make these recipes.

If you're looking for information about individual nutrient groups, this is not the book for you. But if you're exploring the benefits of whole nutrition and searching for an alternative to the everyday notion of food, or for answers about how you can make a difference to the way you feel by eating differently, *Eat Well Live Well with The Sensitive Foodie* is a good place for you to start your own journey to better health.

So, congratulations and thank you for picking up this book. Not only do I hope it helps you understand your relationship with the food you eat and its impact on your health, but also leaves you feeling empowered to make changes to your diet that your body and taste-buds will love.

PART 1
Food and Health

CHAPTER ONE

THE FOOD/HEALTH CONNECTION

Some of us live to eat, others just eat to live. Whatever your preference, food is an integral part of everyday life; it fuels our bodies and is critical to our survival. That's why there is so much debate, disagreement and confusion around what we eat.

All animals, humans included, are programmed for survival. When it comes to food, the human body has an amazing variety of mechanisms to overcome short periods of starvation. But these can only work for so long. Lack of food starts to cause severe problems after just 35 days, death from 45 days. Although humans can survive on just small amounts of food for a time they don't do it particularly 'well', as can be seen in reports of famine and records from prisoner of war camps. Fortunately, most of us will never be in that position. Alongside advances in medicine, a plentiful supply of food has made survival far less challenging for us.

The supply of a variety of different food and food-like products should now mean that malnourishment is a rarity. Unfortunately, it is not. In fact, malnourishment is becoming an increasing problem in the western world. Not from the lack of food overall but from the lack of nutrients contained within that food. To borrow a phrase that sums up the situation perfectly, many people are now 'overfed and undernourished'.

How can that be? The problem lies in the type and amount of food and food-like products that are consumed on a daily basis. Much of our diet is made up of food that is highly refined and processed, packed with chemicals, high in animal products and low in fibre and contains far too little fresh produce.

This way of eating has contributed to an explosion in chronic health problems, which are having a huge impact on many people's everyday lives and are hugely expensive. But despite health budgets and the health (or disease) industry continuing to expand exponentially, the costs of chronic disease aren't just monetary. The real cost is to physical and psychological wellbeing as well as social and emotional problems. As someone with a chronic autoimmune disease, I have experienced those costs first-hand and I don't recommend it!

A continual reel of new reports and statistics reflect the impact of chronic health problems like diabetes, heart disease and obesity, all of which bring with them a corresponding slew of new treatments. In comparison, sadly it is rare that there is similar focus on prevention or reversal. Amazing breakthroughs in medicine improve survival rates from previously fatal events like heart attacks and cancer. We're also living longer, with the average life-span extending continually. Being a centurion is no longer a rarity and it's believed that the first person who will live until 150 has already been born. How mind-blowing is that?

But how 'well' are we living these extended years? Not very. In fact, the number of years spent living in ill-health has also grown. A recent report on the UK population suggests that on average the last 16 years of life are spent battling poor health and disability. And that's an average. While some people have all the luck and experience few problems, others suffer for decades. When planning for retirement, who wants to plan for pain, discomfort and the lack of freedom that comes with chronic health issues?

The steps we take earlier in life have a serious impact on our later years, although that's hard to appreciate when we're young, pain-free and fit. However, life-style is now beginning to impact the health of the younger generation too with an increase in conditions like diabetes and obesity in children; conditions that will need managing their whole lives.

During the time I spent working in a medical intensive care unit (ICU) the majority of the patients I looked after were there due to 'life-style conditions', either as acute presentations or due to secondary complications. It's a real eye-opener when you see the reality of what happens to our amazing, beautiful bodies when we don't take care of them.

Of course, it's ironic that although food is key keeping the body nourished and healthy (particularly in times of stress and illness), hospitals are often the worst places to get food that promotes recovery.

In this chapter, we're going to explore the connection between food and health, but before we do, let's have a very brief look at lifestyle diseases in the UK and at some of the disturbing statistics that surround our poor health.

Understanding Lifestyle Diseases

Lifestyle diseases are conditions that have a multitude of causative factors all of which are related to how and where we live our lives. These factors include poor eating habits, lack of exercise, stress, smoking and excess alcohol consumption as well as contributory social factors like poverty, poor housing, lack of outside space, little or no family support and poor social networks. Added to that are economic issues like long working hours, low pay, lengthy and difficult commutes, the cost of healthy food and factors such as the quality of education, ethnicity, genetic and cultural influences, so it's easy to see that a complex set of factors impact health. No wonder health problems that are increasing continually. None of this is helped by the multitude of conflicting perspectives on the origins of poor health and the subsequent lack of a commonly-accepted solution to the problem.

As a result, it's often the person who's ill that is blamed for their problem, particularly when it comes to obesity. On the surface it appears as if there's an obvious cause – you eat too many calories and are too lazy to burn them off. This attitude equates to a moral judgement that accuses an individual of having a lack of willpower or other character defects. After all, it's easier to blame an individual than look at wider influencing factors. But when examined in more detail, the simple equation for the maintenance of a healthy weight – calories in must match calories used – just doesn't apply.

But what are lifestyle diseases? They're commonly recognised as the big four:

1. Obesity.
2. Type 2 Diabetes.
3. Heart Disease.
4. Stroke (commonly brought about by high blood pressure).

Cancer, or at least some cancers, could be added to this list too as there are recognised factors that can vastly increase the risk for certain cancers, like smoking or obesity. There are also many other illnesses and conditions that are influenced by lifestyle too, not just cancer. These range from allergies, asthma and eczema to Alzheimer's disease, liver disease, kidney disease and autoimmune conditions.

But is it someone's fault they get ill or is it just bad luck?

When I was diagnosed with multiple sclerosis (MS), I asked myself: 'What did I do wrong? Is it my fault that my body decided to start attacking my nerves?' There were times when I felt as if I was to blame because, despite making changes to the way I lived, I'd still ended up with it.

'Fault' and 'blame' are morally loaded words though, and certainly not helpful. In fact, there are a multitude of factors that could have affected why and how I developed MS, ranging from a genetic predisposition to food intolerances and persistent stress. Even doing night shifts seems to be an influencing factor, so nursing doesn't appear to be an ideal profession if you want to look after your health!

I realised that even though I'd developed a chronic health problem, I could and would take positive action to minimise the effects. Creating more stress and worrying about why I'd got ill wasn't going to help. And all was not lost; I could still have a positive impact on my health – as can you. It's empowering to be able to focus on what you can change rather than what you can't.

UK lifestyle disease statistics

Here are a few stats that are worth thinking about:

- Currently, the NHS spends £11 billion a year on lifestyle conditions and this is increasing year on year. It's no wonder our wonderful institution is struggling to cope.
- 27 per cent of the UK population is classified as obese – that's the worst in Europe.
- The number of obese people has tripled in the last 30 years, which is especially worrying because obesity increases the likelihood of developing other health problems.
- Obese men are five times more likely to develop diabetes, three times more likely to develop cancer and two and half times more likely to develop high blood pressure, which can lead to heart disease or stroke.
- Obese women are 13 times more likely to develop diabetes, four times more likely to have raised blood pressure and three times more likely to have a heart attack.

- The NHS currently spends 10 per cent of its annual budget on the prevention, management and associated health problems of diabetes – that's £14 billion a year or £1.5 million per hour on this one condition. Now that's a lot of money!
- 3.2 million people are currently diagnosed with diabetes (so it's not surprising it costs so much to treat). What's even more frightening is that 1 in 17 people are thought to have diabetes (that number includes those who are undiagnosed as well as those already on the list). How much is it going to cost if it carries on this way?
- Heart disease is another biggie on the list. Still the number one killer in the UK, 7 million people are diagnosed with some form of heart disease issue with high blood pressure and cholesterol being top of the list.
- £9 billion a year is spent treating heart disease and related issues, but the actual cost to the economy in terms of premature death, lost days at work and long-term disability is estimated to be a whopping £19 billion a year.

Of course, as I've already mentioned, there are many other 'costs' of health problems, including social exclusion, poverty, chronic pain, depression, isolation and just generally feeling pretty overwhelmed and beaten by life. No wonder so many people seem completely miserable.

Dr Michal Gregor, author of *How Not To Die*, states that 95 per cent of all diseases are influenced by lifestyle factors. Although that might seem like a depressing and negative statistic, it's actually a positive conclusion because if the way you live and eat can make you ill, it can also make you well. You just need to find out *how* to do it. Hopefully this book will give you plenty of ideas.

Eating in the Modern World

I grew up in the seventies, an exciting decade of new technology, social unrest and wonderfully flamboyant fashion. As a young child, my family lived in a small village in the north Essex countryside. We had a large garden surrounded by fields that were owned by a local farmer. I know life can feel easy and idyllic at that age, so I'm sure things weren't as rose-tinted as I recall, but back then it seemed as if all the food I ate was simple, home-cooked and sourced locally.

One vivid memory I have involves a car journey to a local farm that was harvesting peas. You could turn up with your own buckets and fill it with fresh peas to freeze at home. It was a dry, sunny day but I remember having to wear wellies to wade through a thick green sludge that coated the farmyard. The air carried a heavy, pungent pea aroma and I did not like it at all. I had a full-on tantrum right in the middle of the sludge. My poor mum struggled to carry me and two overflowing buckets back to the car, somehow managing not to drop either. Back at home she then spent ages sorting, cooking and packaging these peas to put in our new chest freezer. It was a lot of effort.

At the time, we shopped in the local village rather than travelling further afield. Even though the village was small, we were well-served by a bakery, butcher and general store. We would walk up to the shops most days. When I think back to that time, my clearest memories are of Mum being in the kitchen making our family dinner or slicing bread as thinly as possible to make it last.

I started school in the mid-seventies; it was a big change for me and looking back it was also a time of profound change in our family eating habits. Mum stopped walking to the local shops and instead drove to the nearby town where she could do a one-stop shop in the large supermarket. It saved time and opened up a whole world of new food products that had the benefit of needing a lot less time to prepare. Convenience foods had hit our family.

We pestered Mum to get this or that. It was exciting to try the new products we saw advertised on TV. They were a symbol of affluence and we were ahead of the game. It never occurred to me that I actually preferred the taste of real food to the facsimiles we had. I ate SMASH for so long I forgot what real mashed potato tasted like!

We still ate some fresh fruit and vegetables of course, but these were way outnumbered by meat, dairy and refined carbohydrates, as well as a modern cacophony of chemicals in the forms of additives, preservatives and flavourings. Then as a teen and when I left home, there was the draw of the fast food giants and the novelty of eating with your hands rather than cutlery. It all seemed so radical.

When I moved to London as a student nurse, I had little money and few cooking skills, so I survived on baked potatoes with cottage cheese, chips and beans, and the odd Chinese or Indian take-away – as well as a few slices of cake, of course. On top of that were the cigarettes and alcohol – both of which I enjoyed to the max.

There's nothing unusual in this and my story will have been repeated by thousands of others. I ate to survive; sometimes to enjoy but always because

I felt the need to keep topping up my body with more food. My weight fluctuated constantly because I was always trying out the latest diet. Looking back, I realise I was depriving myself of essential nutrients by living on basic fuel. I overloaded my body with the very food that my body was intolerant to (dairy) believing it was essential. I thought I ate well, but in reality, my meals were packed with refined and processed foods. I was stuck in an addictive cycle.

Dietary changes started long before my own childhood in the 1970s. For thousands of years, most people would have had a direct connection with the food they ate. The agricultural revolution of the eighteenth century became a catalyst for a profound change in life for many ordinary people. Breakthroughs in engineering created mechanical tools that replaced human effort, enabling farmers to create higher yields. Rural populations relocated to urban areas to provide labour for the rapidly escalating industrial revolution. A greater availability of food lead to a corresponding increase in population as well as improved health, enabling the UK and many other industrialised nations around the world to flourish. Of course, this is a major simplification of history and many people suffered, paying the price of progress with their lives.

Today, 83 per cent of the UK population live in urban areas with less than 1.5 per cent working in farming. This means a large percentage of people have no direct connection to the food they eat and it's this disconnection that has led to us directly handing over responsibility for what we eat to the food industry.

Many people don't think this is an issue. Food is food after all. But a combination of technology, the pursuance of food science and the drive to maximise profits has taken the shine off the benefits gained from agricultural innovation. As a result, the vast majority of the population of the Western world has been tipped over the edge to become chemical-guzzling addicts who blindly travel on the path towards chronic ill-health and environmental disaster. This may sound over-dramatic, but it's the reality of the situation. We have become used to having seasonal foods all year round, access to food-like products 24-hours a day and consuming excessive amounts of food-like substances – yet we rarely feel fully nourished.

A recent report found that just over half the food bought by families in the UK is 'ultra-processed', that means food that's been made in factories with manufactured chemicals and additives. As a result, this processed food bears little resemblance to any natural product it might be made with, either in taste or whole nutrition. This is what I refer to as 'food-like'. Sadly, many people don't know how to cook basic recipes because schools are dropping vital life skills like cookery, so they can keep up on an increasingly demanding academic curriculum and cuts in funding.

As humans living in a modern world eating a diet that's dominated by food-like substances that are completely disconnected from their rural heritage, the question is why are we suffering ill-health rather than adapting to these changes? After all, humans have developed and adapted to their environments for thousands of years. Can we no longer evolve? Let's have a quick look at evolution and how we got to be here today.

Slow Learners

I'm constantly amazed by the complexity of the human body. Working in ICU I learnt that every biological system and bodily process works in conjunction with all the others. Even miniscule actions have a back-up. And another back-up. And often another. Just in case. Each one is slightly less efficient but ultimately effective. Programmed for survival, the resilience of human beings is truly beyond comprehension. Even today, scientists are constantly making new discoveries about how we 'work'. Although we seem to know a lot, it's clear that there's a lot we haven't discovered yet.

I remain in awe of the body's incredible powers and find myself reflecting on just how we got to be this way. It's a complex subject, but I'll attempt to make it as simple as possible for the sake of speed and clarity. If you want to learn more, take a look at the recommended reading list on page 306.

When it comes to evolution, there are two major factors that I find difficult to comprehend. The first is the mind-blowing enormity of time and the second is the challenge of differentiating between fact and theory. Just who has got the right answers?

The human brain has an amazing capacity for logical reasoning and understanding. As people, we use our experiences and knowledge to analyse and put things in perspective. The concept of time is relative to our experience. Each year passes much quicker as we get older because each year makes up a smaller and smaller percentage of the time we've been alive. Time is measured in increasingly small units – years, months, weeks, days, minutes and seconds. All are filled with the very busy activities of life. But our individual measurement of time – our lifetime – is miniscule in relation to the bigger picture of human life on Earth. There's an exhibit at the Centre for Alternative

Technology in Wales that explains this with astounding clarity using a model of a skyscraper to illustrate the point.

In this model, the ground floor is the formation of Earth – the point that's believed to be the beginning of the planet. Each floor represents a period of time in Earth's history. Specific events like the Ice Age and the age of the dinosaurs are highlighted as is the appearance of humans (homo sapiens, anyway). Some eras are so long they have one or two floors to themselves. The period representing humanity's existence is so small it's hard to spot it immediately because it's just below the top ceiling! Another way of looking at it is if you measure life on Earth as a 12-hour clock, we've been around for just 2 seconds.

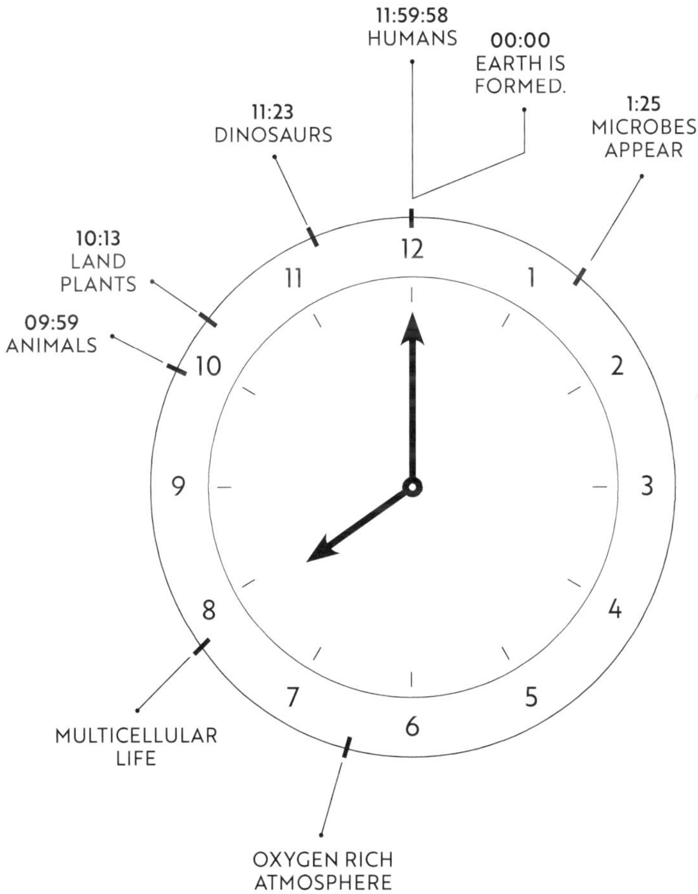

Humans have been around for a miniscule part of Earth's history – just 2 seconds on a 12 hour clock. They hardly register in the lifetime of the planet.

Us human beings are so egocentric that we think our time on the planet is 'it'. But when you put it in perspective, it's obvious that our time is a mere speck in the history of the Earth. The expanse of time is so huge, it's difficult to comprehend. Even when you narrow it down to the period since humans evolved into being, that still covers roughly 200,000 years. That's a lot of lifetimes!

All of which neatly leads onto the second issue: how do we know what is fact and what is theory? Much of the distant past is based on hypotheses backed up by archaeological evidence. Anthropology – the study of humans – is a huge area of research and, ultimately, we can only trust that the experts are right. The problem is that theories change as new evidence is unearthed and so not even the experts can agree on what is the truth.

This is problematic when it comes to understanding our bodies and what we should be eating. Experts have different theories and models that they use to back up their claims. The vast majority of diet books available right now (roughly 30,000) claim to be backed by science, which shows just how much conflict and confusion there is. That might seem an odd statement from someone who has written yet another book about healthy eating, but I think it's important to recognise the reality of the situation we find ourselves in.

Modern humans are very different to our early ancestors, not just in the way we live but in the way we look and behave as well. Life span, brain power, social circles and physiology like height and weight have all changed over thousands and thousands of years. The food we eat has also changed massively, but that's happened in a much shorter period of time, and this is where the problem lies – the rate of change in our bodies can't keep up with the rate of change in the rest of our lives.

The food we eat in the West has changed massively in the last 60 years or so, and now less economically developed countries are catching up too. The change has escalated since the end of the Second World War.

During the war, the UK and US governments used subsidies as incentives to encourage food producers to increase productivity. After the war, and when rationing and austerity measures ended, new technology and the development of new foods led to a massive change in the way food was produced. Looking back, it's easy to see why food changed so dramatically. Along with the advent of consumer marketing and advertising shoppers were persuaded that these new shiny products were much more desirable than the dull, traditional ones of the past.

When time-saving, ready-made meals and fast food outlets started to enter the food market, real home-cooked food almost became a thing of the past. Even though the flavour of mass-produced food and the level of satiety it offered was no match for home-cooked food, burgeoning consumer demand escalated the rate of change so more and more new products were developed.

Even relatively natural products changed in flavour and nutritional profile as raw produce was manipulated to create larger yields or lower overheads and meet the changing tastes of the consumer. When you look back, you'll remember that many staple foods like bread, strawberries or chicken used to taste much better. It's not an illusion, either – they did taste better! I'm always delighted when I eat a humble potato and find it actually tastes like a potato.

Much of the demand for processed food is connected to the discovery of the 'bliss point' by food scientists. As they're essential for survival, humans have evolved to desire fat, sugar and salt in perfect balance. The bliss point is simply the optimum level of tastiness for a product. Too much or too little of one of the essential elements and the flavour is either excessive or bland.

Food manufacturers used this new-found knowledge to the max and it turned out to be good for profits, but not so good for health. The burgeoning waistline of the Western world is the most visual consequence of this sudden change from real to manipulated food-like products. And it's not just adults that are affected, it's children too.

Being overweight is not a new phenomenon. No matter where you live in the world, a percentage of the population will be on the large size, even in the poorest places. But obesity is more than being a bit overweight. To be classified as obese, a person must have at least 20 per cent more body fat than normal. This extra body fat increases metabolic demands and can lead to many of the current chronic health problems we see today.

Worldwide, the number of obese people has risen exponentially. As mentioned above, the UK Department of Health reports that 27 per cent of the population is obese and is set to hit 50 per cent in 2050. In the US, current obesity rates are just under 40 per cent, while in Australia it's around 29 per cent. These are truly scary figures.

So why have humans not evolved to deal with the many 'new foods'? The answer goes back to two key elements: time and data. Not enough time has passed for us to adapt as a species and second, we don't have enough data to be able to accurately identify exactly what influences our physiological response to food. Supporters of a paleo diet – eating in the way they assume our ancestors may have done – would say that farming is to blame and in some ways it is, but not in the way advocates of this movement believe. The problem lies not so much with the original raw products but with what ends up on our plates.

Scientists have physical evidence from archaeological digs about what our ancestors looked like and what they ate, but much of their knowledge is still based on theories rather than fact. After all, how can we truly know what occurred in the far-distant past? Well-founded theories are all we have to go by when piecing together our ancestors' history. And theories can change.

In the 1960s, the population was already starting to get fatter. Scientists were given the task of working out why. Their explanation came in the form of the thrifty gene theory. This theory is based on the hypothesis that being able to build up good fat stores is the key to survival.

As our ancestors travelled out of Africa and populated the rest of the world, major events occurred that seriously reduced population numbers, including epidemics of infectious disease, famine, erratic weather and long, arduous journeys. It was thought that those who could build up hefty fat stores (prior to a long voyage, for example) would have protection against starvation and would cope much better than their skinny brethren. The skinny died, the fat (presumably now skinny) survived to reproduce and pass their super-survivor fat gene onto their offspring. The thrifty gene theory concludes that this gene was positively selected and therefore we all have the ability to stack on weight, even though we now don't need to do that to survive.

This theory seems quite logical and is definitely welcome news for someone who has unfairly labelled as 'fat and lazy'. However, in the survival stakes, infectious disease and diarrhoea were much more common and indiscriminate killers at that time (as can be seen today in the developing world) than long journeys. It also assumes that only just enough food was ever available, otherwise our ancestors would have become fat from over-indulging in times of plenty.

If true, obesity and all its related health problems would not actually be a problem in the current day but be completely 'normal'. Anthropologists also have evidence that hunter-gatherers often ate an abundance of food, so availability might not have been the issue.

The thrifty gene theory has been disputed by many, including the scientist who first came up with it! It's deemed unlikely that a 'fat gene' would have been positively selected. As early humans were still hunted by other animals, a gene that promoted the retention of fat on the body was not likely to promote survival. Carrying too much body weight meant you were not going to move fast enough to escape. Not only that, you would be the most attractive prey being sweet and tasty with lots of meat to munch on. It's more likely that a fat gene would be evolved out, not in, as suggested by the thrifty gene theory.

But being skinny was not ideal for survival either. Fat reserves were still needed for times of scarcity. John Speakman, a British biologist, has mooted that fat genes are there due to genetic drift (hence 'drifty gene'). In other words, it's only there by chance rather than being positively selected. It's now suggested that our early ancestors had an internal regulation system with upper and lower limits as being too fat or too thin was not conducive to survival. It's almost like a 'Baby Bear gene theory', just right. As humans evolved and developed other ways to survive, this upper limit has become less important. The genes may be mutated or have drifted into the genetic pool, leading to an increase in susceptibility to obesity, particularly in populations with excess food intake as we see in the modern Western world.

So, which theory is right? It could be either of these or one of the many others proposed over the years. But no matter whether a theory is correct or not, one thing is for certain – our bodies are struggling with the speed of change. Modern humans (homo sapiens) appeared about 200,000 years ago. Since then, the type, volume and quality of food eaten by humans has changed radically, but the rate of adaptation has been slow. Our genes are slow learners and they take time to acclimatise – much longer than the 60-odd years since the start of the sweeping changes in the manufacture and production of the food and food-like products we eat today. We might not be able to wait a few thousand years for our genes to get a grip on things. If we don't start making major changes to what we eat right now, despite all the medical advances we have made, we might not survive.

Fortunately, all is not lost.

First of all, we're beginning to recognise that our eating is going haywire so we're able to make changes for the better. Secondly, there is a part of our biology that's able to adapt more rapidly: the microbiome, which is the vast population of bacteria that live in the gut.

Scientists are only just beginning to understand the influence that our individual internal eco-system has on our overall health. Even more significantly, they've realised that it can be changed – for better or worse – through the way we live and the food we eat. So, although our genes may be slow learners and our bodies take time to adapt, we have a back-up team fighting for us in the short-term. The question for all of us is whether we're going to choose to look after our microbiome or ignore it. More about that in the next chapter but for now, let's look at what's in our food and how it affects our health.

What's In Our Food?

There's an apple tree in our garden that produces a sweet and tasty crop every year. Apart from prudent pruning, the tree and its crop require no assistance from us. There are no 'food miles' involved in getting them to us and as there's no fresher fruit than one that's just been plucked from the tree, the apples taste delicious.

However, our apple tree is not a perfect fruit-producing machine. The yield varies from year to year, depending on the weather in the spring. An unexpected late frost or snow can wipe out the early blossom and when there's no blossom, there's no fruit. But that's not all …

For a start, there are the birds to contend with. Annoyingly, they like to nibble the flesh of the lower-hanging fruits (the ones we can reach easily) and ignore the ones higher up (that we can't reach easily and that they're welcome to dine on). Some years, the wasp population takes over the tree, laying their eggs in the fruit or enjoying the exposed flesh of the bird-pecked apples.

On top of that, when there is a good crop, the apples all seem to ripen at the same time, so we're inundated with them for a month. No matter how much you love an apple, there are only so many you can eat at a time! We give them away, make crumbles and cakes, freeze slices or purée them for later in the year. Finally, many apples can be stored, but not ours. Once the crop is over, it's back to sourcing our apples from elsewhere.

That means our fruit tree would never be commercially viable – at least not without some interference. So, although we may prefer naturally grown fruit, the weather, pests and nature make that unfeasible and we can't rely on its annual yield. However, there are actions we could take to improve the situation. The weather is out of our control, but the tree could be cross-bred to be hardier or to flower later so there's not so much risk from frost. We could just plant a different type of tree that's more reliable and give up with the unreliable one, making our tree the same as everyone else's. We could use pesticides to deal with the wasps, fertilizers to increase the yield. We could even replace the shed with an air-sealed storage facility to keep the apples for later in the year, having first sprayed them with fungicide of course, in case there's a bad one in the pile.

Fortunately, I'm not a commercial apple grower. I love my apple tree the way it is and I'm grateful for the gloriously delicious and quirky fruit it produces. I just need to find a way to train the birds! Shop-bought apples are a different matter. Bright, shiny apples stacked high in the supermarket may look totally natural and very appealing to the eye, but they're one of the most chemically saturated fruit you can buy. In fact, its number 4 in EWG's (Environmental Working Group) Dirty Dozen, a guide to the twelve most chemically laden produce. Even organic products have been modified in some way in order to keep the fruit viable for sale.

The hard reality of economics is that ultimately, the aim of food producers is to make a profit. Without a financial return, their business is not sustainable and they simply wouldn't be able to get their product to market. The economics of food requires both supply and demand; food producers are essential. Most of us are not self-sufficient producers of our own food (my little apple tree being evidence of that), so we need farmers to grow it for us. Part of a government's responsibility is to ensure there is an ongoing supply of food to the population. To achieve that, farmers in Europe and the USA are given subsidies to incentivise them to produce the right food.

As already mentioned, financial incentives were established in the UK during the Second World War when overseas supplies were interrupted. Food subsidies were a scheme developed to support farmers to ensure they produced enough food for the country. The use of subsidies, along with rationing, manipulated consumer choice and set a precedent for the development of policies in the future.

Once farmers made the investment to grow specific crops and adapted to new industrial farming methods, they were able to continue to supply food at the same rate as during war-time. However, to sustain this level of supply, they needed ongoing support from government grants. It was difficult for the government to revoke financial support and guarantees once they had been given, especially given that farming is such a powerful lobbying force. French farmers are particularly well-known for their active protests against any action that might hurt their income.

Rationing during the Second World War is very interesting from a dietary perspective too because it was during this time that nutritional guidelines were established to ensure the population consumed a healthy, balanced diet. Dairy, meat and wheat products were restricted as supply was limited, but vegetables were available in abundance. Nutritionally, the population was the healthiest it had ever been, even if it wasn't the most satisfied. (For more information, check out *The Ration Book Diet* in the references section).

Once rationing was finally abolished in the 1950s, it left a generation who believed they 'deserved' to have sugar and fat once again and this seeded the perfect breeding ground for the development of the modern diet. There was a sudden explosion of processed foods to meet that demand and the result was the development of a consistently expanding supply of processed foods.

Food subsidies are still in operation today and in Europe it's the Common Agricultural Policy that supports farmers' incomes. However, the focus of subsidies has changed in recent years. They now target wider rural issues rather than just setting output targets. This is largely because of the excessive stores of unused products that built up as a result of farming subsidies. Production quotas were in excess of consumer demand leading to the infamous butter and beef 'mountains'.

In the US, farmers receive subsidies for large yields of specific crops like corn, wheat and soya. Again, the quantities produced are often in excess of demand. Much of this is used for animal feed. In fact, a staggering 70 per cent of arable crops in the US are processed for feeding farmed animals destined for the meat market. In his book *The Omnivore's Dilemma*, Michel Pollen explores how farmers can only survive by getting subsidies to grow certain produce and how growing a non-subsidised crop is often not financially viable.

When crops like corn are over-produced, the market becomes saturated with them and their price falls. This super-cheap produce is a food-manufacturers dream because it can made into a multitude of refined products, like high-fructose syrup and maltodextrin, familiar ingredients on processed food packaging.

Michel Pollen has written extensively about the food industry and as a result, he's frequently quoted. He has created mottoes like: 'Eat food. Not too much. Mostly plants.' And 'If it came from a plant, eat it; if it was made in a plant, don't.' This second one raises an important question around how much of what we eat is 'real'?

It's hard to avoid chemicals, even when you believe you eat a healthy diet. Real food can spoil rapidly or have a short shelf-life. Most processed foods contain some form of food additive, whether it's a preservative, colouring or flavouring. That could be in your loaf of bread, pot of hummus or glass of wine. Some preservatives and flavourings are truly natural, like salt or spices. Some have been used for years, like sugar and citric acid. Many products boast natural additives, which make the consumer feel more comfortable. We all prefer natural products, right?

But not all 'natural' additives are as natural as they seem. For example, citric acid, which most of us probably assume comes from lemons, is grown on yeast in a lab. It appears that when the lemon supply from Italy was disrupted during the First World War, scientists discovered it could be grown on yeast, and so it has been ever since. Many people wouldn't see this as a problem, but for people like me with a yeast intolerance – or for anyone with poor gut health – it can be a huge problem because citric acid seems to be in everything! But it's not just citric acid that causes a problem, many other 'natural' additives are also grown on yeast. And, of course, yeast itself appears in a whole host of processed foods. This makes eating processed food nigh on impossible for me, which as it turns out is a good thing.

'Natural' additives are partnered with a plethora of chemically derived and food-like substances, each of which is designed to enhance the food we consume. Once processed, fresh produce becomes a big loser – of colour, texture, flavour and most importantly nutrients. Most produce starts to deteriorate as soon as it's harvested. The more time that passes between being picked and eaten, the lower the level of vitality and other benefits it can give us. A freshly-plucked apple from my tree is incomparably tastier, more nutritious and packed with greater vitality than one that has been picked, stored and then transported from New Zealand, for example. Freshly picked produce also looks inviting and glows with its own natural energy. The tired, transported ones tend to need a quick spray to make them 'glow' and look more appealing.

It's not just additives that are an issue with food production, though; other chemical substances sneak through the outer layers of fresh produce to reside in the flesh. The residue of chemical fertilizers and pesticides routinely sprayed on crops can be found in most fruit, vegetables, grain and cereals as well as in all forms of animal produce, often in concentrated amounts. Manufacturers of these widely-used chemicals dispute health concerns, saying everything has been tested for safety. But most chemicals have only been tested singly, not in combination with others. The way in which these build up over time is untested and should be a cause for concern.

Residue also builds up in the soil leading to nearby waterways becoming polluted by run-off from these chemically treated areas, which affects the whole of the local ecosystem. Washing produce may remove pollutants from the skin of the produce, but most crops will have absorbed the chemical into their core, as it's stored it in all parts of the plant. There is genuine concern that many of these chemical concoctions have become environmental pollutants, building up over time and possibly contributing to the massive increase in allergies, intolerances and autoimmune conditions.

Organically farmed produce can overcome some of these problems, but currently it's still more expensive and less available than intensively farmed produce. Many dismiss organic farming as a new age fad, yet just 100 years ago, all farming was organic. The wide use of chemicals and intensive farming methods are the new kid on the block, not the traditional farming methods that respect the countryside.

Some parts of the world have more stringent controls when it comes to the use of certain chemicals. EU restrictions are much tighter than those in the US, for example. Even so, a concoction of chemicals still ends up in the food and yet its long-term impact on health is rarely questioned. Banning the use of many commonly used chemicals and derivatives would, I believe, have a huge impact on preventing and minimising the impact of many chronic health problems, although I'm realistic that this is highly unlikely to happen. So, if you have an allergy, intolerance, autoimmune condition, cancer or any other health challenge, you may want to look more carefully at what's in your food.

One other thing to be aware of when it comes to refined and processed food is the extent to which the natural ingredients are altered. History tells us that Mother Nature generally knows best when it comes to survival; plants have developed to survive as much as animals. We've evolved to consume those plants, absorbing maximum benefit from their naturally developed goodness. But from a commercial perspective, elements of natural chemical compounds inconveniently spoil or turn rancid in a short space of time. This makes them either more difficult to process or less cost effective. To counter that, structures and chemicals that occur naturally are removed and others added in to replace them, creating combinations that just don't exist in nature.

Wheat is the perfect example of this. Wheatgerm contains a number of essential fats and minerals, while the wheat bran contains fibre and protein. Both are removed as part of the processing method, leaving the central endosperm; the bulky, starchy, nutrient-deficient part. As a result, while highly-processed white flour might have a long shelf life, it has little nutritional benefit – apart from short-lived, quickly-absorbable sugars.

Of course, there are always fortified grains to fall back on. The problem with these is that when minerals and vitamins are added back in, the balance and amount of nutrition they contain is changed. More is not always better. As you'll see later in the book, chemicals and nutrients found in plants work together as a team. When the balance is upset, we end up with a product that is different to the one we have evolved to tolerate, putting our immune system on high alert. This could well be contributing towards ongoing inflammation, a key contributor to chronic health problems because our bodies have not had time to adapt to them.

Wholegrain

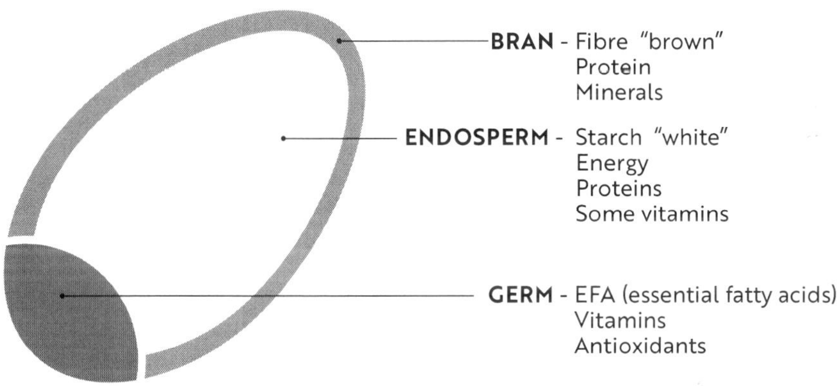

Refined grain

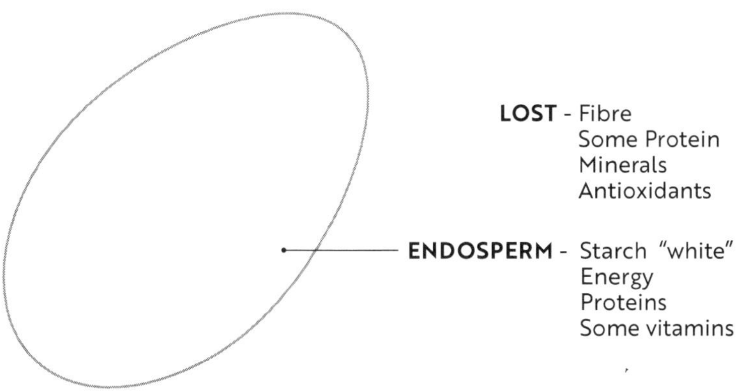

Essential nutrients are lost when wholegrains are refined.

We'll explore the contribution of inflammation in more detail in the next chapter. For now, there's one more element to consider in examining the food we eat and that's the way in which the combination of refined foods are designed to hit our pleasure centres, ensuring we want to come back for more, and more, and more. This is the 'bliss point' I mentioned earlier, the triad of pleasure giving flavours that makes us want to eat. We evolved to desire fat, sugar and salt, all key components for survival. To ensure we ate them, humans also evolved a reward mechanism in the form of tiny chemicals called endorphins.

Endorphins ping opiate receptors found in the brain and gut. It makes us feel good. So good, that we want to feel it again, and again. When food is scarce, this is a good thing. Scarcity is a thing of the past for the majority of people in the developed Western world, but the desire for fat, sugar and salt is still there. And it wants to be satiated.

Natural whole foods contain a bountiful supply of these pleasure-giving molecules but it takes more time for them to be released because sugars and fats are bound up in complex fibres. Refined food that have had their fibre removed, give an immediate 'hit'. Combine two or more together and it results in full-on pleasure heaven.

Triad of flavour 'highs'

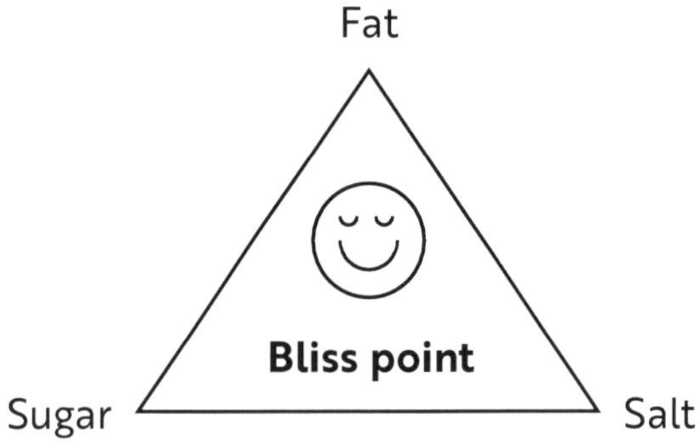

A combination of flavours hit our pleasure centres.

When we've enjoyed something once, we want to go back for more. Over a relatively short period of time, opiate receptors become saturated and increase in number, needing a higher amount of the pleasure-giving substances to achieve the same level of satisfaction. Sound familiar? This is the same process as drug addiction – and it's easy to get hooked without even realising what's going on.

Food manufacturers know this and use it to their commercial advantage. But it's not as simple as just loading products up with a shed-load of salt, sugar or fat (or all of them). That's because refined sugar, salt and fat are not pleasant to eat on their own. Not many people will sit and eat a teaspoon of granulated sugar – it's ridiculously sweet, grainy and sticks to the mouth. A little is more than enough. It's the same for cream. On its own, it's bland and coats the tongue. Not much pleasure there.

But combine them, add a little flavouring (like vanilla), freeze it until it's solid and *voila* – ice cream! And who doesn't love ice cream? In this form, fat and sugar are much easier to consume in large amounts and those pleasure centres are pinged every time.

But you don't have to taste it to 'know' it. Ice cream is ubiquitous and strongly associated with comfort, a 'fact' that's demonstrated through glamorous adverts and a message given to us subliminally through TV and film. How many times have you seen a character in a sit-com work their way through a tub of ice cream whilst lamenting over their lost love?

Combine all three elements – fat, sugar and salt – and the product becomes even more compelling, even if it's not that palatable. Take a moment to look at the long list of ingredients in a flavoured deep-fried snack. In it, you'll see salt, fat and some form of sugar in a deliberate formulation that is made to keep you eating. Pringles weren't joking when they coined the tag line, 'Once you pop you can't stop.' They mean it!

Sugar and salt can be used as a preservative, but too much spoils the taste. That's why processed foods are made to hit the 'bliss point' to ensure the consumer wants more. This doesn't work on everyone, but some people are more susceptible than others; these are the people who are more likely to overeat once exposed to the pleasure power of processed food.

This may sound a bit depressing that dark, outside forces are manipulating our very way of being, but it's not all bad news. Once you're aware of what's going on, you can make some informed choices about what food you eat – and choice is power.

Making a Decision

Once I discovered my food intolerances, I decided to make a choice. The first was to sulk. All my favourite foods – cheese, cake, bread, wine – were making me feel ill and it really pissed me off! Like anyone accustomed to having regular endorphin hits, I didn't want to miss out on these little pleasures in life. I stopped sulking once I realised that I had the power to stop my migraines and start feeling well. After that, my positive choices felt empowering.

Of course, I could have chosen to do nothing and just kept taking the pain killers (as advised by my GP) and put up with it. But I didn't want to do that. I knew from my nursing experience that this would just lead to other problems. So, I chose to make a huge change and started my roller-coaster journey to where I am now – dragging my family along with me for the ride.

I'm so glad that I made that choice – and that I made it when I did. Looking back, it's obvious that the onslaught of migraines I was experiencing 10 years ago was the first symptom of multiple sclerosis. By radically changing the way I ate, I improved my nutrient intake and removed a key protein associated with harming the immune system (butyrophilin in milk). This dampened down the inflammatory fire that was damaging my nervous system. The research that forms the foundation of the Overcoming MS programme validates this and is the perfect example of how food can both harm and heal.

Like me, you have a choice about what you eat. You have free will and you have the power to manage yourself. Your choices will make a massive difference to your health, so choose well. Empowering yourself to take responsibility for your own body can be a daunting but thrilling decision. If you're reading this book, I think I'm safe in assuming that you're either ready to make a choice or have already made one, and I applaud you for that – I'm truly delighted. Knowledge is power, and I'm writing this book to empower you to change the way you eat.

Before we go any further, I want to mention an important point: we're all different and that means we each respond to foods differently. Some may thrive on a purely plant-based diet, switching overnight and never looking back. Others take time or may choose to include some animal protein or fish for whatever reason. That choice is yours, and yours alone to make. Base your choice on clear, independent research. There is a huge amount of information available but be aware that much of it is funded by food industry bodies who have a vested interest in the results. Question everything you read but take action too; confusion is a tool used by powerful lobbyists to stop individuals making changes that will damage their profits. Remember, any change you make, no matter how small, will make a difference. Your mind and body are connected after all, so make the choice, feel the power and enjoy the benefits.

Before we look in detail at how the biological functions of your body are connected, let's find out how wonderful your body is and how the way you eat impacts it. But a word of warning – once you know something, you can't 'unknow' it. Awareness has a habit of growing. I started my plant-based journey focusing on health, but soon it expanded to cover environmental concerns and animal welfare. Once you start to question what you 'know', you soon realise there's a lot more to learn.

CHAPTER TWO

OUR AMAZING BODIES

I developed many things whilst working as a nurse, including a warped sense of humour, immense patience and a bad back. But the most important thing I learnt was an unending respect for the human body. We're all amazing! No engineer or scientist could ever create something as complex and intricate as our bodies; they're sleek, wonderfully dynamic feats of nature – and yet we tend to take them for granted.

The human body is incredibly intricate so I can't cover every aspect of it in this book. So this chapter briefly explores the fact that our bodies prefer to live an easy life in the middle lane. I also look at two important contributors to our health – inflammation and the microbiome.

Why We're So Incredible

How often do you take a moment to appreciate how many different processes are taking place in your body each time you take a breath? Or how many nerve endings are being stimulated when you have that thought? It's rare for most of us to take time to contemplate the delicate biological balance that keeps us alive or to recognise the impact of our choices on our bodies.

Essentially, we're programmed to survive and reproduce. Actions like making a decision, eating and drinking, having sex, looking after our offspring – they all take time and energy. If we had to think about breathing, making our heart beat, digesting food or warding off infections there just wouldn't be time to do anything else. So, these essential functions happen automatically.

Because we don't have to make a conscious effort to make our bodies work,

I believe we've developed a lack of appreciation and understanding about just how amazing they are. Our bodies have every right to feel unappreciated and taken for granted. Sometimes they protest and demand attention because even though they have enormously complex methods of maintaining a satisfactory equilibrium, when pushed too far they start to unravel.

The Middle Way

Human beings have evolved to operate within biologically stringent parameters that favour the 'middle way'. Achieving this involves a mind-blowingly large number of minute chemical reactions that happen at a cellular level every second. Scientists estimate there are 37.2 trillion cells in the human body, each of which has a specific function – and sometimes multiple functions. That's a lot of cells working hard every second of the day. No wonder we feel tired sometimes!

Each cell requires the right amount of energy, oxygen and co-factors to do their job. Energy and many of the chemical co-factors come from food. Other co-factors can be manufactured by the body itself, combining many bits of different nutrients that have already been broken down. That's why our bodies need a good supply of fuel to power all those metabolic processes.

Working as a nurse in intensive care, I soon realised quite how much the body needs to be kept within these tight metabolic boundaries. In fact, when you begin to realise what's involved, it's pretty amazing that we've survived this long. Nursing a critically ill patient is all about trying to keep that person's body working within specific parameters so they stay alive. And when it comes down to it, there's not much leeway.

The body can be likened to Baby Bear's porridge in the tale of Goldilocks and The Three Bears – everything has to be 'just right'. That applies to temperature, carbon dioxide levels, blood glucose levels, blood acidity, mineral and vitamin levels – everything, in fact. Some parameters are tighter than others, but all are important. The body functions as a whole, not as separate parts. If one process shifts outside the middle way, it affects the whole body.

For example, if the acid level of the blood increases (i.e. the pH drops), cells throughout the body cannot function properly as it's not the right environment for them to survive. The same is true of body temperature. If you've ever had a fever, you'll know how awful you feel when your body is too hot. That's because the body operates within a very tight temperature range and gets very unhappy if it rises too high or sinks too low.

By keeping us within the Baby Bear parameters, our amazing bodies utilise 'essential toxins' and use them as key activators for a wide range of processes. Carbon dioxide is the perfect example of this. The waste product of breathing, carbon dioxide (CO2), is toxic in our blood stream above a certain level. The mechanical process of breathing draws in fresh oxygen and expels harmful CO2. However, we need a certain amount of CO2 in our blood because if we don't have enough, we forget to breathe. Even though it's a toxin, it's CO2 that stimulates us to take the next breath, but it's a delicate balance between not too much and not too little.

Baby Bear body parameters

Too low	Just right	Too high
Work harder ←	Temperature	Work harder →
Shut down	Acidity	Get sicker
	Blood sugar	
	Electrolytes	
	Oxygen	

Glucose is another example of an essential toxin. A simple molecule, glucose is used for energy in cells, especially in the brain which is super-hungry and uses about 25 per cent of all our glucose intake. Low blood glucose levels can cause the body to go into emergency shut-down mode when back-up mechanisms don't kick in fast enough or levels are not rapidly restored. However, if large amounts are left circulating in the blood stream other problems start to develop. High blood glucose levels make the blood more acidic (not good) and starts to damage essential protein structures. Fortunately, in health, there are a myriad of metabolic processes in place to maintain glucose levels within the right parameters and ensure this essential toxin doesn't get out of hand.

All these complex processes have back-up processes, and the back-ups have their own back-ups because it's essential that these tight parameters are maintained in the face of changing or challenging circumstances. Every metabolic process requires different chemical combinations and enzymes using a selection of nutrients that come from the food we eat.

These processes are designed to work efficiently. The first way is the most efficient. Back-up processes require more energy and more micronutrients but create more waste, which means the body has to work harder. That's fine every now and then, but once this becomes the norm, it creates ongoing and persistent stress on our system. And stress is not good for us – or at least, not the chronic type.

Because our bodies are so good at what they do, it can take a while for a problem to become apparent. And once the problem becomes 'normal', it's hard to recognise when it's not normal. That can be anything from feeling tired and sluggish to ongoing pain or the gradual slide into a chronic health problem.

As I mentioned earlier, it's difficult to know how good you *can* feel if you've never felt it before. Even small changes to the way you eat, like making sure you get at least five portions of fresh veg a day, can make a huge difference. The benefits build up over time, so you might not notice them until you slip off the wagon and go back to your old ways of eating. It's only when the old 'normal' returns that you realise how good 'good' feels. That's the true lightbulb moment. When that happens, it's easy to see how good your new normal is. And how easy it is to feel good just by changing your diet.

It's not just me who's experienced this; time after time people who have been on my Eat Well, Live Well course report that when they slipped back to their old ways it made them feel awful and spurred them back to their new eating patterns. That's because once you start giving your body what it needs it doesn't want to go back to having to work hard again. Deep down, our cells just want an easy life!

But how can you tell what to eat to keep your inner Baby Bear happy? Looking at how the body is set up is a great place to start because it has evolved over thousands of years to become super-efficient and effective. And when it comes to food, the basic structure of the digestive system gives us the biggest clues.

Eating by Bodily Design

The digestive system is lengthy and complex. Hidden away from sight, it still holds many secrets that are only just starting to be uncovered.

Digestion is a process that requires some conscious effort from us – or at least at the beginning and end. We participate in the enjoyable activity of eating at the beginning and the less enjoyable yet equally essential removal of waste products at the other end. That's generally the total engagement required. Apart from a few rumbles, we tend not to give our digestive system much thought – or at least, not until things start to go wrong. Indigestion, bloating, cramping pains, flatulence or diarrhoea can all pop up from time to time. But for some it's a daily occurrence and that's a sign that all is not well.

As a self-confessed foodie, I love everything about food. I spend hours thinking about dishes I want to cook and exploring magazines and cookery books for inspiration. Preparing, cooking and then eating is all pleasurable for me – it's just a shame about the washing up!

Even thinking about flavour combinations, textures and colours makes my mouth start watering. That's the digestive process in action. It starts in the brain and is stimulated by thought, images, sounds and smells. The brain then sends messages to the mouth and stomach so they start secreting digestive enzymes long before the first forkful arrives. A rumbling stomach or watering mouth shows you're prepared for what's coming next. This is why eating as a mindful, engaged activity is an important part of the digestive process. Grabbing food on the go or rapidly wolfing down a meal will impede the whole process from the beginning.

Digestive system

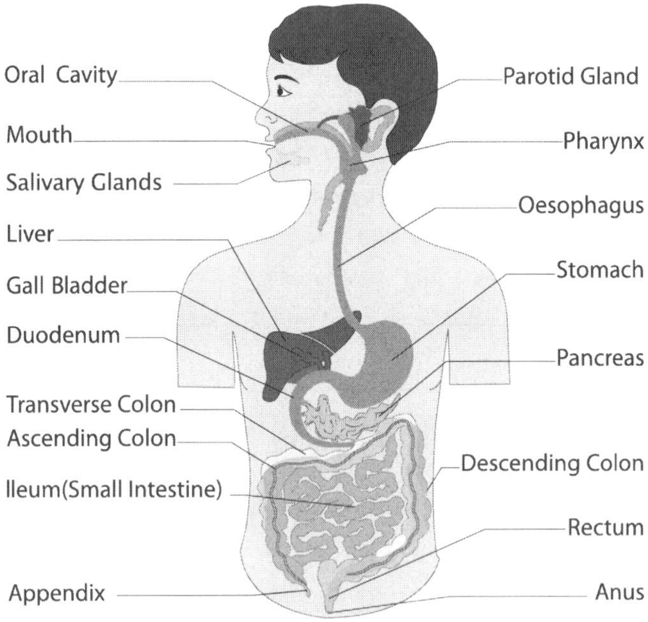

A view of the digestive system from top to bottom.

Digestive enzymes excreted in saliva in the mouth start to break down the main macronutrients – protein, fat and carbohydrate. These are released through chewing and grinding. Human's mouths are developed to do this efficiently with a range of different types of teeth and a jaw that moves from side to side as well as up and down. Animals designed to eat large amounts of meat have a more rigid jaw structure that's built for strength so they can tear into flesh, which is then gulped down rather than chewed. Our 'canine' teeth are not strong enough to do this and are better adapted for biting into softer textures, like fruit.

Moving on from the mouth, partially broken-down food products head south into the stomach, moved along in the oesophagus aided by gravity and a muscular process called peristalsis. A highly acidic fluid awaits the delivery of the latest meal in the stomach. A mixture that includes hydrochloric acid and bile, this fluid continues to break down your meal, particularly protein structures, and kills off pathogens like bacteria, viruses and fungi that may be lurking there. This green acidic stomach soup (chyme) is pretty foul and just one of the reasons why vomiting is so unpleasant. But as long as the pH level is right, it's very effective.

A low pH is needed in order to digest proteins. If the pH is raised (by taking antacid medication for example) these proteins may not be fully broken down, which can lead to partially digested proteins being released into the intestines. This is particularly significant later in the digestive process and is linked to both inflammation and poor gut health.

Once the chyme leaves the stomach it moves into the small intestine, which isn't small at all at seven metres in length. A huge amount of the digestive process goes on in here. Enzymes continue extracting nutrients in the upper section making them available for absorption into the bloodstream. Most of this is done in the ileum, the last section of the small intestine, which is lined with tiny finger-like projections called villi. These massively increase the surface area within the small intestine, so much so that if the small intestine was spread out it would cover a tennis court. That's quite impressive for something deemed 'small'.

Although the stomach contents are highly acidic, the pH changes quite radically when it enters the small intestine by reducing to a neutral pH. In the ileum, it changes back to a slightly acidic pH of 4.0-7.0. That's a good thing, as friendly bacteria flourish in a more acidic environment and happily carry out their cleaning and maintenance jobs, keeping the villi healthy and perky so

Villi

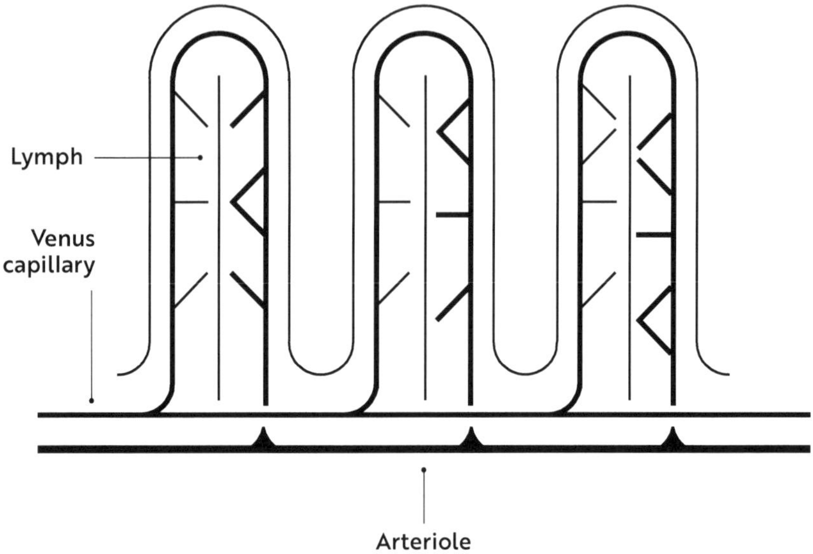

Tiny finger-like projections called villi line the gut wall.

they can absorb the right nutrients. (*See* The Magical Microbiome on page 49 for more details.)

Waves of peristalsis help to move the digestive contents along the long tract. Fibre from food also helps to keep things moving along. The speed of movement has its own Baby Bear parameters. Too fast (diarrhoea) and there's not enough time for absorption. Too slow (constipation) and the gut lining gets irritated by bad bacteria and toxic by-products of digestion. Interestingly, fibre can help minimise both diarrhoea and constipation, keeping things moving along at just the right speed. It's one of the reasons why eating fibre in good quantities is so important.

Fibre is only found in whole plant foods, which is a key indication as to why we're not designed to consume large amounts of animal products. Meat, dairy, eggs and fish contain no fibre and linger in the gut longer. This is not good as they also contain forms of bacteria that can irritate the gut lining and damage the villi. Guts that are designed to eat large amounts of animal flesh, like the intestines of dogs and cats, are short so that the toxic by-products and putrefactive bacteria found in meat are rapidly ejected from the body.

When most of the nutrients have been extracted from the food in the small intestine, the insoluble fibre, waste products and a lot of water pass into the large intestine. Ironically, this is much shorter than the small intestine at just five metres in length, but it's wider in diameter. The first part, the colon, is where the largest colony of gut bacteria lives. Up to 50 per cent of insoluble fibre is consumed and fermented here and the remaining nutrients and most of the water absorbed back into the body.

Finally, after your first active participation in the digestive process – around 18 to 24 hours previously – it's time for you to get involved again. Once the final remains of the meal enter the end part of the large intestine – the rectum – it's time to expel the leftovers.

This wonderful, complex process has evolved over thousands of years and has been shaped by the best food available to support our amazing bodies. Although my explanation is brief, I hope you can see how balance is key; mess around with the pH, consume the wrong amount of fibre or upset the balance of bacteria and things can go haywire. Ignoring our physiology by consuming a large amount of animal or highly-refined processed foods containing low levels of nutrients and fibre wreaks havoc within the gut.

By now, it's becoming clear that the gut is critical to our health and that our food choices have a direct impact on it, and on the magical microbiome. The food we eat can either create or reduce inflammation, both locally in the intestines and throughout the body. This is why each one of us has the power to directly influence how we feel by choosing what we eat, so let's explore this in a little more detail.

Inflammatory Issues

Inflammation is the body's inner guard dog. It's a complex system of protection that turns on and off again in order to achieve the overall goal of keeping us well and promoting survival. The immune response is easy to see in action when you cut your hand or have a cold. There's heat, swelling and gunk, all essential parts of the process. Then once healing is complete, all of these go away and the affected area goes back to normal. Healing involves many different types of cells, messengers and chemicals and occurs throughout the body. When we're in good health, it's super-efficient, but there's a lot that can go wrong

External factors like invading bacteria will trigger an inflammatory response as well as internal irritation to specific molecules or even by-products of our own metabolism and cell activity. It appears that the gut lining is particularly vulnerable to inflammation, which can lead to pesky partially digested proteins leaking through into the blood stream. Food intolerances, allergies, skin conditions, chronic fatigue, autoimmune disease and inflammatory bowel disease can all be directly linked to an inflamed, leaky gut.

This is a very simple explanation of an incredibly complex process. In an ideal world, it all works perfectly – but of course, we don't live in an ideal world. We have to make many choices every day based on the situations we find ourselves in and that's when silent inflammation contrives to make this protective process problematic for us.

Silent inflammation

Thought to play a role in the development of every chronic degenerative health condition, silent inflammation is the constant low-grade stimulation of the inflammatory process that never settles down. There may not be any outward sign of it, but researchers have found that it's connected to a wide range of health problems, including heart disease, allergies, type 2 diabetes, autoimmune disease, cancer and Alzheimer's disease.

Inflammation can be identified with blood tests. The most common, and therefore cheapest, is to look for an inflammatory 'marker' CRP (C-reactive protein). This spikes rapidly following acute injury or as a result of infection but then goes back down to its base level.

Some doctors argue that CRP is unreliable and only shows acute inflammation. But the real issue is that the test is not sensitive to lower levels and that some people's base level is consistently higher than it should be. Even a continual, tiny increase can have a deleterious effect – this is silent inflammation – which sits there in the shadows, unnoticed.

The other issue about CRP and other commonly used inflammatory markers is that it doesn't tell you what the problem actually is, just that it's there.

Despite this difficulty, a number of different factors have been identified as contributing towards silent inflammation.

These include:

- Insulin resistance and obesity.
- Stress – both emotional and physical.
- Environmental toxins (air pollution, pesticides etc.).
- A lack of anti-oxidants from food.
- Increased exposure to free radicals, particularly through smoking.

- Chronic infection.
- An imbalance in dietary fats.
- An increase in gut permeability.

It's interesting that many of these are connected to the food we eat every day. There are also connections between silent inflammation and the speed of the ageing process, which is why many health problems develop in our later years as our system gets damaged and is less able to cope. Again, there are incredibly complex processes involved in this, many of which have been integral to recent research breakthroughs. It seems that silent inflammation is causing damage at the core of our being; our cell DNA. To understand this, let's delve deeper and explore the fascinating roles of anti-oxidants, free radicals and telomeres.

Anti-oxidants and free radicals

Free radicals and anti-oxidants are just two of the many buzz-words to pop up regularly in media reports and product promotions. But what exactly are they? And do they deserve the hype?

To answer this, let's take a moment to think small – infinitesimally small. If we consider our bodies, activities and surroundings at a purely chemical level, everything is a collection of atoms and molecules held together in specific chains. Tiny chemical processes happen at every moment. Atoms have an electrical charge and like to travel around in pairs. If separated during a chemical process however, they become unstable and pesky, rushing off to find something else to pair with. These are free radicals. Desperate to find a new friend, they will hook up anywhere, including gaps where they shouldn't be. This creates the wrong molecular structure and this in turn is what causes oxidative damage.

Free radicals are released normally after every molecular process. The body is a huge seething mass of these with numerous processes going on all the time within each cell. If we put our body under pressure with work-related stress, toxic chemicals like cigarette smoke, a poor diet or lack of sleep, it has to work even harder to stay within the Baby Bear parameters. More free radicals are created, ready to wreak havoc, putting the body under even more stress.

To get things under control, the inflammatory response is triggered. But this involves even more processes that produce even more free radicals, and so the cycle continues. Over time, the metabolism heats up, the body starts to

Valiant antioxidants stabilise pesky free radicals.

struggle and health starts to deteriorate. Certain molecules are targeted more than others, like the fats found in cell membranes, protein structures or our DNA.

Fortunately, a group of hero molecules anti-oxidants, come to the rescue to keep these pesky free radicals under control. These molecules are so stable they're able to neutralise rampaging free radicals. Often described as free radical scavengers, I imagine them to be like Pac Man with a cape, scooping up manic molecules as they whizz around the body. Anti-oxidants can also prevent free radicals from being formed in the first place and can repair and even remove altered molecules.

While our bodies can produce some of their own anti-oxidants, most are introduced via the food we eat. Humans evolved eating a wide range of fresh foods that contain a variety of anti-oxidants, so the body out-sourced the role. Found in fresh fruit and vegetables, many anti-oxidants are familiar, like vitamins C, E and beta-carotene (the plant precursor to vitamin A). Tiny phytonutrients also act as powerful anti-oxidants (more about these in Chapter 3).

Unfortunately, anti-oxidants are delicate. They start to deteriorate once fresh produce is harvested; cooking, processing and refining all increase the rate of this decline. Highly refined processed foods are practically devoid of natural anti-oxidants. This is why the five-a-day message is so important; unfortunately, it appears to be fairly ineffective as only 25 per cent of UK adults reach this low target.

To visualise the whole free radical/anti-oxidant process, think about how an apple starts to brown once it's been cut open. Exposure to oxygen in the air causes an explosion of molecular reactions, changing its appearance. The anti-oxidants in lemon juice stop this process by mopping up the free-radicals and stabilising the molecular surface.

Dealing with free radicals should be simple: free radicals are produced, our body deals with them using the anti-oxidants in our diet, and balance is maintained. But it's not simple at all, especially in our modern era. The sheer volume of free radicals around us means the body is under constant attack while at the same time, the level of natural anti-oxidants we're consuming in our highly processed Western diet has plummeted.

Many chemically synthesised food preservatives have anti-oxidant properties that can actually contribute towards silent inflammation rather than suppress it. Synthetic anti-oxidants can be made from dubious substances, even 'natural' ones like ascorbic acid (synthetic vitamin C). Made from a series of chemical reactions using fermented corn, ascorbic acid is far from natural and can be a source of added irritation for anyone with a yeast imbalance. These substances are benign compared to others, like synthesised vitamin E (tocopherols), which are derived from petroleum or rubber.

The reason why anti-oxidants have become so marketable is because, as well as reducing inflammation and fighting disease, they help to slow the ageing process. But how, exactly? The answer appears to be through tiny guard-dog DNA strands called telomeres.

Telomeres

Every precious cell in our body has an important function but the genetic coding found in cell DNA is even more precious. Without it the cell cannot renew itself and continue working. Held together in chromosomes, our unique coding is protected by telomeres, little bundles of DNA segments found at the end of each chromosome.

Discovered by Dr Elizabeth Blackburn and her colleagues, telomeres appear to be key to ageing and help answer the question about why some people seem to age better or worse than others. Telomeres can be compared to the little plastic ends of shoe-laces – once these are broken and lost, the shoelace is almost impossible to rethread, the lace unravels and becomes useless. This is what happens to our telomeres – once they become too short or get worn away completely, the cell can no longer divide and do its job,

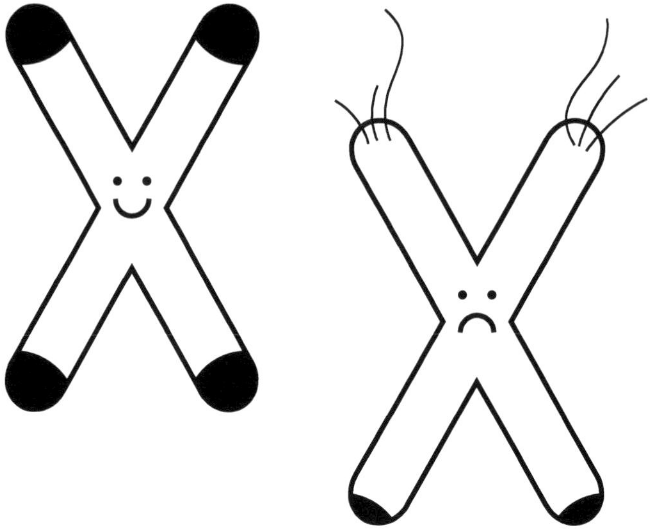

Telomeres protect chromosomes but can get worn away.

becoming defunct. Once damaged, the cell starts to leak inflammatory substances into the surrounding area before it eventually dies.

There are a multitude of complex factors that shorten telomeres including genetic make-up, lifestyle, diet, social and physical environment and emotions – all the things linked to free radicals, oxidative stress and silent inflammation.

Telomeres naturally start to wear down every time the cell divides. As we get older, the body slows down and eventually dies. It's the quality and speed of ageing that impacts health. If telomeres are rapidly worn away, health problems can occur. We may be alive, but in poor health. No-one wants to live for a long time in an incapacitated state, that just leads to a poor quality of life. But unfortunately, that's increasingly becoming the reality for many people.

The good news is that it's possible to protect telomeres from being attacked by free radicals. It's even possible to lengthen them, even if they've suffered a bit of a bashing. A whole-food plant-based diet is packed full of anti-oxidants and phytonutrients that mop up free radicals and minimise the damage they do all over the body. That's one of the reasons why eating this way has so many positive side effects. Even though you may start out changing your diet to deal with a health issue, you'll probably find that your hair becomes thick and glossy and your skin becomes clear and glowing too

– I call these 'beneficial side-effects'.

Reducing inflammation, minimising free radicals and looking after telomeres enables each one us to directly influence the quality of our health. Eating fresh, health-giving food, giving up smoking, getting regular exercise and controlling anxiety using mindfulness all contribute to this. Empowering yourself to feel better is a great way to start the healing process and wave goodbye to silent inflammation.

Imbalance in dietary fats

There's one other important issue that's worth looking at here and that's the balance of essential fatty acids: omegas 3 and 6. The body formulates many fatty acid chains itself but not all, so some need to be obtained from food, hence the reason they're called 'essential'. The ratio of these two fats is important when it comes to health, especially in relation to inflammation.

The inflammatory process is varied and complex. It needs to know when to respond and when to calm down. On a very simplistic level, omega 6 is involved in switching the inflammatory process on and omega 3 helps to switch it off. This is very important because without an on-switch the body wouldn't know when to respond to danger and equally without an off-switch the body wouldn't know when the danger had been contained, allowing it to return to its resting state.

We evolved consuming a fairly equal balance of omegas 3 and 6, generally on a 1:1 ratio.

- Omega 3 fatty acids are volatile oils found mainly in nuts, seeds and fish but also some vegetables and grains.
- Omega 6 oils are also found in nuts, seeds and fish, but also all animal products as well as crops like corn and soy.

Due to their volatility, products high in omega 3 oils deteriorate rapidly once processed. This is a problem for the food industry as longevity is required so cheaper products have a longer shelf life. This is why much of the omega 3 is removed or lost during the mass-production of food, leaving many foods higher in omega 6 than omega 3. On top of that, refined oils like vegetable or sunflower oil contain much higher levels of omega 6 oils than they would normally have in their natural state. And, of course, animal products are mainly omega 6, although some fish have a better 3:6 profile.

Omegas 3 and 6

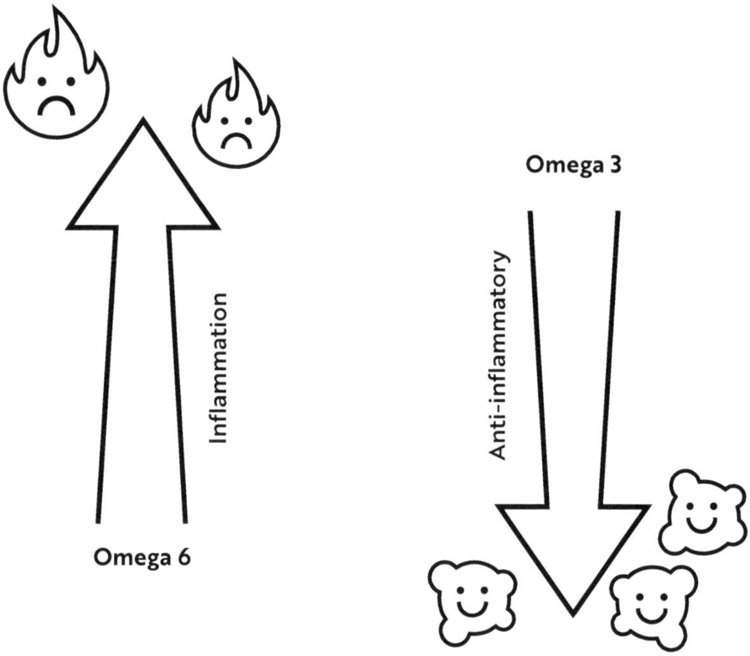

Omega 6 and 3 help switch inflammation on and off.

Eating a diet low in whole-plant foods but high in animal products and refined products results in a huge discrepancy in the omega 3:6 ratio, moving it from the balanced 1:1 ratio that we evolved eating to an average of 1:15 to 1:20 over the last 50 years.

This high level of omega 6 fatty acids promotes an inflammatory state. However, by reducing omega 6 dominant foods and increasing the amount of omega 3 fatty acids we eat we can help reduce inflammation. Consuming more omega 3 fatty acids helps to switch on our natural anti-inflammatory responses, particularly in the brain. This is why these fats have been associated with improving a whole range of health problems, including allergies, auto-immune conditions, heart disease, mental health problems and even conditions such as ADHD and dementia.

Next, let's explore my other favourite topic – the microbiome – and see how it's also inextricably linked with inflammation.

The Magical Microbiome

It's strange to realise we may be more bacteria than human. If that thought makes you want to grab the nearest anti-bacterial wipe, then think again. As more is discovered about the bacteria that live in our gut, the clearer it becomes that bacteria are an essential part of living a healthy life.

As you now know, the number one function of the gut is the digestion, absorption and expulsion of food. But it does many more amazing things as well. Listed below are just a few of them.

- The gut acts as a huge protective barrier again sickness, disease and environmental toxins. In the same way that the skin acts as a layer of protection on the outside of us, the digestive tract acts as a similar guardian on the inside. As the skin can be seen, we know when it's been damaged. If you have a cut, it gets covered to protect it from infection. A rash or area of irritation is treated with a soothing cream. Being on the inside, the gut can't easily be seen, so it's hard to know when it's damaged or inflamed and even harder to help it heal.
- The gut and microbiome work together to support the immune system. For example, the lymphatic system is involved in producing white blood cells that fight infections, viruses and other toxins. Areas of lymph tissue, called Peyer's patches, are found in the small intestine. They secrete pathogen-fighting cells and are a key part of our defence system. When a young child is feeling unwell, they generally say they have stomach ache even if it's not a stomach problem; that's Peyer's patches hard at work, activating an immune response.
- The microbiome influences the brain. A whopping 90 per cent of serotonin, the main chemical neurotransmitter associated with mood and depression, is produced in the gut. In fact, there is a whole nervous system that connects the brain and the gut called the enteric nervous system. It's fascinating stuff. Check out *The Second Brain* by Michael D Gershon if you want to know more.
- The microbiome produces hormones. Some are directly involved in digestion, but surprisingly hormones like oestrogen and progesterone are also secreted here.

Protective activity of bacteria on the gut lining

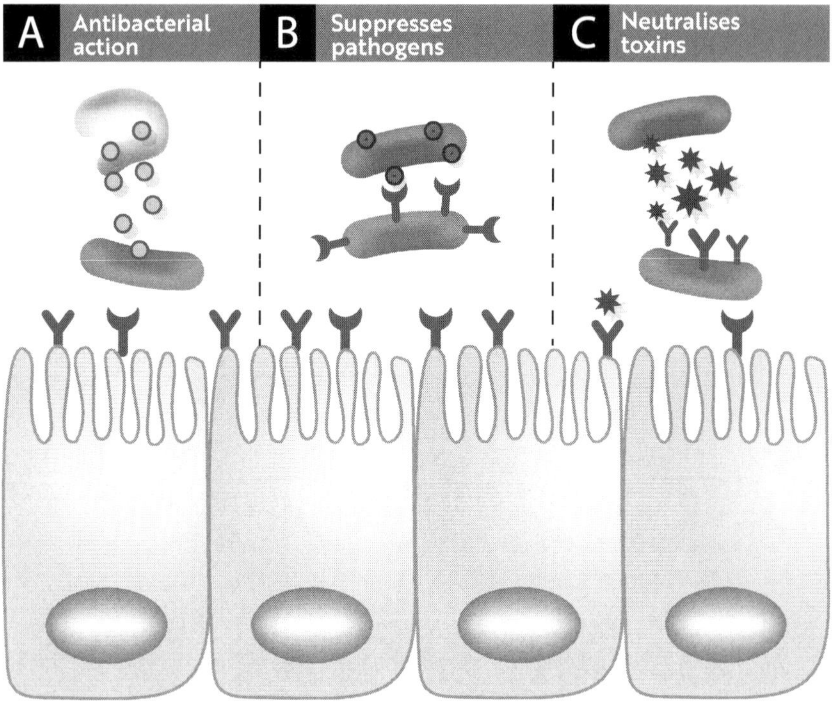

How bacteria are involved in protecting the gut wall.

There are more too. In fact, gut bacteria are an integral contributor to our well-being. Poor gut health is now thought to be a significant factor in many chronic health problems, including obesity, diabetes, heart disease, allergies and autoimmune conditions – the list goes on. A happy gut is key to health. But what exactly is the microbiome and what has happened to upset it?

We are not alone!

Essentially, the microbiome is an internal ecosystem that's populated by billions and billions of bacteria that are found within the digestive tract. It's a symbiotic relationship that has evolved over thousands of years. It appears that bacteria are a key part of the human health team. We need each other to survive. This relationship is so intricately developed that we have even out-sourced some functions to them. That increases the body's capacity for performing other functions, but means if the healthy bacteria are lost, so are the essential functions they carry out, which has an impact on health. This is a particular concern with regards to the current obesity epidemic and questions are now being asked as to whether poor gut health is to blame. Other parts of the body have an ecosystem too, including the skin and armpits. But the largest is the microbiome, hidden away in the dark recesses of the gut.

The microbiome is populated by a variety of bacteria, viruses, fungi and yeasts. Some are friendly and contribute to keeping us healthy, others are unfriendly (or putrefactive) and do not. An overgrowth of unfriendly ones can lead to inflammation and a whole host of health problems. Whilst bacteria can be found throughout the gut, they are focused in two main areas – the ileum and the colon – and each has a specific role.

As I mentioned earlier, the ileum is lined with tiny finger-like projections called villi. These villi have a thin, fragile cell membrane so that tiny nutrients can pass through into the blood stream. Friendly bacteria are involved in caring for the villi, keeping them clean and protecting them. One of the problems with these helpful bacteria is that they're easily wiped out (by antibiotics, for example) or overwhelmed by bad bacteria. Once they're wiped out, it can be hard to re-establish them. We'll look at this in more detail below.

The colon, found in the first part of the large intestine, hosts the majority of the microbiome. As well as absorbing water and any remaining nutrients, this is the area where the friendly bacteria carry out their outsourced functions. Feeding on insoluble fibre that cannot be broken down elsewhere in the gut, these bacteria produce hormones, self-made antibiotics and special short-chain fatty acids (SCFA), all of which play essential roles in the body.

While both friendly and unfriendly bacteria live within the gut, as we've seen elsewhere in the body, it's all about getting the right balance, but this is proving difficult in the modern world.

Gut health history

Gut health starts when we're born. Before that, a baby's gut is sterile. As a baby's nutrition is obtained via the mother's umbilical cord there is nothing passing through the gut.

Our microbiome is born when we are – literally on the way out. Once a mother's waters have broken, the baby is no longer held within a sterile environment. Being born through the birth canal immediately exposes it to a variety of bacteria. We tend to see exposing babies to bacteria as a bad thing, but these are specifically designed to start colonising this brand-new microbiome. Once the baby is out in the wide world and starts to breast feed, other microbes found on the mother's breast and in her milk also provide a good start for the baby's gut.

Of course, it's not as simple as that! Natural childbirth at home is generally a thing of the past; medical interventions save lives but also interfere with this long-evolved gut colonising process. Increasingly, babies are born via caesarean section which means they by-pass the birth canal, missing out on this initial seeding opportunity. And although breastfeeding is positively promoted now, it wasn't that way for a long time, so many babies missed out on getting their guts off to a good start; many still do.

This puts them at a disadvantage right from the start, and health issues can start early on because of this. This is one of the reasons why allergies and intolerances have consistently risen in children. For example, up to 85 per cent of children are affected by eczema by the age of five, (according to Allergy UK). That's a huge and disturbing number.

I wish I'd known all this when I had my children; one was born by emergency Caesarean, the other naturally. Both were premature, cocooned in a sterile environment early on, so breastfeeding was just too difficult. Both had asthma and eczema as children and both have dairy intolerances. But knowledge is power and it's never too late to improve the situation by eating healing food.

Apart from what happens when we're born, gut health is also affected by a number of other factors, including medications like antibiotics, chronic stress, environmental toxins and of course the food we eat.

Let's have a look again at the digestive process and how that affects gut health both positively and negatively.

Gut health or gut harm?

When it comes to gut health, what we eat is critical. We have seen that digestion is a long and complex process that relies on:

- A good amount of fibre.
- The right pH.
- A happy balance of bacteria.

It doesn't take much to muck it up though, and we seem to have become very skilled at doing that. Let's have a quick look at each of these contributors to gut health in more detail.

Fibre

Fibre is essential for encouraging the elimination of waste products from the body and feeding the friendly bacteria beavering away deep inside. Only found in whole plant foods, there are two types – soluble and insoluble (more about this in Chapter 4). Different plants have different types of fibre, so variety is important as is the amount consumed. It sounds simple – eat some food, feed the bacteria, all is well.

The problem is that fibre is lost once a food has been refined. Flour is a great example. Most cakes, bread or pasta are made with white flour rather than wholegrain. Look again at the diagram on page 29. White flour is the starchy centre of a wheat grain. The fibre is found in the outer bran, the essential nutrients in the oily wheatgerm end. Wholewheat flour is harder to process and cannot be stored as long as white flour because the essential oils go rancid and spoil the product. White flour provides bulk energy but minimal nutrients and fibre.

The same goes for all refined products – most of the essential nutrients and all their wonderful benefits are lost as a result of processing. Not only that, but refined food that has had all its fibre removed still contains all the sugar, which is now in a simple and easily released form. This sugar gets absorbed into the bloodstream much more rapidly so the body has to work much harder to deal with this sudden influx.

Only plant-based foods contain fibre. A diet that's high in meat, eggs, dairy or fish and low in complex whole foods creates a lot of waste products. That results in a lot of bad bacteria hanging around in the gut because there's little to keep it moving. When waste products linger, the gut lining becomes irritated, creating inflammation. Beneficial bacteria soon become overwhelmed by the hardier and more aggressive putrefactive ones. Sluggish bowel movements or constipation from lack of fibre is not conducive for a healthy gut. The current popular low carb diets seem to conveniently forget about the natural long and circuitous structure of the gut, the need for large amounts of fibre and the delicate balance of the microbiome.

pH

As you're aware by now, if friendly bacteria are to proliferate, the environment has to be just right for them. The stomach contents are highly acidic in order to ensure proteins can be broken down and pathogens destroyed. Anything that affects the acidity in the stomach and the first part of the small intestine has a knock-on effect elsewhere in the gut, especially when it comes to protein.

Many drugs affect gut acidity. Antacids for example are taken to lower acidity and ease the pain of indigestion and heartburn. Proton-pump inhibitors (PPIs), prescribed to counteract the potential side effects of blood thinners (like aspirin) or non-steroidal anti-inflammatory painkillers, alter the production levels of stomach acid. Many people take these for years, even though they were designed for short-term use. Some people naturally suffer from low stomach acid – hypochlorhydria – which can lead to digestive problems, and others have had surgery that directly affects the stomach's actions. So, as you can see, there are many interventions that can affect gut pH, which creates a perpetual circle of dysfunction.

Digestive enzymes work more effectively in the right environment; the wrong pH means they cannot work as well. Changing the pH can enable bad bacteria to proliferate in the wrong part of the intestines, creating pain and dyspepsia (indigestion or heart burn) and the 'need' for more drugs.

When there's reduced acidity in the stomach, proteins may only be partially digested, which as we know, can impact the entire gut. If the gut lining is already irritated and 'leaky' (see below) this causes even more of a problem because a leaky gut lining allows larger, partially-digested proteins to sneak through into the blood stream, triggering a systemic inflammatory response. As the friendly bacteria in the microbiome proliferate in a slightly acidic environment, if the pH is even slightly raised, they'll fail to thrive.

Balance

Every environment in the gut needs variety to stay healthy. Too much of any one thing can become unhealthy, even the good stuff!

Bacteria is introduced into the gut via the food we eat; stomach acid should kill off the dangerous, infectious ones, leaving a whole range of beneficial and not so beneficial bacteria to proliferate. The problem is that the bad bacteria are sturdier than the good ones and can easily become dominant if they're given the opportunity. A course of oral antibiotics generally wipes out most of the bacteria in the gut, both good and bad. But as the bad are hardier, some will survive. So, unless a new source of friendly bacteria is introduced either in fermented foods or probiotic supplements, the bad bacteria will multiply and dominate.

Our obsession with cleanliness also impacts gut bacteria. With cleaned produce, anti-bacterial washes and high cooking heats, good bacteria are obliterated before they've had a chance to do their work. For both children and adults, playing outside and getting a bit dirty is good for the gut. But a lot of people, especially children, spend a huge amount of time indoors, playing on computer games or watching TV. And that's a problem.

Eating a range of different foods is also essential to maintaining the balance of good and bad bacteria in the gut. Meat and other animal products contain more bad bacteria. Raw milk contains friendly bacteria, but this is killed off when pasteurised. On the other hand, plant foods provide different sources of bacteria and pre-biotics as well as an abundance of fibre, which friendly bacteria love to eat. This helps promote a more positive balance in the gut.

Another key contributor to balance in the gut is variety. Too much of the same type of food means that there will only be a limited range of bacteria available for the gut to use. Scientists have discovered that our ancestors ate up to 130 different types of food. This created a hugely diverse colony of bacteria living in the microbiome, all carrying out a different role. Shockingly, a refined Western diet has only four main food sources: meat, dairy, wheat and soya. And when you look at what many people survive on – cereals and milk for breakfast, ham sandwich for lunch, pizza for dinner – it's easy to see that diversity doesn't get a look in.

The highly refined, low-fibre and chemical-laden Western diet creates the most hostile environment for the microbiome you could imagine. The nutrition industry that focuses on the large macronutrients has overlooked the importance of the microbiome and the result is a general decline in the health of the population.

The Microbiome and Our Health

So just how does an unhealthy gut environment impact the rest of the body? This is a huge question. Lots of research is being undertaken right now and we're only just beginning to understand the connection between the microbiome and our health. But a few of the ways a poor microbiome affects our health include:

- Impaired digestion, which means micronutrients are not fully available in the first place.
- The gut lining is irritated or coated with gunk. This means the ability of the gut to absorb nutrients into the bloodstream is impaired, which in turn results in metabolic processes being impaired.
- The lack of certain types of fibre means that bacteria are under-nourished and as a result don't have the right raw materials to perform their roles.
- Bacteria that undertake a specific role such as producing a hormone or SCFA are not able to survive, which is connected to problems like obesity and depression because there is no back-up process available to fill the gap.

A healthy microbiome with a good balance of bacteria takes care of the gut lining, keeping it clean, well-nourished and in top condition so it can function well. This is particularly important in the ileum with its lining of villi. There are gaps around each villi so that it can maximise its absorption area and the membrane wall is ultra-thin to ensure nutrients can be easily absorbed. Friendly bacteria keep these gaps between the villi clean and protect this essential membrane.

The problem with friendly bacteria is that they're a bit lightweight and can be easily overwhelmed by bad bacteria like yeast or fungi. When that happens, the gut lining becomes irritated and inflamed and the villi may start to wilt, leading to a reduction in the absorption area. On top of that, the irritation kicks off the inflammatory response.

There are a multitude of events in this incredibly complex response. One is to send out white blood cells to locate, identify and start dealing with the inflammation. The lining of the gut has blood vessels that has tiny holes dotted along it so that safe, small compounds can pass through as needed. However, white blood cells are bigger so part of the inflammatory response is to make the holes bigger too, so the emergency help can squeeze through.

This results in a leaky gut. When the holes in the membrane enlarge to allow the white blood cells through, many larger molecules can sneak through the bigger holes too. This includes those partially digested proteins mentioned earlier. And because they're foreign to the internal world of the body, they create another immune reaction, and so the cycle continues.

Leaky Gut

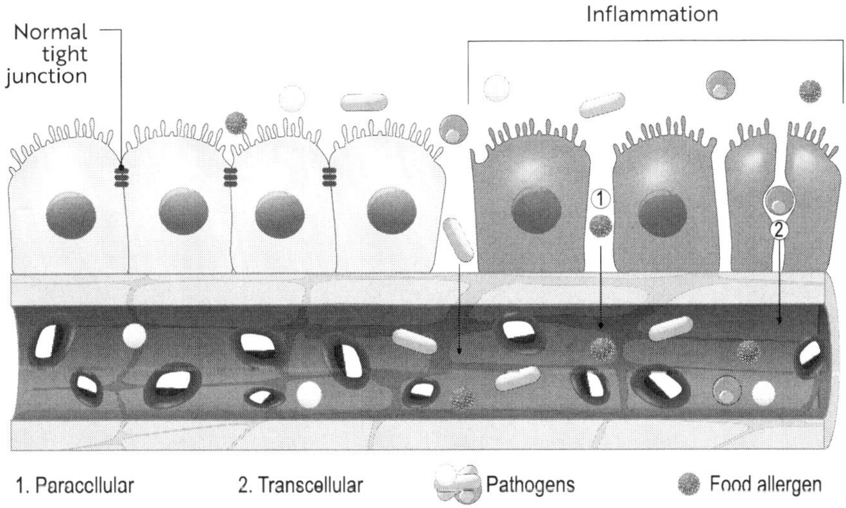

Healthy gut wall in comparison with an inflamed and leaky gut wall.

Gut Healing Plan

If you want to heal your gut, you can take a number of simple actions to help your microbiome get back to full health and maximum functionality. Here's a summary of what you can do:

- Eat a diet that's high in whole foods and fibre, and low in refined sugars and oils in order to minimise the source of bad bacteria – i.e. eat a whole-food, plant-based diet!
- Repopulate the gut with friendly bacteria by taking a course of pro and/or pre-biotics and eating lots of different types of fruit, vegetables, grains and legumes.
- Include some fermented foods in your diet as they contain natural forms of good bacteria.
- Minimise your intake of chemicals by eating organically grown food and minimising the amount of processed food and food-like products, which have lots of added chemicals.
- If possible, minimise the number of damaging medications you take, such as antacids and pain killers (although *never* stop taking a prescribed medication without consulting your doctor first).

- Reduce your stress levels. The stress response diverts blood away from the gut because it's needed elsewhere. Without a good blood supply, the villi will struggle, the gut will have to work harder to function efficiently and less nutrients will be absorbed.

As your gut heals and the microbiome re-establishes itself, your entire body will benefit. Now, that's magical!

It's clear to see how easily the body can get stuck in a perpetual circle of decline. Unfriendly bacteria, yeasts and fungi continue to proliferate, they wipe out the beneficial bacteria and this leads to the gut lining becoming more and more inflamed – and more and more leaky. This means essential functions and nutrients are lost which continually triggers the immune response, leading to a demand for even more nutrients. But as they can't be absorbed properly, they become increasingly scarce.

It's not all doom and gloom, though. The microbiome can recover and become re-established. It may take a while, but once the friendly bacteria get back to work the gut can heal. This means nutrients are more readily absorbed and the outsourced functions start working again. The microbiome is also able to adapt to its environment, so unlike the rest of the body, it can evolve much more rapidly and cope with change more easily.

When I discovered my food intolerances, I realised that yeast was a big problem for me and that I was stuck in a negative cycle. Every time I had a glass of wine or a sugary snack, I fed the yeasts in my body and encouraged their proliferation. It's taken some time to make the right changes, but by doing so, my microbiome is well on the way to recovery.

CHAPTER THREE

EVERYTHING IS CONNECTED!

After a life-time of eating a food that just didn't suit me, it was obvious that it would take time to get back to normal – or rather, discover my new normal. Eliminating dairy and yeast products made a huge difference. But at that time, I knew little about a plant-based lifestyle and the power of plants, so I reluctantly returned to eating meat again, as it seemed the simplest and least processed food to add back into my diet.

It was great to make changes to my diet, but deep down I wanted to be well too. Little did I know that I would have to travel 5000 miles and live on another continent to find the answers I'd been looking for. I learnt so much during our time in India and much of it forms the basis of this book and my courses and workshops. The key message I came to understand was that everything is connected.

What I Discovered on My Indian Adventures

The relocation of our family to Bangalore, India was life-changing for all of us in many ways. The children learnt, at a formative age, how to be global citizens and all of our eyes and minds were opened to many different possibilities and experiences. I expected a lot to happen while we were there but finding my true purpose was an unexpected added bonus.

When we left the UK, I had been eating a dairy- and yeast-free diet for 14 months. I was still coming to terms with living without cheese, bread and wine. Fortunately, when I got to India, these were either not readily available or were pretty unpalatable so I soon realised I wasn't missing out. What also helped was that we discovered the delights of South Indian food, much of which was vegetarian. It was simple, delicious food.

Having time on my hands enabled me to attend different types of cooking classes and seminars. I was experimenting with dairy-free recipes and was delighted to go along to a workshop about dairy-free eating. This is where I met Dr Nandita Shah. The workshop turned out to be about so much more than a dairy-free diet; it was my first introduction to plant-based eating.

Nowadays, there's a lot of information on the internet about the problems caused by dairy in relation to health, the environment and animal welfare. Much has changed since I attended that workshop, but back then, it was all new to me. Up until this point, my focus had been on my food intolerance. Having been bought up believing that dairy products are natural and necessary for human health, I was suddenly exposed to new information that told me otherwise. And it blew my mind!

Looking back, it seems obvious that animal milk is not designed for human consumption – at least, certainly not in the amount and ways it's used in the modern Western diet. That's not to say it's nutritionally bereft. After all, a mother's milk is designed to provide optimum nutrition for her baby. So, milk contains lots of protein, fat, sugar (in the form of lactose), vitamins, calcium and iron. The main role of protein is growth and repair, so milk is the perfect source for babies at a time when they're growing and developing at the fastest rate in their whole life. However, cow's milk has three times the amount of protein and twice the amount of fat as human breast milk. That's because calves grow rapidly, doubling their weight in just 47 days, reaching a whopping 540kg in weight when they're just two years old.

Despite what we're led to believe, we simply don't need that level of protein at any time in our life. There are swathes of research projects that connect dairy to a range of inflammatory-stimulated and chronic health problems, including heart disease, cancer, autoimmune disease and allergies, to name just a few. (There's much more about protein and the other two macronutrients, fat and carbohydrate at www.thesensitivefoodie.com/book-links.)

As well as the excessive nutrition, milk introduces other unwelcome elements too. As it's a bodily fluid, milk retains many of the chemicals circulating inside the animal that produced it. Cow's milk contains female hormones (natural and synthetic), plus residues of pesticides or herbicides from cattle feed and antibiotics. Milk also contains pus (as many cows suffer from mastitis) as well as viruses and other bacteria. Many of these are destroyed through pasteurisation, but not all.

But pasteurisation creates problems too. The high heat causes protein molecules to clog together, making them difficult to break down and absorb in the gut. It also kills off the beneficial bacteria that is naturally found in all breast milk, as well as some of the vitamins and helpful antibodies.

After hearing all this, I was really glad I'd stopped eating dairy! But how has it become so embedded in our way of living? Looking back, at some point our ancestors would have had a much closer relationship with animals than we do now. A shortage of food and a seemingly natural supply of it from another animal would have made perfect sense; it would have been essential for survival. The cows would have grazed on clean grass with no chemicals, their young at their side, content and living in a mutually beneficial relationship with humans. That's the image we're still sold today, but the reality of intensive dairy farming is far from this ideal. This is not the place to go into more detail, but if you want to know more see the Chapter 3 resources in the reference section on page 302.

One other issue about dairy is the lack of fibre; remember how essential fibre is for gut health? Dairy is fibre-free and has lost its beneficial bacteria unless consumed raw. A large percentage of the world's population are intolerant to it, particularly the milk sugar, lactose, and yet it remains a dominant food source throughout the world.

Listening to Dr Shah and seeing how she created amazingly tasty dishes using only plant-based products was fascinating. On top of that, I was mesmerised by her as a person – she just oozed health. Her skin and eyes shone brightly and she was brimming with energy and passion. I realised how much I didn't know and quickly signed up for more of her workshops.

In her 'Peas vs Pills' workshop, Dr Shah introduced me to the amazing healing properties of food. This affirmed the power of plants and I began to understand the connection between food and health, including the detrimental effect that a highly refined, high animal protein diet has on the human body. But I also began to see how simple it would be to reverse that damage by eating a whole-food, plant-based diet.

Everything she taught was backed up by research. She introduced me to the amazing work of Dr Esselstyn and Dr Ornish, pioneers of 'lifestyle medicine'. They helped patients with advanced heart disease to not only survive but to reverse their conditions. These were patients who were too sick for mainstream medical procedures. By using a purely whole-food, plant-based diet containing no oil and adding stress-reduction activities like meditation and exercise, these patients became well again.

Dr Shah also introduced me to the work of other researchers and writers. The first was Dr Campbell, who is the author of The China Study, a result of research undertaken 50 years ago which connected diets high in animal protein with cancer. Another was Dr Neal Barnard of The Physicians Council for Responsible Medicine. He uses a whole-food, plant-based diet to reverse diabetes and other chronic health conditions. What inspired me even more was that these doctors practised what they preached and used the power of plants to keep themselves healthy as well as their patients.

There is an ever-increasing number of medical practitioners who now advocate the benefits of whole foods for health. In fact, junior doctors are demanding training in nutrition and lifestyle medicine as they too see the beneficial impact of this amazing way of eating. But we're a long way from using food as medicine.

Hearing all this amazing information armed me with the facts I needed to connect the dots around my own health challenges and I decided this was the way forward for me. This was the day that my, and my family's, way of eating changed profoundly.

What Exactly is a Whole-food, Plant-based Diet?

When someone discovers I eat a plant-based diet, the response is 'oh you're a vegan' so they're rather surprised when I say I'm not. A whole-food, plant-based diet contains whole plant products. That's unrefined and unprocessed food, which means no food-like products, ready meals or fast food. It's all focused on the quality of the food.

Veganism is a movement, mainly focused on animal welfare and the morality of eating sentient beings. This is something I support, but a vegan diet isn't necessarily a healthy one. There's a huge amount of fake and junk food that's also labelled as vegan. In the last year alone, there's been a 61 per cent increase in vegan products, most of which are highly refined or fake foods. I've come across some astoundingly unhealthy vegans who never consume a fresh vegetable!

A whole-food, plant-based diet is just as it sounds – plant foods that are whole and unrefined. So, what does that mean?

- Fresh produce not fake – I'd eat a strawberry rather than something strawberry flavoured (i.e. made from chemicals and never been near an actual piece of fruit).
- Wholegrains rather than refined – wholemeal pasta rather than white, wholegrain rice not white.
- Whole fats rather than refined or chemically altered – sunflower seeds rather than sunflower oil or margarine.
- Whole fruits rather than juiced – eat an apple rather than juice it (it takes the juice of 5 apples to fill an average glass).
- Whole beans and legumes for protein – not manufactured protein powders.
- Whole foods that are sweet but have their fibre intact, such as dates or raisins, rather than refined white sugar.
- Baked rather than fried foods.
- Freshly prepared home-made meals rather than those that come out of a packet or off the supermarket shelf.

It's amazing how many people I upset when I first changed to a whole-food, plant-based diet. It brings up many emotions in people, ranging from sadness and defensiveness to being dismissive or angry. The fact that I was doing it to solve a health problem made it easier and gave it justification. I sometimes wonder if I would have made the change without my food intolerances to spur me on. I like to believe that, once I'd learnt about the power of plants, I would have taken the same positive step with my diet.

Some people assume I don't like food, but they couldn't be more wrong because I love it! I love thinking about food, planning meals and enjoying eating them. In fact, I enjoy food even more now as I know that whatever I put in my mouth is helping me to heal. My taste-buds have changed and I now appreciate flavours and textures far more than I used to. I marvel at the wonderful rainbow colours of the fresh produce that can be used to create beautiful dishes. Good food and the pleasure of eating are the founding principles of my business, The Sensitive Foodie Kitchen.

After changing the way I ate, I soon realised that the only way to silence the critics was to prove them wrong and be the evidence that living a life powered by plants was the best way to be. That's why one of the reasons I love creating new recipes and dishes is so I can share them with others and pass on my passion.

Fortunately, times are changing. Plant-based eating is the fastest growing food movement in the West. Whether people choose to go all-in or are 'meat-reducers', eating a plant-based diet is a growing trend. It shows that people are beginning to wake up to the terrible effect of a highly processed and nutrient deficient diet.

A whole-food, plant-based diet is based around five groups of food:

1. Fruit.
2. Vegetables.
3. Beans and legumes.
4. Whole grains and cereals.
5. Nuts and seeds.

There are hundreds of different types of food in these five groups and I'll explore them more in the next chapter. I believe there's far more variety, choice and freedom in plant-based eating than with a diet mainly based on animal-products. It's really quite exciting!

Whole-food, plant-based eating is a remarkably normal way of eating too. Many populations all over the world have traditionally consumed a mainly plant-based diet for cultural, social, religious or economic reasons. Historically, animal products (certainly the amount freely consumed in the West today) were reserved for special days and holidays – or for the rich. History is littered with tales of excess animal consumption and its subsequent health problems – think King Henry the Eighth as a model for the consequences of a high-animal, low plant-food style diet. Admirers of the ever-popular high protein or low-fat and low-carb diets really should take note.

Economics and disposable income play a huge role in influencing the traditional diet of populous countries like China and India. As middle-class affluence rises, so does meat consumption and with that comes chronic health problems. India is currently facing an epidemic of diabetes and hypertension, which has been directly linked with rapid changes in diet and lifestyle. Reverting back to more traditional dishes or following whole-food, plant-based programmes like Dr Shah's can reverse these health issues and slow the expansion of Indian waistlines. This is a challenge in itself though, as carrying a little weight is still viewed as a sign of wealth and prosperity.

That's not to say that communities that live under the poverty line all are bouncing with good health – malnutrition due to lack of the availability of high-quality food is still a major problem for over 11 per cent of the world's population. But there's also a certain irony that the over-availability of food has led to malnutrition and, as identified earlier, many people are most definitely overfed and undernourished.

Much of the information we're bombarded with about which food we should or should not eat is based around ensuring we get a full range of nutrition from set of specific nutrient groups, some large and some small. First, there are the larger macronutrients, which include protein, fat and carbohydrate. Opinion on how much of these we should eat seem to change on an almost daily basis. Second, there are the smaller micronutrients made up of vitamins and minerals, which we need in different amounts. There's no doubt that eating from all these groups is essential to our health and well-being. In fact, the discovery of all these elements has led to the eradication of many health problems that were once common.

The problem is that once these nutrients are isolated or given different levels of importance, they no longer work together as they do in their whole, connected and natural form. Processing and refining also destroys more delicate nutrients, like vitamins and some minerals such as potassium and chromium. Processing also creates an imbalance in the macronutrients themselves, which means that the minute cellular processes going on in our bodies may not be supported by getting the full balance of chemicals they need to work.

All nutrients found in food, no matter how big or small are made of combinations of compounds and molecules, such as hydrogen, carbon and nitrogen which are all held together in different forms. These are the same compounds and molecules that we too are made from.

The importance placed on the bulk nutrients – protein, fat and carbohydrate – makes it appear as if these categories are real entities in their own right. Meat is often referred to as 'the protein' on cookery programmes – but there's more than just protein in it. Rice is called a 'carb', but wholegrain rice contains fat and protein too.

On top of that, these bulk nutrients are just made up of smaller chains of molecules in different forms. Protein is made from different chains of amino acids and fat contains fatty acid chains. Carbohydrates contain a variety of carbon chains called saccharides. Digestion breaks down these bulk nutrients into smaller constituent parts so they can be used as needed. So, as long as we eat a range of foods that contain this variety of molecules, our amazing body will do the rest.

When the importance of one specific molecular formation is raised above the others, it automatically creates an imbalance. For example, protein contains lots of nitrogen compared to carbohydrate, which contains more carbon and is the basis of fibre. Diets that promote the importance of protein over carbohydrate tend to feature large amounts of animal products. This results in a low intake of fibre, which upsets the microbiome and creates an imbalance in the type of molecules available in the body. The same can be said of any diet that promotes the high intake of any single nutrient over another. And as we have seen, imbalance upsets our Baby Bear parameters and can lead to inflammation and ill-health.

If you stop focusing on the constituent parts and look at food as a whole, you'll see that food – and in particular whole-food – contains all the constituent nutrients that we need and in the right balance, which makes life so much easier. So, don't focus on eating 'a protein', 'carbs' or even a specific vitamin – just eat real whole food.

Whole-plant foods give the body the nutrients it needs to carry out the numerous cellular processes and functions that have allowed us to evolve and survive both efficiently and effectively. Whole foods support the whole body as they are packed with the tiny chemicals and molecules our bodies are designed to use. Not only that, the complex fibre contained within whole foods, whether vegetable, fruit, grain, legume or nut, cares for the microbiome, enabling it to function at full capacity. Having said that, there is one specific nutrient that can be difficult to find in a plant-based diet today and that's B12.

An essential vitamin that has to be obtained from food, B12 is formed by microorganisms – basically the bacteria in food. Due to food hygiene guidelines, there are not many bacteria left on plant foods (consumers don't like mud with their potatoes!) whereas many animal-based foods contain a variety of bacteria. Plus, the animal has already either manufactured its B12 or eaten it in fortified feed.

B12 is really important as it acts as a co-enzyme for many cellular processes including cell energy production and nervous system functioning.

A deficiency in B12 can result in blood disorders or general symptoms like fatigue, muscle weakness and confusion. Some plant-based foods like milks or nutritional yeast are fortified with B12, but for some it may be wise to take a supplement on a regular basis. If you want to know more about this, please visit www.thesensitivefoodiekitchen.com/book-links for more information.

But there's one other tiny but powerful group of chemicals found hidden within whole-plant foods – phytonutrients. Let's look at them next.

Fabulous Phytonutrients

One of the things that gets me really excited about eating a plant-based diet is the magical properties of phytonutrients. They're tiny chemical structures that are found within every item of produce you can get your hands on. Every fruit, vegetable, legume, whole-grain or any other group of plants contains these magical properties. In fact, they're the real reason why we eat them. Phytonutrients complement both the macro and micro nutrients in foods, but they also have wonderful roles of their own, making them the nutritional icing on the cake – whole-food and unrefined of course.

You may have heard the message about eating a rainbow every day – I certainly bang on about it all the time. Each coloured produce has its own wonderful array of phytonutrients that will support and benefit the body in some way. So why are we only realising this now?

The truth is, we're not discovering anything new. Our ancestors may not have known why it was good to eat something, they just would have done it and oral traditions would have been used to pass down the message through the generations. The use of plants as medicinal remedies has been recorded as far back as 60,000 years ago. And if you eat what's available in each season, you naturally consume the phytonutrients most beneficial for that time of year. Rosehips in winter provide high doses of vitamin C to support the immune system in cold weather. Dandelions promote cleansing and liver detoxing in spring, a time of new growth and regeneration.

This knowledge has always been available to us, but it's only recently that scientists have started to break foods down into their constituent parts as they look for the next big thing or the magical cure. Whilst eating a whole-food diet ignores the parts and looks at the bigger picture, it's good to have a look at what phytonutrients are, why they're so essential and how they work to support our health.

One of the wonderful benefits of eating a whole-food, plant-based diet is that you automatically consume a large amount and variety of phytonutrients without even thinking about it. That means you're naturally nourishing your body while eating amazingly tasty food – effortless health through enjoyment. You can't go wrong with that.

Phytonutrients are tiny chemical compounds that, once absorbed into the body, support a whole array of metabolic functions – the essential processes we're rarely aware of. Many of them are found in colour pigments within the plant. Basically, they help make our bodies work efficiently, effectively and effortlessly. This is how we have evolved and how our bodies are designed to be supported. It's completely natural and necessary for health and vitality.

This is why I get so frustrated when the power of plants is denied or a highly processed and nutrient-deficient way of eating is promoted. Plants are essential to our health, otherwise we would have evolved and developed differently. It's also why the five-a-day message is so ineffectual when it comes to promoting optimum health. Five portions of fresh fruit or vegetables really doesn't hit the spot when it comes to food for health. It's another thing you don't have to think about when eating a whole-food, plant-based diet – the portions just come rolling in with minimal effort. You just eat great food and reap the benefits.

Scientists don't yet know how many phytonutrients there are because there are so many different plant foods around the world; many of them are still undocumented. Each plant has an array of different chemical structures, even plants that have traditionally been seen as nutritionally poor, like yams. To date, over 25,000 phytonutrients have been documented and new ones are being discovered all the time.

As there are so many different phytonutrients they're too numerous to list here. Some are well known, like beta carotene and lycopene, but others like adiponectin, not so much.

Phytonutrients work best when eaten in their whole, natural form, working together as a team. Each one has its own special action, which is supported by the work of others around it. It appears they mainly act as anti-oxidants, mopping up pesky free radicals circulating in the blood looking to cause damage. This not only keeps health problems at bay, it also slows the ageing process, as we saw in Chapter 2.

Other roles for phytonutrients include acting as co-factors for enzymes, cell energy and precursors for other essential nutrients. They benefit our bodies in numerous ways, and they taste and look good too. Their vibrant colours make them attractive to the eye, and if it looks good, we naturally want to eat it.

Phytonutrients are delicate things and deteriorate as soon as the plant is harvested. Any form of processing hastens this process, as does exposure to light and for some, heat is damaging too. Imagine the effect that food

Phytonutrients

Group name:	How many	Found in	What it does
Carotenoids	>600	Orange veg – carrots, squash, sweet potatoes Green veg – kale, spinach, Red fruit/veg – tomatoes Fruit – cantaloupe melons, apricots, citrus fruit	Pre-curser to vitamin A Anti-oxidant activity Supports immune system
Coumarin	>1300	Orange – carrots Purple – beetroot Pale green – celery, fennel Fruit – citrus	Supports the immune system Stimulates anti-oxidant pathways Some anti-tumour properties
D, G and T (dithiolthiones, glucosinolates thiocyanates)	>150	Brassicas – broccoli, brussel sprouts, cabbage, kale etc	Aids body detoxification Can protect cells from being damaged by cancer causing compounds
Flavonoids	>6000	Fruit – berries, cherries, citrus Red veg – tomatoes, peppers Orange veg – peppers Yellow veg – peppers Green veg – peppers, greens Legumes – peas, lentils	Antioxidant properties Can support the immune system Anti-tumour properties
Isoflavonoids	>200	Soy beans Legumes	Block oestrogen receptors
Lignans	>150	Whole grains Nuts Seeds, particularly flaxseed	Can modulate hormone receptors Anti-oxidant effects
Limonoids	>300	Fruit – citrus Pale green – celery	Support detoxification Block carcinogens
Polyphonols	>500	Tea – green tea Brown – chocolate Red – grapes (wine!)	Anti-oxidant effect Can block carcinogens from forming Modulates hormone receptors
Sterols	>200	Legumes – soya Nuts Seeds	Can block carcinogens from being produced Modulates hormone receptors

Different types of phytonutrients and where you can find them.

manufacturing and refining has on them – it's easy to see why most processed foods have lost their magic along the way.

Even when a food product is marketed as being healthy – let's say a diet vegetable lasagne – all the ingredients have been highly processed and cooked at high temperatures. It's also possible that the produce itself could have been harvested a long time before it gets processed and put on the shelves. There's not much chance that the fabulous phytonutrients will survival that.

Go to a fresh fruit and vegetable market though, and the produce looks positively radiant, glowing with an energy our subconscious minds instantly connect with. Why do you think supermarkets tend to place the fresh produce section at the front of the store? Because we're naturally drawn to the rainbow colours provided by fabulous phytonutrients.

Connecting the Dots

The sheer volume of information now available about the possible positive and negative effects of certain foods means that, for many, advice has become white noise, so it gets ignored. Beliefs about food can be as strong (if not stronger) than religious or spiritual beliefs; people get defensive if they feel that their food choices are being criticised or labelled as erroneous. In fact, I would suggest that the new social guideline for appropriate conversations should be 'never discuss politics, religion or dietary choices'.

After attending Dr Shah's workshops, I understood so much more about food and its impact on the body. I realised that working in healthcare meant I'd been trained to focus on the symptoms rather than the cause. In fact, healthcare in the Western world really is symptom and disease management, it's rarely about promoting health. By understanding the benefits of eating a whole-food, plant-based diet, I realised my food intolerances were not the real issue; they were merely a symptom that my body wasn't getting the type of food it needed.

For the first 40 years of my life, I'd been putting my body under immense stress, asking it to deal with proteins that were not right for it. I created constant inflammation and overworked my cells by asking them to function without providing the extra micronutrients they needed to cope. On top of that, my poor gut health was being made worse by eating refined foods that contained less healthy fibre. I was also eating yeast products and sugar (in many guises), which together just perpetuated my yeast over-growth. Talk about daft!

Once I had my light bulb moment, I finally understood that changing the way I ate was about giving my body more of what it needed to be well, not missing out or excluding food I enjoyed, like cheese and cake. Much of getting on board with eating for real health is about changing your language and perspective around it. Changing how you talk about what you eat makes it much easier to alter life-long habits and go from feeling resentful and deprived to grateful and fulfilled. To me, continuing to eat as I had been eating most of my life was like being a car driver who continued to put petrol in their diesel-engine car knowing the car would break down every time and cost a lot of money to put right again.

Whilst the body is much better at coping with the wrong fuel than a car, it still does it harm in the long run, which is why it's much more cost effective (in terms of health and well-being) to stop putting in the wrong fuel in the first place and take on board the good fuel instead.

Which is why, in a delightfully ironic way, I'm profoundly grateful for my food intolerances, because without them I would never have started on this journey to feeling great. As it turned out, my light-bulb moment came at a vital time, enabling me to dampen down the chronic inflammation that was damaging my immune system.

Up to this point, I thought I knew all I needed know about food and health, even though I was constantly on diets which only worked in the short term. If I 'failed' a diet, I told myself it was due to my lack of willpower or grit – it was a personality defect not a dietary one.

No more diets

One of the first benefits of eating a plant-based diet was that I lost weight. Not only that, it stayed off and I haven't had to 'go on a diet' since. Diets always made me feel deprived, even though it was a short-term sufferance. But using plant-power as a way of life gave my body everything it needed, allowing me to cut out all the foods that made me overweight and listless. It was a wonderful positive side-effect. People who meet me now find it hard to believe I ever had a weight problem, even though they see how much I eat.

It's not just me who has experienced this though. There are some amazing transformations detailed on the special book website link (www.thesensitivefoodiekitchen.com/book-links). Most people who move to a whole-food plant-based way of eating find their body weight and shape change. Best of all, it's natural, gradual and happens without any effort. I still get excited when I tell people they need to eat more to lose weight – more whole plants that is!

That's because whole-plant foods are packed with more water and fibre and less calories than most processed foods or animal products. On top of that, they contain all the wonderful tiny nutrients that support metabolic processes, resulting in efficient and effective energy (calorie) absorption and utilisation. It's hard to overeat, partly because it takes longer to chew your way through a plate of vegetables than a hamburger and partly because the large fibre content makes you feel full faster and for longer.

On top of that, your brain recognises that the meal has delivered a shed-load of nutrients – and in the right configuration for the body to use. A benefit of this is that you won't feel hungry for some time after each meal as your nutrient levels are fully topped up. Hunger messages are often signals that your body still requires particular nutrients, so it puts in another order for food.

We're all responsible

Coming from a nursing background, I'm very passionate about health and wellbeing. I believe that each of us has a personal responsibility to care for our own health. But I've noticed that many people expect or accept health problems as inevitable, unaware that nothing is pre-determined and they have the power to change the quality of their health.

Working in intensive care, I observed this first hand, listening to heart felt regrets on numerous occasions. One particularly sad tale has always stuck in my mind. It's about two brothers, both of whom were in their early 40s who had a clear family history of severe heart disease and early death. Both brothers were given the same advice: make huge changes to your diet and lifestyle or you'll suffer the consequences of heart disease and death at an early age.

One brother heeded this warning, the other didn't. Sadly, the one who failed to take his doctor's advice suffered a devastating stroke at the age of 42. Newly married and on a successful career path, he survived, but only just. But even with immediate treatment and a prolonged period in intensive care, his physical capacity was hugely diminished and he found himself unable to communicate verbally or even turn in bed without assistance. His brother carried the guilt that he didn't do more to help his sibling make changes in his lifestyle. But it wasn't up to him.

Our genetic makeup is seen as playing a significant role in our health, but for most chronic 'lifestyle' diseases, the way we live has a far bigger impact on our health. In fact, it takes some effort to switch on the genes that result in poor health, although it's hard to be specific about how this happens. But what it does give us is power – nothing is set in stone and we can take positive action to prevent these genes from ever being activated. It is important to remember that everyone is different, this is not a blame game. For some there is a clear link between their health and their genetics but they often get glaring warning signs from their family history, genetic testing and ongoing monitoring.

Plants give you a second chance

The wonderful thing about adopting a whole-food plant-based diet is that even if you do develop a health problem, it'll probably be less severe or develop more slowly than if you hadn't made the switch. Even better, if you already have health problems, it's not too late to change the situation. If nothing else, taking control of your health by changing your diet and lifestyle choices will help you feel more of a person and less of a patient.

Following my diagnosis of multiple sclerosis, this has certainly been my experience of continuing to use food to keep me well. Feeling empowered to make decisions and eating food that calms the raging inflammation that's damaging to my nerves makes a huge difference. Handing my health over to someone else just isn't an option for me, proving that nurses really do make the worst patients!

I was devastated when I was diagnosed with MS. I thought I had failed. Yet in hindsight, I can see that the changes I'd already made had given me a fighting chance of managing my condition. I have since realised that my migraines were early signs of MS, although there was no way of knowing that at the time.

Health is influenced by many factors, including the triad of wellness: diet, exercise and stress management. If the Baby Bear is out of balance in any of these areas, it can have an impact on your health. Even if you've been handed a diagnosis and a selection of medication so you can 'manage' your symptoms, it doesn't mean that's the end of the story. Never allow yourself to be defeated – I believe that any health challenge can be positively improved in some way. It may not be the complete cure you're looking for, but this healthful approach can provide the opportunity to promote wellness.

I now follow a diet and lifestyle programme called Overcoming Multiple Sclerosis (OMS). Founded on evidence-based research, the programme focuses on maintaining the triad of good health as well as making some other important health choices too. It was developed by Dr George Jelinek, an Australian Professor of Emergency Medicine who also developed MS in his forties. While he was off work, he explored all the medical research to determine the best course of action to minimise the effects of the disease on his body. His conclusion was to create a plan that consisted of a low-fat, whole-food, plant-based diet that was rich in Omega 3 fatty acids and vitamin D, plus exercise, stress management using mindfulness or meditation, and medication (if needed). Twenty years on, Dr Jelinek is still working, still researching and is relapse-free. Anyone with MS can follow the programme for free. To find out more about OMS, check out the website details in the Online Resources and Article References section on page 302.

But MS is just one health condition that can be influenced by a change of diet. As mentioned above, there is a wealth of evidence-based research that promotes using a whole-food, plant-based diet to manage, and more importantly prevent, many health conditions. In fact, anything that is connected to the ravages of inflammation or an imbalance in our metabolism, can be positively impacted by choosing this way of eating and living.

There is another wonderful benefit of eating a whole-food plant-based diet too – and that's the fact that it doesn't just improve one health condition as medication may (or may not), it impacts a range of conditions. That's because nutrients travel to wherever they're needed and can improve cellular function from the top of your head to the tips of your toes. It's not unusual for people to change to this way of eating because of one health problem and find other issues also improve. There is a Buddhist expression for this called 'turning poison into medicine'. If you want to read some inspiring real-life examples of this in action, check out the case studies on my website.

Plants taste good

Another dot connected on my journey to discovering the power of plants was just how much pleasure I could get from eating real food, especially in comparison with how dieting made me feel. Real, whole, plant food tasted delicious and I loved eating meals that made my taste-buds tingle with delight and my body shimmer with health. I always felt deprived on a diet because the food was so insipid and dull – where's the joy in that? Being able to eat amazingly tasty food without restriction now means I never feel deprived.

The other problem with diets is that they tend to be focused on what you can't eat rather than what you can. This always pressed my self-sabotage button so I'd eventually give in to a slice of sugar-laden cake – and then have another slice because I'd already 'failed'. Then I'd feel guilty and berate myself for being weak-willed or pathetic. Sound familiar?

Negative self-talk is one of the hardest things to overcome when you're trying to lose weight but I find that with a whole-food, plant-based diet, that isn't a problem. The food is so satisfyingly delicious and the positive effects are felt so quickly, that I don't need to feel bad about anything I'm eating. On top of that, as your gut health improves, so does your mood, because all the right neurotransmitters are being produced effectively. And if you do fall for the odd cake or hamburger, don't worry about it. You'll have given yourself so many wonderful nutrients up to that point that your body will cope. Just get back on board with your new way of eating as soon as you can and move on.

Of course, switching to a plant-based diet does mean you'll need to avoid eating certain foods. Some are easy to bypass, others aren't. Cheese can be a big issue for some people; it certainly was for me. I used to find myself nibbling bits I'd cut for the children's sandwiches without realising what I was doing. I hadn't realised quite how addicted I was to cheese. When I went on Dr Shah's course, I connected another dot: milk, or mother's milk, is naturally desirable. It's all to do with survival.

That's because babies need more than just hunger to encourage them to want their mother's milk. They need to have desire too. The protein in milk – casein – creates this desire. As this protein gets broken down, it forms another protein called caseinogen that is small enough to cross the protective blood-brain barrier. Once circulating in the brain, it pings the pleasure centre (the dopamine receptors), giving the baby just enough pleasure to give the baby a small-scale addiction so it keeps coming back for more. Mother Nature is very clever!

Cow's milk has a higher concentration of casein than human breast milk, therefore giving a bigger hit than we're naturally designed to cope with. Then when you consider that there's 10 times more caseinogen in cheese than milk, it's no wonder that it's so hard to give up. We're naturally addicted to it, so it takes time to free ourselves. But it's not just cheese this applies to, though. Have you ever wondered why there are so many forms of milk in processed foods, particularly ones where there's no apparent need for it? It's because the milk panders to our natural addiction, so we keep eating it – and buying it. So our addiction is good for profits, even if it's not so good for our health.

The good news is you can wean yourself off this addiction. Going cold-turkey may work for you or you may choose to gradually reduce your intake over time. It's important to do your own thing as that gives you the control – and the responsibility – you'll need to succeed. After all, it's your health, so it's your choice. And it's a wonderfully tasty choice to make!

The environment and animals

Since starting on my plant-based journey, I've discovered another important benefit of eating this way: it supports the environment. I've always been concerned about the environment and tried to follow the principle of the 3Rs – Reduce, Reuse, Recycle – but never felt it made much of a difference.

However, I've since learnt how much of an impact the food industry has on the environment and I've started to think again. Manufacturing certain food products uses up huge swathes of natural resources like land and water, while at the same time producing polluting gases and waste products. We all have to eat, of course, so growing plants in their various forms is bound to use a lot of natural resources. But eating a whole-food, plant-based diet puts far less pressure on the environment than either processed food or animal-based products, particularly when it comes to land use and intensive farming methods. Here are some not-so-fun facts about the environment and animal farming:

- It takes 2400 US gallons of water to produce one pound of meat (this is over 6 months).
- 70 per cent of the grain grown in the US is used to feed animals, not humans.
- 17 billion livestock are farmed for meat production requiring vast amounts of land, feed and water, and producing a large amount of emissions.
- 60 per cent of all mammals on the planet are livestock.
- 70 per cent of all the deforestation in the Amazon is the result of cattle ranching.

Connecting the dots between the food I ate and its impact on the environment suddenly made changing to a whole-food, plant-based way of life even more positive because it was not only good for me, it was good for the planet too. (In fact, if you're interested in the environment, this is the most direct and effective action you can take to support it.

My light-bulb moment has helped me to connect one more important dot – the one between humans and animals.

I grew up eating meat – I knew what it was when it was on my plate and it seemed perfectly normal. But now I question why. And not just that, but also why it's only some animals we eat and not others. For many people, there's a huge disconnection between the animals they see in a field and the slab of meat on their plate. We pride ourselves on being a society of animal lovers, yet we readily consume the remains of those same animals we see grazing in the countryside. Added to this, many of those animals will have lived a fairly miserable life, maybe on a farm using intensive farming practices. They're often kept inside, have their movement restricted and are fed an unnatural diet, all so they can be hauled off to the abattoir at an early age. That's the reality of the life of many animals that end up as cheap meat in the supermarket.

There are still farmers who lovingly care for their animals, maintain high welfare standards and provide lush pastures for their flocks and herds to roam. But even so, their money is made from the animal – whether it's through products like milk or from its meat.

There also seems to be an inherent hypocrisy around the animals we consider suitable for food. It's okay to eat a cow, but not a horse, although it's acceptable in France, for example. And eating a dog is even less acceptable. However, pigs are as intelligent as dogs, yet they're readily consumed in many countries. Dr Melanie Joy talks about how humans justify meat eating and it makes fascinating reading. (*See the Online Resources and Article References section on p302.*)

The more I thought about this, the more I realised it's my choice and my responsibility what food I eat. I would never kill an animal myself as that would be taking a life, which is something I inherently oppose. So how could I justify eating an animal that had been killed by somebody else? Not only that, but it is now known that animals experience acute fear and stress just before they're slaughtered. This leads to stress hormones being released into the meat, which are therefore consumed. If stress hormones contribute to inflammation then animal products cannot be conducive to an anti-inflammatory way of eating.

Once all these dots had been connected, I realised that incorporating lovely whole plants into my way of eating was about more than the food I ate. It connected my health and my actions with the wider world. No man (or woman) is an island. Everything is connected. And once my mind had been opened to this, it couldn't be closed again.

CHAPTER FOUR

THERE'S MORE TO IT THAN LETTUCE

I hope by now you're on board with the idea of a whole-food, plant-based diet and can see that it's healthy and packed full of wonderful nutrients of all shapes and sizes to keep our amazing bodies well. And don't forget all that fabulous fibre that supports the marvellous microbiome, which in turn supports us back.

But in a world of fast food, pinging bliss points and instant gratification, maybe a whole-food, plant-based diet is just a bit too dull and virtuous to enjoy in our modern age.

Isn't it a bit … boring?

No! It's far from boring. I've discovered a whole new selection of flavours, textures and aromas that delight my taste-buds and satisfy my body better than ever before. It's an exciting and innovative world with fewer constraints than traditional animal-based eating – and it definitely includes a lot more than lettuce.

Diets are certainly boring. Or rather calorie-counting diets with flavourless food that leaves you feeling deprived is boring. I've been on so many diets in the past and have 'failed' every time. Diet plans focus on calorie restriction for short-term weight loss. It's all about taking focused action to get fast results. There's always an element of deprivation, martyrdom and yearning for a time when it's over. These diets are all nigh on impossible to continue in the long term. Lack of variety, taste and satisfaction add up to a lack of enjoyment. And that definitely is boring!

An Abundance of Food on Your Plate

One of the biggest problems with weight-loss diets is that they require you to restrict or give up the very foods your body has been designed to need for survival: sugar, fat and salt. It's not so hard in the short term, but when you cut them out for too long, your programmed survival instinct kicks in and you end up with a deep craving that builds and builds until you finally crack. How many times have you started with a will of iron that's been eroded over time? For me, I would eventually give in, splurging on cake or a packet of biscuits or anything else that would give me a quick fix.

Instantaneously satisfying, the guilt would soon follow – along with horrid, negative self-talk. I'd failed. I wasn't strong enough. I had no willpower. But it wasn't me that was 'bad', it was the quality of the food that was just not giving my body what it needed

However, it's not just calorie restriction that can lead to these feelings of deprivation. Any diet that focuses on one macro-nutrient and eliminates another has the same effect. High animal-product diets like Atkins or Ketogenic diets that eliminate complex starches and carbohydrates have the same effect. Our bodies are designed to desire sugar. So, no matter how many times you read that ketone bodies work the same as glucose molecules, the truth is they just don't.

As we saw in Chapter 3, a whole-food, plant-based diet is different because it's packed full of whole, natural foods that contain all the nutrients the body needs and desires. It hits the bliss points with the perfect balance of sugar, fat and salt. After time, when the messages become clearer, you can tune in and let your body tell you what it would like to eat each day. And believe it or not, once whole-food, plant-based eating has become your new normal, you actually start craving it. Yup, you read that right! Move over cake, you can crave carrots just as much.

If that sounds just too crazy to be true, I'm here to assure you it's not. When you saturate your body with wonderful nutrients from whole foods, it soon misses them when they're gone. Even a sudden change from a moderate fruit and veg intake to none can set off the 'feed me veg *now*' alarms. And it's not just me. My son, who would say he prefers junk food to fresh, experiences veg cravings. It only took one weekend away at scout camp, where the only veggies on offer were the fried onions on the hamburgers, for him to start craving the green stuff. Returning home, ravenous as usual, all he wanted was a huge plate of vegetables. I was one happy mum.

Once I started to embrace this way of eating, I was surprised and delighted to discover that whole plants were far from boring. Instead they were:

- Full of variety and choice.
- Exciting to eat.
- Easy to cook with.
- Filling and satisfying.
- Super-quick to use (after I came up with some short-cuts).

Variety

There are an amazing number of plant species in the world – somewhere around the 400,000 mark and new ones are still being discovered. Not all of them can be eaten by us, though roughly 200,000 are edible. But despite this, only around 200 are cultivated for human consumption.

Incredibly, less than 20 different types make up more than 90 per cent of the food eaten around the world. This connects back to the issues around gut health and the lack of dietary diversity as covered in Chapter 2. Anyone who eats a standard Western diet will mainly consume only four types of food: meat, dairy, soya and wheat.

Once you move away from this highly processed and refined way of eating and start to consume more whole food products, the variety of foods you'll consume will increase enormously. And if you have variety, you won't get bored.

The wonderful thing about eating more whole, plant-based foods means there are always fantastic alternatives, so you never have to miss out. Take milk, for example. There are generally three types of animal-based milk available to buy. Cow's milk is the most obvious as well as being the most common and cheapest. But there's sheep and goat's milk too.

When it comes to plant-based 'milk', there are far more than three different types available, especially if you make them yourself. The range includes everything from soya to nut-based milks, such as almond and coconut as well as oat or even seed-based milks. There truly is something for everyone. Each has a unique flavour and texture as well as different nutrient and tolerance profiles. Some work better in cooking or hot drinks than others but you can use more than one. I usually have two, sometimes three, different types of milk in the fridge. I tend to prefer organic soya milk in my tea, almond milk on cereal and oat milk in cooking.

The plant-based milk market is rapidly expanding, having more than doubled between 2010 and 2018. You can also buy more unusual versions now too, like hazelnut or hempseed. The demand for almonds for making nut 'milk' has grown particularly rapidly. So much so, in fact, that it's sadly creating environmental issues in drought-hit California, where most almonds come from. There, large areas of land have been given over to growing almonds but, because their cultivation requires large amounts of water, it's making the situation with the drought worse – which shows why variety is good. By comparison, oats are thought to make the most environmentally-friendly plant-based milk – and it tastes good too.

If variety is the positive side of plant-based milks, the downside is additives; shop-bought versions may be convenient but contain preservatives in some form or other in order to prolong shelf-life. And in a whole-food diet, milks generally have minimal or no fibre. Fortunately, many milks, like nut or oat, are easy to make at home, removing the need for added chemicals. A bit of fibre also tends to slip through too, which is an added bonus. Check out the section on plant-based milks in the recipe section – you might just be surprised about how great they taste and how easy they are to make!

Variety is good for the planet and it's good for our taste-buds and gut bacteria too. Once you start experimenting with different recipes, you'll be surprised just how many different types of fruit, vegetables, grain, pulses and nuts and seeds you'll eat in one day. Recent research released by Tim Spector and his team at the British Gut project suggests that people with the healthiest balance of gut microbes ate 30 different types of plant in a week – and that's a minimum. Miguel Toribio-Mateas, a nutritionist specialising in brain health, recommends eating 50 different types.

Everyone can get stuck in a rut when it comes to meal times, especially when time restraints, convenience, cost and personal preferences all influence choice. If you make a batch of soup and there's only one or two of you eating it, monotony kicks in pretty quickly. It takes time and energy to think of new ideas, especially if you're new to eating a whole-food, plant-based diet.

Creativity for me is exciting! I love coming up with new ideas, experimenting with different ingredients and working out how to adapt a favourite dish to make it whole-food and plant-based. Professional chefs are coming on board too, and with the same enthusiasm. Suddenly a whole new larder is opening up to them, bringing fresh challenges that stimulate their ingenuity and test their culinary skills. Many top chefs are transitioning towards plant-based cooking; there's even a fully vegan Michelin-starred restaurant in central London offering an eight-course tasting menu – foodie heaven!

But you don't have to be a Michelin-starred chef to flex those creative muscles. One of the great things about eating plant-based is that you're less likely to give yourself food poisoning! And if, like me, you're a messy cook who doesn't like following the rules (which is why I failed cookery at school), then it's perfect for you because there aren't really any – even baking is less restrictive. One lady who attended my Eat Well course reported that her grandson loved using my baking recipes because they're so quick and easy. He didn't have to spend time 'creaming all that white stuff' (butter and sugar). He loved the simplicity of tipping one bowl of ingredients into the other and stirring fast. Much easier.

Quick and easy

When I say that eating plant-based is quicker, I generally get quizzical looks. On the surface, cooking with whole-foods from scratch does look like a lot of hard work. And to start with it can be, but then learning any new skill takes time and effort. But once you get it, it's easy – trust me.

Once you learn how to approach it, let loose with your creativity and keep an open mind, it's surprising what you can achieve. Remember, I'm not a professionally trained chef – far from it in fact. All the recipes in the second half of this book are designed to make your life easy and your body happy. True, some take a bit longer than others (especially the posh dinners) but overall, I think you'll be surprised just how easy it is to create delicious and enjoyable food in a fairly short space of time.

Being organised is key, but not in an obsessive or restrictive way. Start to think ahead and have a rough plan for your week. This ensures you don't get stuck with a choice between eating junk food or nothing. Following my top tips in Chapter 6 will help with that.

Shopping is definitely quicker and easier. Navigating the supermarket becomes simple. I spend most of my time in three sections: the fresh produce section, the tinned or dried goods section and the 'free-from' section (where I can get dairy-free products). That's about it. Even eating out is easier, because unless you're going to a fully vegan restaurant, menu choices are usually limited to one or two options, so you don't have to spend time choosing.

Filling Fibre

Another thing the people on my courses find difficult to comprehend is just how filling whole-plant food can be. A key part of my Eat Well, Live Well course is that I provide a full meal made with some of the recipes handed out that week. After saying how tasty the food is, the most common response is surprise because everyone feels satiated – but not uncomfortable. As they would put it, 'pleasantly stuffed'. That's another benefit of a whole-food, plant-based diet: you don't feel uncomfortably bloated – even if you eat a lot. This is because it's packed full of nutrients, as well as large amounts of fibre, so your body knows when it's had its fill and you know when it's time to stop eating. But how?

- Whole fats and sugars hit those bliss spots, releasing energy at a stable and sustained rate.
- Fibre fills your gut with bacteria-friendly fodder.
- Macronutrients are broken down and absorbed through a healthy gut lining.

When the digestive system is enabled to work effectively, your body gains all the nutrients and energy it needs to function. No more sugar lows. That's a huge relief!

When I was young my mum always seemed to be on a diet. I remember her weight constantly fluctuating – yoyo dieting is not a new phenomenon! In the early 1980s, she discovered the F-plan diet, and 'fibre' soon become a common word in our vernacular. Being horrible pre-teens, my brother and I would tease her about the sensory stimulating after-effects – flatulence – and of course renamed it the 'Fart-plan'.

In a world of reductionism, fibre becomes an entity of its own. It can be extracted, made into supplements with premium prices and used as a marketing tool for processed food products. We all know fibre is important, so any product with the tag-line 'high in fibre' must be good, right?

In the world of whole-food, plant-based eating, no additional tag-line is needed. Fibre is part of the basic structure of plants. Everything is high in fibre – unless it's processed and taken out.

So, what actually is fibre and why is it important? In a nutshell, it's the components of plant cell walls. At the time of the F-plan diet, it used to be referred to as 'dietary fibre', the indigestible part of the plant that moved through the gut. Its role and why it wasn't digested was unclear, but it was good for us as it promoted good bowel function i.e. it helped us poo! Since then, discoveries about fibre have expanded. We now know:

- There are three main components of fibre: insoluble, soluble and lignans.
- Insoluble may be indigestible to humans, but not to our microbe guests deep in the bowel – for them, it's dinner!
- Diets low in fibre effectively starve friendly gut bacteria, which leads to health problems.

As a general guide, plants cell walls are made up of 35 per cent insoluble fibre, 45 per cent soluble fibre and 15 per cent lignans, although every plant wall has a different composition of the three. And remember, fibre is only found in plants, not animal-derived foods, so be aware of how much fibre is lost on any programme that claims to be low carb.

As with the nutrients in all plant power foods, the three types of fibre found in plants work together as a team – one is not necessarily better than the other. They all have important roles to play and they perform them best when they're in their natural state. Variety is key – too much or too little of any can have a negative effect. And as we are all individual with different gut biomes, we all react differently to varying amounts of the farty stuff!

Let's have a quick look at the three main components of fibre before exploring the benefits of eating good amounts of it in all its forms.

Insoluble fibre

This is mainly a substance called cellulose and is made up of complex chains of sugar molecules that are bound together. As the name suggests, insoluble fibre doesn't dissolve in water but it does bind with it, acting as a bulking agent. Basically, it's what makes up the structure of poo. If you've ever seen the bulky, fibrous poo made by elephants, you'll understand! They eat a large amount of insoluble fibre that comes out pretty similar to how it went in. In fact, it's so fibrous, some enterprising places around the world are turning it into paper.

Despite secreting various digestive enzymes, humans cannot break down insoluble fibre, so anyone whose alarm bells went off when reading 'sugar molecules' in the paragraph above can relax – the body cannot access it. But gut microbes can; friendly bacteria found in the large intestine love it – it's a veritable smorgasbord of delight. Scientists believe that approximately half of the insoluble fibre found in plant-based food is broken down by beneficial bacteria, helping those good bacteria to proliferate rather than the toxic, harmful bacteria.

But that's not all. Whilst our friendly bacteria are happily dining on insoluble fibre, they're also creating short-chained fatty acids (SCFA) like butyrate that nourish the cells in the gut wall, promoting cell health and optimum absorption of nutrients. It's a win-win once again.

Soluble fibre

This is fibre that dissolves in water. This type of fibre is real plant power, with even more beneficial effects on the gut plus medicinal effects on the body. There are a few types but the main ones are:

Hemi-cellulose: This is a starch, like cellulose, but dissolvable. It helps to increase the amount of water in stools, so contributing towards a good transit time, that is the time between when the food goes in and the waste come out. It is also digested by beneficial bacteria and makes SCFA. But it has another trick up its soluble sleeve. Hemi-cellulose binds with excess cholesterol in the gut, preventing it being absorbed into the bloodstream. Instead it escorts it out of the body where it can do no harm. Oats are the best example of this and are scientifically proven to help reduce heart disease.

Gums and mucilage: This is the seed portion of plants. As the name suggests, this is the sticky, gluey part of plants that contain powerful gel-forming fibres. Like all types of fibre, this gel aids transit time, helping things slide along. It also helps remove toxins and other harmful substances from the gut. They have been found to help with weight loss and the management of blood sugar levels.

Chia seeds and flaxseeds are a good example of this type of fibre but they also have many other fabulous properties – mixed with water they swell and make a sticky gloopy mess that can replace eggs when baking, amongst other things. Okra is another great example. When cooked, it releases a thick gummy texture that some find unappetising, though I love it. The word mucilage always makes me think of snot – over-cooked okra can have a similar texture. You have been warned!

Pectin: Anyone who has ever made jam will know the importance of pectin levels in fruit. It's what helps the jam set. As the fruit is cooked, water and pectin are released and at a certain temperature the pectin binds with the fruit sugars and hey presto, it's jam. Or at least, that's the idea; I've made some very runny jams by miscalculating some element of the formula!

Pectin is found in the cell walls, skin and rind of both fruit and vegetables in varying amounts. Like oats, it helps to reduce and remove excess amounts of cholesterol in the gut and also binds with bile acids that may contain fatty substances that need to exit the body. It's also a favourite dining extravaganza for friendly bacteria; stewed apples are a great way of supporting your gut health. Add oats as a topping and you can make apple crumble into a health food.

Lignans

Lignans are health-promoting compounds found in high-fibre foods. Whilst not a fibre themselves, they are an important part of the whole fibre set-up. Found in various seeds, grains and legumes, lignans change into fabulous protective compounds once in the gut and have anti-cancer, bacterial, fungal and viral properties. This protection is the way we can naturally defend ourselves from all sorts of diseases.

Fibre keeps us regular – remember we love to be in that Baby Bear state, not too much and not too little. It promotes a healthy transit time of food through the gut, enabling it to be digested and nutrients absorbed but also moving things along fast enough to prevent harmful substances causing inflammation and damage. Too much fibre, or only one type of fibre, can be harmful, contributing to an unhappy and failing microbiome.

So, what is the right amount of fibre? Over 50 grams a day is thought to potentially create nutrient absorption problems, although this has not really been researched. Government guidelines suggest about 30 grams a day. Most people have much less than this, even people who think they have a healthy diet. One of my clients was shocked to see that after following what he thought was a good dietary regime he only managed to consume an average of 12 grams of fibre a day, mainly due to the fact that his diet was made of more animal-based foods than plant-based ones.

Counting grams of fibre eaten in a day is not practical for most of us, but you don't need to do any calculations when you eat a plant-powered diet that includes a variety of vegetables, fruits, pulses, grains, nuts and seeds as they are all packed with fibre.

When it comes to fibre though, there is one thing I haven't mentioned – the flatulence potential. For some people, certain types of fibre can be just too flatulent-inducing, to the point where it's painful. This is particularly true for anyone suffering with IBS or other gut diseases.

Gas, wind, farts, flatulence – whatever you want to call it – it's a natural part of the digestive process. Gut flora ferments fibre to break it down and this produces SCFA, energy and gas. If your microbiome is struggling, then certain types of fibre will produce rather volcanic eruptions. I used to suffer from wind big-style; my kids were always complaining about the various noises and aromas wafting their way. But I had a very unhealthy gut with a yeast overgrowth and years of eating dairy, which I was intolerant to.

My transition to a plant-based way of eating was gradual, and as time went by my gut health improved and my legendary eruptions subsided. I can even eat Jerusalem artichokes (or fartichokes as my kids called them), something that previously left me curled up in a corner surrounded by a noxious fug! Fibre is one element where one size does not fit all; fibre is important, but you must listen to what your body is telling you and eat the right amount for you.

Where do I get my calcium (and other minerals) from...?

If you're worried that a plant-based diet can't supply the nutrients you need, the table below should put your mind at rest. It lists 18 easily available foods and whether they contain four key minerals you need for good health. As you can see, each food is rich in nutrients, and even if there isn't a tick in the box, it doesn't mean that food lacks that vitamin or mineral, it just means it may only be there in smaller amounts. As long as you eat a wide range of foods, you won't need to worry about nutrition.

	Calcium	Iron	Magnesium	Zinc
Almonds	✓	✓	✓	✓
Avocado	✓	✓		
Brazil nuts	✓	✓		✓
Cashew nuts		✓	✓	✓
Chia seeds	✓			✓
Chickpeas	✓	✓	✓	✓
Edamame/soya beans		✓	✓	✓
Greens	✓	✓	✓	
Kale	✓	✓	✓	
Kidney beans	✓	✓	✓	
Lentils	✓		✓	✓
Oats	✓	✓	✓	✓
Pumpkin seeds	✓	✓	✓	✓
Quinoa		✓	✓	✓
Sesame seeds	✓	✓	✓	✓
Spinach	✓	✓	✓	
Sunflower seeds	✓	✓	✓	
Whole wheat	✓	✓	✓	✓

Essential minerals are found in a variety of fresh foods.

As I said before, there's definitely more to a plant-based diet than lettuce. In fact, there's an amazing abundance of gloriously delicious foods to include, some of them you'll be familiar with, others maybe not so much. So, let's have a look at what could be on the menu.

Veggies

There are so many wonderful varieties of vegetables to eat throughout the year, it's surprising that there's time to eat anything else! Many people stick to a few familiar options like peas, carrots and (if they're feeling extravagant) broccoli, but there's such an abundance of veggies available that it's a shame not to explore them more fully.

Vegetables have a bad history in the UK. Many people have memories of soggy, flavourless mush from school dinners. Or maybe going to granny's and being served cabbage that's been boiled to within an inch of its life, leaving behind sulphurous aromas and not much else. Being forced to eat boring or poorly cooked vegetables can bring back bad memories. For many, vegetables were the centre of emotional battlegrounds when they were children, leaving a lasting impact in adulthood.

But veggies are amazing, if treated right. One of my aims for running my supper clubs was to showcase just how delicious a swathe of amazing produce could be. And there's no chance of getting bored, because there are a surprising number of different groups of veggies to try, with a number of varieties within each group. So there's lots to hold your interest at any time of the year.

Cultivated plants that we call vegetables can be linked together into different groups. Most people are surprised by just how many there are. I believe there's such an abundance of choice, even those limited by intolerances, health issues or bad experiences can find a whole slew of options to choose between. All that's needed is an open mind and the willingness to try.

Explore the list below so you can see what's on offer. Not every vegetable is listed and many more can be found in different areas around the world. That which will give you something to look forward to if you're lucky enough to travel.

Brassicas

While all veggies are important and have their own magical combination of micro and phytonutrients, brassicas are a particularly powerful group when it comes to health benefits. Their sulphur-containing compounds are the key and this is what gives this group their slightly bitter taste.

These compounds may be responsible for releasing farty wafts during the cooking phase, but they also have powerful anti-cancer properties and can help reduce heart disease. Brassicas also contain certain phytonutrients that are good for eye health and can help reduce overall inflammation within the body, which as we saw in Chapter 2 can only be a good thing.

Most of the research on the benefits of brassicas has been done with broccoli. However, it is thought that the benefits can be applied to all veggies in this group with a little variation in total nutrient content. But remember, when you eat a variety of whole foods, you automatically consume a wide range of nutrients.

Brassicas is a large group that includes roots, stems and leaves. How many of these could you nibble on every day?

Types of brassicas include:

- Brussels sprouts
- Romanesco broccoli
- Cabbage
- Kale and other greens
- Kohlrabi
- Hot leaves – rocket and mizuna
- Swede and turnip
- Radish
- Watercress
- Hot stuff – mustard, horseradish and wasabi

Some of the veggies in this list contain different varieties. Cabbage, for example, has many different colours (red, green, white), structures, sizes and flavours. Some might also define kale or spring greens as cabbage, although I have listed them separately. Each variety has a different flavour, culinary use and nutritional profile. With cabbage, rainbow eating is easy because you could have three different colours of cabbage in one day.

One of the interesting things about brassicas is that most sections of the plant can be eaten. With cauliflower, we tend to eat the 'flower' (it's in the name after all!), but the leaves and stems can also be just as good, and the same goes for broccoli. Brassicas sneak into all the vegetable groups – leaves, stems and roots – as well having their own special gang.

I was surprised to discover vegetables like turnips and horseradish are in the same family as cauliflower and cabbage. This is partly due to the fact that parts of these plant aren't usually available to buy. The leaves of all these plants are edible, but unless you grow your own or are able to buy them direct from a farmers' market, you might struggle to find them in a supermarket. Sprout tops are one example of this as this part of the plant would have been discarded in the past. However, some shops are now increasing their variety of seasonal greens, which is good news for the whole-food eater.

I was surprised to discover turnip leaves for sale in a Portuguese supermarket but they're a common staple in some local dishes. This is fantastic, as the leaves are packed full of amazing nutrients, much more than the bulb or root that we tend to focus on in the UK.

Some brassicas such as kale and greens have a bad reputation when it comes to thyroid health. Some of the phytonutrients could be goitrogens – a thyroid antagonist. What that means is some of the natural chemicals could combine with iodine receptors on the thyroid gland surface, blocking the uptake of iodine in the blood and leading to low thyroxine levels. Some people may be particularly susceptible to this.

There has been a lot of hype on the internet about this, but from what I understand, this is only a problem if you eat an excessively large amount (10 kilograms or so) of *raw* kale in a day. That's a lot! Maybe if you're a serious green juicer it could be an issue, but for most people eating even 100g of kale would be too much. Goitrogens can be disarmed by cooking, so if you're concerned but still want to eat an elephant's portion, pop it in the steamer first.

As mentioned above, brassicas contain amazing protective and beneficial phytonutrients, particularly sulforaphane. There is an issue though. Sulforaphane is locked up in the cell walls and is only released when activated by an enzyme called myrosinase. This occurs when the veg is cut or bitten into. All good so far.

The problem is that myrosinase does not like heat and is deactivated if the veg is cooked. Eating some raw veggies is a good thing, but most of us prefer to have our cruciferous veggies like broccoli and cauliflower cooked. So how can we get the benefit and still have cooked veg? The solution is to chop and leave – prepare the veg then leave it for 30 minutes before cooking.

Once released, sulforaphane is heat-resistant so won't mind being popped in a steamer for a few minutes.

Some people find it hard to absorb other nutrients from brassicas, so to make the most of them, try adding a squeeze of lemon juice just before serving, especially if you're using them in a soup or stew. The vitamin C aids the absorption of iron and magnesium in the body – and it also lifts the flavour slightly, a good thing if you're not used to the earthy, sulphurous flavour of brassicas.

One final point to mention about brassicas is their fibre. Brassicas tend to contain equal amounts of soluble and insoluble fibre; great for keeping you regular, maintaining an intact gut lining and of course giving those beneficial bacteria something tasty to nibble on. No wonder research shows they're particularly good for people with colon cancer.

Leafy greens

You may think all things green have been covered by brassicas, but no! Although there is some cross-over (after all, we eat the leaves of some brassicas), leafy greens have their own category, and a very important one it is too.

The leaves of plants carry amazing nutritional properties. Their greenness comes from chlorophyll, the compound found in plants that is instrumental in all their chemical processes. Without chlorophyll, photosynthesis cannot occur and essentially there's no plant.

In biology lessons we're taught that humans can't process chlorophyll and gain no benefit from it. However, new research suggests that's not true. It appears that red light-waves penetrate the body and if you have recently eaten greens (and therefore chlorophyll) you can create energy from it. That's mind-blowing stuff! Greens also work deep at the cellular level – as long as you get out in the sun that is, so it seems that sunlight is useful for doing more than just making vitamin D.

In fact, the leaves of most veggies are edible. You can even make soup or pesto with carrot tops, though you need to make sure you use only young fresh leaves for this as they become rather woody when they're older and larger.

There are a few leaves that definitely cannot be eaten though. Tomato, rhubarb and parsnip leaves are poisonous so please don't be inspired to give them a go.

Leafy greens include:

- Spinach
- Chard
- Lettuce – all types, including romaine, little gem, radicchio (it's red, but green!)
- Curly endive
- Bok choi
- Fresh green herbs like parsley, coriander and mint
- Watercress
- Rocket and other peppery leaves
- Kale
- Turnip, radish and beetroot tops
- Pea shoots
- Celery leaves
- Dandelion leaves – tender when young and free food if you pick them yourself

With such a wide range of leaves, different greens are available all year round. Sadly, many of these are hard to find in the shops. Beet leaves for example are super-tasty, but once picked they wilt quickly, creating a logistics issue for supermarket chains. Equally, if too many leaves are harvested while the plant is still growing, it won't be able to survive, which would limit their availability.

My family think I'm obsessed with adding greens into my cooking. They may be right. They're always looking for the hidden spinach or kale, and often find it! If you add a handful of leaves into curries, pasta sauces, soups, pie mixes – anything really – it elevates the nutritional profile without you having to munch through a pile of raw leaves. They add to the flavour too, particularly strong peppery leaves or fresh herbs.

One way of helping your body absorb more nutrients from leafy greens is to pair them with a whole fat. Nut-, seed- or avocado-based dressings and creams are a super-tasty way of making sure both your taste-buds and body benefit. There's a whole selection of simple sauces to try in the recipe section. Alternatively, you could just sprinkle some whole nuts or ground flaxseed over your leaves, or drizzle over some cold-pressed flaxseed oil.

Finally, try to make sure your leafy greens are as fresh as possible. If you're able to, grow your own; even a few pots of leaves on the patio can keep you going for a while. If that's not possible, look for freshly harvested options at the market or supermarket. Even better, try a veg box scheme that delivers seasonal fresh leaves throughout the year.

Fruit vegetables

If you're not sure of the difference between what makes something a fruit or a vegetable, you're not alone. Research by a gardening website revealed that many people were confused. There's a surprising amount of produce we think of as vegetables that are botanically classified as fruits. Most people know that tomatoes are a fruit – if you've ever grown your own it's fascinating to observe how the little yellow flowers develop into tiny green orbs that swell, grow and finally ripen red (or whatever colour tomato is being grown). That same process happens with many other veggies, and of course fruit. Anything that is a seed-bearing structure that develops from the ovary of a plant is botanically a fruit. So, think of a veg that contains seeds and you'll discover it's a fruit.

There's a huge range of fruit vegetables to choose from. They're a colourful bunch and they help make rainbow eating a wonderfully tasty option.

Types of fruit vegetables include:

- Tomatoes and tomatillos
- Peppers – bell, chilli
- Pumpkins, squash and gourds
- Cucumbers
- Aubergine/Eggplant
- Okra
- Olives
- Avocado
- Courgette and marrow
- Sweetcorn
- Peas and beans (for this section, that includes mange tout, runner beans etc. More on beans and legumes later.)

Just writing this list has made my mouth water! There's such a variety here, all containing wonderful powerful phytonutrients and anti-oxidants that support cell health.

Stems, bulbs, tubers and roots

Another big group of veggies, this bunch tend to be the staple for many people around the world. In the northern hemisphere, many bulbs, tubers and roots can either be harvested in the winter or stored to provide a steady food supply in the less productive months. Root vegetables, in particular, tend to be associated with 'comfort food' – warming soups and stews that are perfect for keeping the cold at bay.

Contrary to some popular beliefs, this group is far from nutritionally poor. Our ancestors would have picked stems and dug up roots and bulbs they found whilst foraging for food. Many of this group have strong medicinal properties, particular the alliums, like onion and garlic. And many of these are particularly popular with friendly microbes in the gut, acting as pre-biotic fodder to keep our bacteria happy and healthy.

Types of stems include:

- Asparagus
- Celery
- Bamboo shoots
- Chive
- Leeks
- Rhubarb (not a fruit!)

Types of bulbs include:

- Garlic
- Onions and shallots
- Tubers – Jerusalem artichokes, potatoes and sweet potatoes

Types of roots include:

- Carrots
- Turnips and swede
- Celeriac
- Radish and daikon
- Beetroot
- Parsnip
- Ginger

Rainbow veggies can flourish, even when grown under the ground. Some of these, like asparagus, have a very limited season, but many others can be grown all year round. And whilst some veggies, like potatoes, have a reputation for being nutritionally poor, much of that is due to the way they've been adapted for growing and processing. A baked potato – either the sweet or normal variety – is the ultimate simple supper. It's what you put on top that makes the difference.

Fungi

My husband once had a very drunken debate with a friend who declared that mushrooms shouldn't be part of a plant-based diet as they're not a plant. Now of course that's technically true, but then they're not an animal either. Being fungi, they're in their own special category, but have traditionally been treated as a plant in cooking.

Fungi have always featured in the human diet, and rightly so. They contain a wide array of vitamins, minerals and phytonutrients, and have been used medicinally for thousands of years. The Romans called mushrooms 'the food of the gods' and in Egyptian times they were reserved for the Pharaohs. More recently, there has been an increase in the development of medicinal mushrooms as researchers have uncovered some of their mysteries and unlocked the chemistry of their healing properties, particularly anti-inflammatory and anti-cancer.

I love mushrooms, but many people are not keen, and some are intolerant or allergic to them. Many people who have a gut imbalance and yeast overgrowth need to avoid them too. Fortunately, they didn't seem to affect me negatively, despite my yeast problem, which was a relief.

The texture of mushrooms can also be a problem for some people, particularly if they're overcooked or past their best. Being fungi means they can become slimy and taste a bit mouldy, which is enough to put anyone off if they've had a bad mushroom experience. But don't be put off. When they're delicately cooked, they have a great flavour and give a wonderful texture to many different kinds of dishes.

There are thousands of different types of mushrooms that can be used in food. Foraged, wild mushrooms are particularly sought after by top chefs and other foodies. It's no wonder experienced foragers are secretive about their favourite patches of tasty fungi. Some fungi are poisonous though, so never go mushroom picking on your own unless you know what you're doing.

Even though there are many types of mushroom that can be eaten, my local supermarket stocks a pretty limited choice. Most are cultivated rather than wild and the range is usually limited to button, chestnut and Portobello mushrooms. Although these might seem a bit boring and unimaginative, I love them and try to add them into my diet in some form most days. One of my favourite breakfasts is mushrooms with spinach and avocado. Quick, simple and super-tasty.

If you fancy some more exotic mushrooms and your supermarket doesn't provide them, try going to a Chinese supermarket instead as they often have a wider range. Trumpet mushrooms are really worth a try. With thick stems and a small cap, they look like mini trees and have an incredibly meaty texture. If fresh ones aren't available, you can always use dried mushrooms instead. Remember to keep the soaking water for stock as the flavour and nutrients will pep up any broth or soup.

Sea vegetables

In the past, if you grew up by the sea then sea vegetables like dulse and samphire (sea asparagus) would have been a regular part of your diet. Laverbread, which is nothing like bread, is puréed laver (a type of seaweed) that was traditionally eaten for breakfast in Wales. You can buy it online if you fancy trying it out (*see the Online Resources and Article References section on p302*). If you know what you're looking for, you can still go foraging for sea vegetables today, but for many of us, they've become part of food history.

Sea vegetables are not really veg but algae and, like mushrooms, not all of them are edible, so it's not a good idea to nip down to the nearest rock pool to munch on a bit of bladder-wrack. You may get more than you bargained for!

Samphire has become popular now; I discovered it by watching one of Rick Stein's cookery programmes. Even though I knew it came from the sea, the first time I ate it, I was surprised by how intensely salty it was. Having done more research, I learnt that I needed to soak it before I cooked it in order to draw out some of the excess sodium. Once you get past the salt challenge, you'll discover that it has a fabulous texture and flavour, although it's not cheap to buy.

Do try to include some form of sea vegetable in your diet every now and then. Black, red and green algae all contain amazing nutrients, especially minerals. Iodine, which is quite hard to get elsewhere, is abundant in sea vegetables. This is essential for effective thyroid function and there is growing concern that many people consume inadequate amounts.

Sea vegetables also have amazing phytonutrients that have a whole array of health benefits. If you want to know more about this, check out the links in the Online Resources and Article References section on p302.

Of course, another amazing way to eat sea vegetables is to get yourself some sushi. Nori and kombu are sea vegetables that are mainly found near Japan, and they're key elements of sushi rolls. Many restaurants now offer a wide selection of vegetable sushi options which is very useful if you travel a lot. You could also try incorporating wakame into miso soup.

If you want to have a regular intake of sea vegetables but can't find any locally, dried sea-vegetable flakes are a useful alternative. There are a number of organic options available on the market. These can be used as a general seasoning instead of salt and pepper. They not only enliven any dish but also give an extra nutritional dimension.

If you suffer with bean-induced flatulence, add a piece of dried kombu into the cooking water. Not only will it help the beans to cook faster, it reduces some of the compounds within the beans that make you fart. Great advice for top trumpers!

Fruit

Humans are naturally drawn to fruit – it must be our monkey genes! Advertising experts know this. Supermarkets often display images of vibrant red strawberries or sun-ripened peaches to entice us through the door. Vividly bright so it catches the eye, fruit is sumptuously sweet on the tongue, hitting many of our comfort and satisfaction buttons. And rightly so, because fruit is packed full of amazing nutrients and phytonutrients that support our bodies in many ways, helping us feel great and live well.

Yet recently, fruit or at least the sugar in fruit, called fructose, has been given a bit of a bad name. Although fructose is a simple sugar (like glucose), it can muck around with blood sugar levels if it has been refined and denatured. However, the fructose found naturally in a whole fruit is partnered with another key ingredient, fibre, and that makes all the difference.

Fruit really is a key battleground in the world of refined versus whole foods. If you consume whole fruit, fructose is delivered in moderate amounts and – along with all the vitamins, natural oils and phytonutrients that the body loves – can be absorbed into the bloodstream at a slow and steady rate. As soon as you extract the juice from the fruit and consume it on its own, you're heading into the danger zone because you're likely to consume two if not three times the amount of fructose than in the whole fruit and, of course, you'll get none of the fibre.

Take orange juice as an example. Eating an orange takes time. First you have to peel it to get to the juicy segments inside. Then you have to remove any excess pith because it tastes bitter. Next, the segments have to be separated and possibly some seeds removed. Finally, you get to eat it. But when you do, each segment is packaged in a fibrous coating that takes some chewing to break down. As a general rule, one orange is enough.

Unless you're squeezing your own orange juice, it takes no time at all to pour juice into a glass and drink it. It's rare that you'd pour the small amount of juice that is extracted from one orange. Usually it's two, three or even four oranges freely flowing into the stomach and again, with the fibre and essential oils missing that just becomes a super-instant sugar shot.

The natural fruit sugar, fructose, is also associated in many people's minds with the manufactured product called high fructose syrup. This mega-sweet gloop is one of the many by-products of processing corn. It's a very cheap sweetener made for the processed food industry. High fructose syrup pings the brain's pleasure receptors so it's not surprising that it's in a high percentage of manufactured food products. There are no nutritional benefits from this type of fructose; it only causes inflammatory harm.

The best way to get your fruit sugar hit is from fresh, whole fruit. Many of my cakes include some form of fruit because it helps to reduce the need for other forms of sugar, while also adding nutritional benefits. I like the idea of cake being health food!

Dried fruit is also useful for baking and many raw desserts contain dates and other forms of dried fruit. But it's important to remember that these are concentrated forms of sugar. They may contain all the fibre of fresh fruit, but because the water has been extracted (or vastly reduced) it makes each fruit smaller so it's easier to eat many more of them in one go. Think about how easy it is to knock back a few handfuls of raisins. And yet they're just dried grapes. You may think twice about eating that many fresh grapes in one go, even if they're very moreish. I'm not telling you to avoid eating dried fruit, it's just worth being mindful about how much you consume in one sitting. This is particularly pertinent when it comes to dates.

Dates are the ultimate sugary snack food for the whole-food diner. Super-sweet and sticky, some dates have a deep and complex flavour that's reminiscent of fudge. When eaten whole, it's easy to lose track of how many you're consuming although, to be honest, they're so rich it's hard to have a huge amount all at once. Having said that, my husband's colleague did manage to polish off a big bag in one day when he went on a diet. He must have consumed more sugar in that bag than he would normally have done in a whole day! And as for all that fibre, I hate to think of the outcome.

It's that rich sweet flavour and chewy texture that makes dates the perfect ingredient in raw desserts and snacks. The only issue is that they need to be broken down in a food processor and blended with other ingredients. No fibre is removed, but the processing reduces the amount of digestive effort required so the sugars are released more readily. Also, you may well end up eating a lot more than you would if you were nibbling on a couple of whole dates.

Now, I'm not saying don't eat dates. Indeed, they are a key ingredient in many of the desserts in the recipe section. They taste wonderful! Just be aware of how much you're consuming particularly as everyone will tolerate and process dates at different rates. The fibre content will slow the release of their natural sugars, even when blended, increasing the feeling of satiety, helping you feel fuller sooner and for longer. It's definitely better to eat dates than consume lots of refined sugar.

The bright colour of fruits is a sign that they contain powerful phytonutrients like flavonoids and carotenoids. They're also a fabulous source of vitamin C. All of these nutrients have anti-oxidant effects in the body.

Although each fruit has a season, most are available all year round in shops because they're either forced under cover or flown from other parts of the world. Eating fruit in season is much better for you; it's fresher, more local and provides you with the best nutrients for that time of year. That's why it's no coincidence that citrus fruits, which are high in vitamin C to support the immune system, are in season during the winter. Or that summer-fruiting berries contain anti-oxidants to protect the skin from sun damage. Mother Nature is very wise.

One of the problems with extending the growing season or sending fruit on long journeys is that it can spoil, so to prevent this, large amounts of chemical sprays are used. Indeed, strawberries and apples are on the list of the most chemically-laden produce you can buy. These are the chemicals that can harm our microbiome. Try to consume only organically grown fruit or grow your own, if possible.

Some fruits like strawberries have natural yeasts on their surface and when you combine that with the natural sugar content in the fruit itself, it can cause a problem for anyone with a yeast over-growth. If your gut is in a particularly poor state, you may find yourself bloating after eating berries and melon, or you may find it hard to heal your gut. If that's the case for you, abstain from these fruits for a while and stick to more gut-friendly varieties that contain pre-biotics, like apples and bananas.

Another good habit to develop is eating fruit at the start of a meal rather than at the end and having it as a snack in between meals. Fruit is digested more quickly than other heavier, more complex and fibre-filled foods so it'll start to ferment if it's held up in the gut. It's much better to let it go first and have free run of the gut.

Many fruits contain pectin. This gel-forming part of fibre is what helps jam to set, but it also provides nourishment for friendly bacteria and contributes to gut health. Apples and even bananas contain large amounts of pectin, which is why they can act as a replacement for eggs in cakes and as a sweetener. Two jobs in one! In fact, apples have many amazing properties that support our bodies – the saying 'an apple a day keeps the doctor away' is pretty much spot on.

Legumes (beans and pulses)

If you're still wondering where you're going to get your protein from, look no further than legumes. Packed full of wonderful fibre, minerals and other phytonutrients, legumes have always been – and still are – the world's main source of protein.

Derisorily known as 'the poor man's meat', legumes and more specifically beans, are the oldest known form of cultivated plants and have been found in prehistoric archaeological digs. Not only are they cheap and readily accessible all around the world, they also have amazing health benefits with a wealth of scientific evidence to prove it. Who can forget the classic childhood rhyme guaranteed to annoy mums everywhere?

Beans, beans are good for your heart,
The more you eat, the more you fart,
The more you fart, the better you feel,
So, eat baked beans at every meal!

Now I'm not sure about the logic of connecting farting with feeling good, but this rhyme is certainly right about them being good for your heart. They can also help balance blood sugar levels and have also been connected with a reduction in cancer rates.

The farting is an issue for some people, although for many, beans don't have as bad an effect as their reputation suggests. Research shows that on average humans pass flatulence 14 times a day. What a project to work on! Half of that comes from swallowed air; if you talk while you eat or gulp your dinner down, you'll swallow more air than food and suffer the consequences later. Gut bacteria produces most of the rest, creating gases as they dine on insoluble fibre in the colon. Aromas come from high-sulphur foods like eggs and meat, although bad bacteria can contribute some pretty offensive wafts.

If you suffer from IBS, legumes can have an even more potent effect on the gut resulting in excessive wind, bloating and sometimes crippling spasms. Taking action to improve your gut health should help reduce these problems, but it can take time and perseverance. Some people react more strongly to one type of bean than another, which could be the result of an intolerance born of a leaky gut, so it's important to be aware of how different foods affect you.

Beans and pulses can be made more tolerable and digestible with good preparation. Proper soaking and cooking can help too, including cooking with a little bicarbonate of soda. Soaking and sprouting can also make things better as this helps to release the wonderful nutrients found inside the bean and make them more available for absorption in the gut. Dried beans contain phytic acid, a phytonutrient that keeps the inner nutrients locked up until the right environment comes along – in this case, warmth and water – which is why the right preparation makes such a difference.

There are so many different types of beans and lentils it's hard to get bored with them, which means it's easy to ensure you get a good variety of them to keep your gut bacteria happy and healthy. Buying dried beans and cooking them at home can be cheaper than buying them tinned, although once you include the cost of the fuel needed to cook them and the time they take to prepare, tinned versions are often much more attractive. After all, plant-based eating is not about being a slave to the kitchen and tinned beans can be used to create quick and delicious meals.

Try to buy tinned beans in unsalted water, but if you can't, remember to rinse them well so you can get rid of as much of the salt as possible. The other bonus about unsalted beans, particularly chickpeas, is that the brine can be used as a replacement for eggs. Chickpea brine or aquafaba is an amazing discovery that has a multitude of applications in plant-based cooking – far too many to go into here. If you've not come across it yet, have a look for it on the internet as there's lots of great information and many recipes to try.

My friend says she associates beans and lentils with hippy figures like Neil from the TV show The Young Ones, but these days they're more hip than hippy! There are lots of suggestions about how to use them in the recipe section. Personally, my favourite pulses are yellow or red split lentils as I love dal, and black beans because they have such a great texture.

Grains

Grains are a major feature of almost every diet around the world, yet they've gained a bad reputation in the last few years. Despite this, extensive research (including enormous lengthy studies with thousands of participants), conclude that they're extremely beneficial for our health. So, what's the problem?

The problem is us – humans! The majority of the grains eaten in the Western world are refined, white and quite frankly just not what they used to be. Intensive farming and changes to the grain to ensure they have an extended shelf life has leeched the nutrients out of the soil and destroyed the beneficial compounds from them. On top of that, cross-breeding aimed at maximising yield and minimising cost has created a hybrid product that isn't what we're accustomed to. Remember, our bodies are slow learners and modern wheat, for example, appears to be having a negative long-term effect on them.

Eating wheat and whole-grains is not new, despite the fact that some say otherwise. A recent archaeological dig discovered evidence of our pre-historic ancestors consuming Emmer, an early variety of wheat.

Of course, grains are more than just wheat. In fact, this huge group includes cereal crops and pseudo-grains such as:

- Rice
- Barley
- Oats
- Rye
- Millet
- Quinoa
- Buckwheat
- Teff
- Amaranth

Some of these crops include a wide range of varieties, but our supermarkets only tend to stock a limited selection. When I was in India, I discovered a plethora of different types and colours of rice, each with their own texture, taste and nutritional profile. Red rice became a firm favourite of mine. Even though it has now become more common in the UK, there are still only one or two types of red rice on offer, whereas I came across many more in India, some of them very local to a specific area.

Up until the early 1970s, it's believed that there were over a million varieties of rice in India. Now though, this number has fallen to just 6000. That's still more than you'd find in the UK, but if variety is the key to gut health, it's easy to see how our microbiome has lost out over the last 40 years or so.

There are many claims made on the internet that grains create inflammation in the body, and yet the science suggests otherwise. Studies monitoring inflammatory markers in blood conclude that consistent consumption of whole grains both moderates and reduces inflammation. However, nutrient deficient grains like white flour that feature in a highly processed, low-fibre diet are certainly not going to offer much benefit.

Gluten has been targeted as the big issue. It certainly can cause serious harm to anyone who has coeliac disease (a gluten allergy) or a gluten intolerance. The rate of those reporting an allergy to gluten or an intolerance of it has increased over the last decade or so, and yet no one really knows by how much.

Many people claim to feel better after excluding wheat from their diet, but is it the wheat that's actually causing the problem? Modern bread is often full of other ingredients as well as genetically-altered, poor-quality wheat.

But if it's not the wheat, then maybe it's the yeast that's the problem. Traditionally, using a natural ferment and slow rise method, it took time to make bread. By contrast, modern day processes minimise the time it takes to make bread by incorporating fast-acting yeast and including additives and preservatives to give the bread a longer shelf life. When you factor in a struggling microbiome, it's easy to see how the yeast alone could create a great deal more gas and discomfort than you'd care for. I've discovered that, since my gut health improved, I can tolerate a traditional sourdough loaf, but if I eat any form of 'plastic' bread my migraines reappear with a vengeance.

One of the other issues with grains, and particularly wheat, is that even in a whole-food, plant-based diet, we tend to consume it in flour form rather than its original whole form. Aside from bread, the most obvious of these is breakfast cereals. Although the packet may gloat about its whole-grain contents, in reality, the final product is far from the original and the sugars are released more quickly due to it already being partly processed.

This is not the case when you're cooking with wholegrain rice, quinoa, buckwheat and millet etc. These too can be milled into a flour, but are much better consumed in their whole form wherever possible. Apart from anything else, the flavour and texture of these products contribute greatly to the enjoyment of the dish.

Some grains like wholegrain rice can take a while to cook. One solution is to soak it in advance – just remember to measure out the rice and water in the morning before you go to work and when you return in the evening it will take only 10-15 minutes to cook. Alternatively, you could invest in a rice cooker with a timer. Other grains, like quinoa and millet take only 10 minutes to cook. As a general rule, rice needs a 1:2 rice to water ratio, other grains need a ratio of 1:3. To make life simple, I always measure amounts of grain and water using cups. So, for rice, I use one cup of rice and two cups of water. It doesn't have to be a formal measuring cup – a small mug will work just as well, as long as you fill it to the top.

If you struggle with one type of grain, don't just dismiss the whole group. Try different varieties and see if it makes a difference to how you feel. Of course, if you have a known gluten allergy then take care to avoid grains like barley and rye that contain gliadin, a protein found in gluten. There are many that don't, so you have a choice. If you have an intolerance, avoid the main offender but keep an open mind because as you improve your diet and gut health, you'll hopefully find you can increase your levels of tolerance. As always, variety is key, so mix it up and keep creating new options for yourself.

Nuts and seeds

While trying to lose weight in my early twenties, I spent a long time following a low-fat diet that excluded all nuts (except for chestnuts) because of their high fat content. Ironically, the diet included meat, despite it also being high in fat. Looking back, it seems 'nuts' that this diet advocated such discrepancies and in hindsight it may well have been a big error following this plan for so long. A study published in 2012 found that a poor intake of nuts (and seeds) contributed to the death of millions of people around the world. So, the good news is that if you eat a small amount of nuts every week it could extend your life by a couple of years.

Nuts and seeds contain different types of fat, ranging from simple mono-unsaturated to poly-unsaturated to fully saturated depending on which ones you choose to eat. They also have different ratios of omega 3 and 6 essential fatty acids too. But there's much more to nuts and seeds than just fat. For a start, there's protein and fibre plus a whole range of micro and phytonutrients that our bodies just love.

All nuts and seeds have their own magic properties both in terms of their nutrient content and their culinary variety. Many can be used to make versions of dairy-free milk, although some are more practical for this than others. Almonds make a delicious and creamy milk, fabulous for breakfast dishes and desserts or for creating a creamy-textured nutrient hit in a soup. But when it comes to creaminess, the cashew nut is king. Versatile and requiring little prep, cashews make amazing sweet and savoury creams and sauces because they lack a strong flavour and so take on whatever flavour you partner them with. You'll see them pop up in many of the recipes in this book.

Pecan and walnuts are also a favourite of mine. Their rich, deep flavours enhance salads and desserts, and both can be broken down and used as a pastry base, their natural oils both binding and enriching the final product.

Despite knowing that nuts are good for me, I still feel rather naughty when I eat too many at a time. And that's one of the problems with them – they're too easy to eat! And when you start blending them it's all too easy to lose track of exactly how many you're eating at any one time. If one of your aims in changing to a whole-food, plant-based diet is to lose weight, you need to be aware that the high calorie content of nuts could make weight loss difficult. Bear in mind that all the research revealing the health benefits of nuts is based on someone eating the equivalent of a *small handful* each day.

The hard shell around the nut shows that Mother Nature is giving us a hint that we need to take care over the quantity of nuts we eat. When a nut is in its shell, it takes time to open it, extract the prize and eat it. By the time you've cracked open the equivalent of a handful, the novelty has worn off – you've had enough. But if you open a packet of shelled (and salted) nuts all the work has been done for you and before you know it half the pack has gone. This problem is compounded when it comes to eating nut butter, especially if it's highly processed with added oils and sugar. Nut butters ping all our dopamine receptors and makes us want to eat even more of them. So, it's wise to be aware of how you consume nuts and make an effort to eat them at different levels of refinement throughout the week.

As well as enjoying nuts, I also love seeds and add them to dishes (and especially salads) whenever I can. Not only do they look pretty, but they add texture, flavour and little nuggets of whole fats and nutrients too. For example, sesame seeds contain good amounts of calcium and can help support healthy bones. I usually toast a handful and scatter them over a green salad or use them as a coating for small falafels or veggie patties. They're easy and quick to use as well as being super-tasty.

Some seeds are amazing sources of omega 3 fatty acids, particularly chia and flaxseeds. Both contain fibre that forms into a gel when mixed with water. This is very useful for plant-based baking because, as well as adding additional healthy nutrients, they can also help stick things together.

Both nuts and seeds crop up regularly in my recipes, either as a main ingredient or a garnish. It's useful to have a good stock in your cupboards, but don't buy them in bulk unless either you're going to use them relatively quickly or you have somewhere dark and cool to store them. Containing delicate oils, nuts can go rancid if exposed to light or heat, making them good for nothing. As with all groups of food, don't just rely on one type but graze on a wide variety as each one has different nutrient and fibre combinations that'll help keep your microbiome happy and healthy.

Finally, flaxseed has a super-tough outer coating and needs to be ground otherwise it will come out the same way it went in. The oils within are extremely delicate and so need to be kept in the fridge otherwise the wonderful nutritional benefits will be lost. The easiest and cheapest way to do this is to buy a bag of flaxseed and grind a small amount at a time, then store the ground seed in a jar in the fridge. That way you don't have to grind the seeds every time you want some and you'll always have a fresh and highly effective supply whenever you need it. I sprinkle a tablespoon on everything – breakfast, soups, stews, salads, vegetables – as it gives anything an extra nutritional kick. You really can't go wrong.

But What About Protein?

If you're wondering if a plant-based diet can supply enough protein, the following diagram should help put your mind at rest. Eating a range of these foods gives you all the amino acids your body needs to function well.

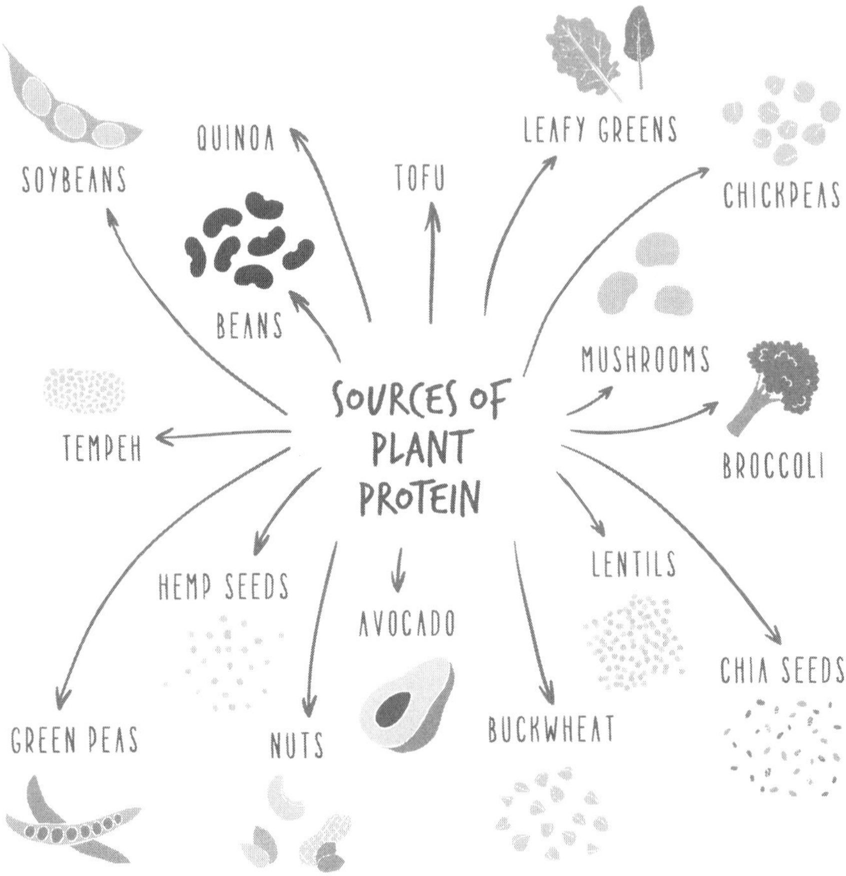

There are plenty of plant-based proteins to choose from.

CHAPTER FIVE

COOKING TECHNIQUES AND EQUIPMENT

So now we have looked at *what* is in a whole-food plant-based diet, let's have a quick look at some specific cooking techniques and equipment that will come in handy. After that, we'll look at the final and very important part in this section – *how* to make it work for you.

On the whole, cooking a whole-food, plant-based diet is pretty simple and easy. You'll know most techniques as they're standard procedures, but there are a few new methods and approaches worth learning. After a few disasters, I've learnt some tricks over the past few years, which I've set out below to create an essential guide to what to do and why. These tips will help prevent you from carbonising your onions or ruining a cake. Of course, if you're anything like me, you'll learn by doing rather than reading, but it's worth taking a moment to look through this chapter before jumping in.

Frying Without Oil

Avoiding refined oils is key to eating a whole-food plant-based diet, particularly if you're dealing with a health problem. Frying with oil at high heats changes the molecular structure of the oil – and that's on top of the changes that have already occurred during the refining process. This makes the oils toxic to the body giving it another metabolic challenge to deal with.

The alternative is to sauté with water or vegetable stock. The key is to use the right amount at the right temperature. This is influenced by what you're cooking and the pan you're using, as well as the type of hob you're cooking on.

When it comes to appliances, a gas hob and a fan-oven are my ideal choices, but those options are not always available, so you need to develop a relationship with your hob. Work out how quickly it adjusts and the best rings and settings to use to get the job done efficiently and deliciously. I prefer gas as it's more flexible and sensitive to adjustments. Electric hobs vary enormously in sensitivity to change – if your pan gets too hot, you may need to take it off the ring completely and let both the pan and the ring calm down a bit before bringing the two back together.

My top tips for frying without oil

- Use a non-stick frying pan or heavy-based stainless-steel pan.
- Pre-heat on a medium setting for a few minutes.
- Drop a tablespoon of liquid into the pan – if it sizzles and bounces, the heat is just right. If it over-reacts and evaporates, cool the pan slightly. If nothing happens, it's not warm enough so wait a bit longer until the fluid starts to bubble.
- Once ready, add your ingredients plus a dash more liquid and stir well. Reduce the heat slightly and pop on a lid. This stops the moisture evaporating.
- Stir regularly so the ingredients don't stick, although a little caramelisation on the bottom of the pan is fine because it adds depth to the flavour.
- If all the liquid disappears, add a little more but not too much as there's a fine line between frying and braising.
- Some vegetables contain a lot of fluid, like tomatoes so they'll help to deglaze the pan and lift off any stuck-on bits.
- Always adjust the heat in response to what's happening on the bottom of the pan.

As with most things, practice makes perfect so don't fret if it takes a few times before you get to grips with it. Once you do, you'll wonder why you were taught to use oil in the first place.

Oven bake, don't fry

Many popular foods are deep fried. It saves time, creates texture and the fat is enticing. It's also the most unhealthy way to cook, particularly if the oil is persistently reheated. If you have an oven, don't be afraid to use it, as many foods that are traditionally deep-fried taste just as good baked. It does take a little more time, but it could also lengthen your life-span so it all works out in the end.

There's no getting away from the fact that the flavour and texture will be slightly different though, but then this whole way of eating is slightly different and once you've eliminated all that greasy oil from your diet, your body will love you for it. You'll also discover that if you go back to eating something that's been deep-fried, it won't taste great or make you feel good. Honest!

Good non-stick baking sheets are a must. Take care of them, because if they get scratched or the coating starts to flake off, you must stop using them. If ingested, the coating will just add to your toxic load. Another option is to use baking paper or a silicon mat to stop food from sticking. The other essential tool is patience. Don't be tempted to try turning a patty or falafel when you've only just put it in. If you do, disaster will strike and it'll collapse into a sad and squashy mess. Have faith and leave well alone. It's surprising how it will suddenly turn light brown from the natural sugars caramelising and firm up on both sides so it's perfect for serving. Once again, practice makes perfect.

Baking Cakes

Life is too short not to have cake; fortunately, even when you're eating a whole-food, plant-based diet, it's easy to make tasty cakes. Of course, they also have the added benefit of being a healthier option. I'm a big fan of cake – I was distraught at the thought of not being able to have it as part of my new dairy-free way of eating. But this minor trauma was significantly lessened once I learnt a new way to bake. It may sound shallow to mourn the loss of cake, but we all need pleasures in life.

Naturally, baking without butter, milk and eggs can seem a huge challenge at first. The science behind baking (lessons at school are not called 'food technology' for nothing!) involves calculations to achieve the correct balance of fat, sugar and flour to create a cake with a light, fluffy texture and wonderfully satisfying flavour. If you've ever watched The Great British Bake Off you'll know how complex and serious it can be.

Fortunately, plant-based baking has fewer rules, which means you don't need to be so precise – definitely a bonus for me given my slap-dash way of cooking. That doesn't mean it isn't sometimes a challenge to get a good rise and a suitable 'crumb', especially using gluten-free flour. The appearance, texture and taste may be different, but that's not necessarily a bad thing. You can still achieve amazing results with a little patience and ingenuity.

The baking session is always very popular on my course, especially for people who are new to eating the plant-based way. I always do a little demo to show how quick and easy it can be to make cakes and biscuits. It helps that I have an abundance of tips and techniques that can make plant-based baking a success. Below is a list of my top tips for helping you get started making some delicious plant-based goodies.

Traditionally, the five main ingredients involved in baking are milk, butter, eggs, flour and sugar. When it comes to food intolerances, these are all high on the list of offenders. There's not much that's plant-based or whole-food about milk, butter (or other refined oils or fats), eggs, refined flour and sugar. The wonderful thing about plant-based baking is that there is a whole cupboardful of healthy options you can use so even if you have food intolerances, there's always an alternative you can use in your cake, which means you can literally have your cake and eat it.

Let's have a look at each of these main ingredients and their main alternatives.

Core Baking Ingredients

Milk

When it comes to choosing which plant-based milk to drink on a day-to-day basis, it's usually a matter of going for the one you most like the taste of and which you can tolerate. But when it comes to baking, there's a bit more science involved. This is because the source of the milk – nuts, seeds or beans – contains different properties and molecular structures that can have an influence on the outcome of your cake. If you choose well, you'll get a light and fluffy result that even Mary Berry would be impressed with. Choose unwisely, and you might be feeding the dustbin instead of yourself.

One of the first things to be aware of is the sugar content of any dairy-free milks. This is because dairy milk is quite sweet, so manufacturers often add refined sugar to make their dairy-free milks more palatable – especially to those whose palates haven't adjusted to having less sugar. Needless to say, refined sugar has no place on a whole-food, plant-based diet and as time goes by, your taste-buds will change so you won't miss it. But if you want to reduce your dependency on sugar faster, avoid sweetened dairy-free milks from the start. In terms of baking, if you use sweetened milk it'll only serve to make your cake sweeter.

As mentioned above, each type of dairy-free milk has different molecular properties that will influence the success of your cake. Here's a list of when and where to use each one.

Soya milk: This is my milk of choice for baking. With a similar molecular structure to dairy milk, soya is stable at high and prolonged temperatures and makes an excellent direct substitute. Choosing the right type of soya milk is important, though, as some have a very strong flavour and chalky texture, plus it is often sweetened. Double check to make sure it is unsweetened and avoid brands that promote a 'whole bean flavour'. Some people are also concerned about buying genetically modified soya products, although this is currently less of a problem in Europe. If you're concerned, buy organic.

Buttermilk: Sometimes cake recipes ask for buttermilk to help get a good rise or a good crumb texture, often bread or muffin recipes. This is not something you can readily buy but it's easy to make as it's essentially just soured milk. To make it, add a little vinegar or lemon juice to soya milk. You can turn soya milk into buttermilk because it has a higher protein content than other plant-based milks and it's this that curdles when the acid is added, turning it to a gloopy, slightly curdled mix. Just what you're looking for!

Oat milk: Light but still has a creamy texture. As it doesn't have a strong flavour, oat milk works well in baking when soya or nut milks are off the menu. On the plus side, its low-fat and low-protein content means it doesn't curdle but, on the down side, it doesn't work so well with the raising agents and doesn't always produce a good rise. Of course, the exact result depends on the recipe as not all cakes are designed to rise, so it's good for these recipes. In general, I use oat milk more in savoury cooking than sweet.

Rice milk: This tends to be lighter and thinner than soya milk, so has a less creamy texture. But it's good for creating bubbles, which means it produces a light, fluffy cake. As it doesn't have much flavour, rice milk won't interfere with the taste of your cake by adding or masking other flavours and it's ideal for anyone who can't tolerate soya or nut milks. Rice milk tends to separate in the carton, so make sure you give it a good shake before you pour it, otherwise you'll end up with a disappointing jug of cloudy water.

Nut milks: Super-creamy and full of flavour, nut milks like almond and cashew are now the most popular dairy-free milk versions available, even overtaking soya milk. The molecular structure of nuts is dense in comparison with oats, rice and soya for example, which means it can be too heavy to use in cakes as it makes it difficult for the raising agents to create enough bubbles to make the mixture rise. Whenever someone tells me their cake didn't work, it's usually because they used almond milk. However, the creaminess of nut milk is perfect for more solid bakes like *Oat and Raisin Cookies* (*see page 284*). These are naturally dense and rich so the almond milk adds to that texture. Coconut milk used straight from a tin is definitely too heavy for most cake recipes and even though you can buy coconut-based milks from the chiller cabinet that are similar to other milks, it's still too heavy to use for baking.

Butter and fats

Unlike traditional cake making, there's no creaming of fat and sugar with a plant-based cake – or not the way I make them. This means cakes are much quicker to make. It also means I don't have any justification for investing in an expensive brand of food mixer to look pretty on my work-top.

For cake, flavourless oils are the fat of choice and I specifically recommend using olive oil or organic rapeseed oil rather than ordinary vegetable or sunflower oil. Although both are still refined they can tolerate higher heats and tend to be slightly less chemically toxic to the body. Cookie and biscuit recipes can be adapted to use a dairy-free butter alternative. As demand grows, so do the number of spreads made from sunflower, soya, olive and coconut oils. The fats in these spreads have been altered and have water added so they're solid and spreadable. This makes them a useful, though not necessarily healthy, substitute for butter.

It's not advisable to use these butter alternatives if you have a health problem or are following an anti-inflammatory, low-fat programme. Nut butters like almond and peanut or tahini also work very well in cookies. Processed but unrefined, they're a great alternative to both dairy and dairy-free butters, adding both richness and depth of flavour. They're too heavy for cakes though, as they make it difficult to get a good rise.

If you're using food to help reverse a health problem or do not want to use any refined oils at all, then fruit and vegetable purées can act as a fat alternative. Apple sauce is particularly good for this as it's light and relatively flavourless when combined with other ingredients. Mashed banana is also a good option but will flavour the cake, which is perfect if it's a banana cake. Puréed sweet potato is also worth a go and can even be a star ingredient; it's used as a base for a chocolate cake frosting in the recipe section (*see page 282*).

However, one of the drawbacks of using a purée in place of an oil or fat is that the cake tends to stick to the tin. It's important to line the tin properly with a quality non-stick baking paper or you'll find yourself picking bits of paper out of your teeth.

Baking is not just about cakes and cookies – there's pastry too. Finding a suitable whole-food, plant-based pastry to buy is impossible. Some ready-rolled pastry products are 'accidentally vegan', using cheaper refined vegetable fats and shortening instead of butter. Gluten-free pastry is equally difficult and often has the disadvantage of including egg in place of gluten to help bind it together. So, it really does come down to making your own.

If refined fat is not an issue for you, then you can directly replace butter and lard with dairy-free spread and shortening. This works just as well with wholemeal and gluten-free flour.

But if refined fats are off the menu for you, there is good news. You can still make pastry, although it's a little different. Nuts make a great fat-replacement option in pastry, just as they do with cookies. Once ground into a powder, nuts can be combined with your flour of choice along with a magic ingredient – ground flaxseed mixed with water. The ingredients can all be mixed together to form a ball and then either pressed or rolled out and baked the same way as normal pastry. It's very forgiving too; if it cracks or tears, a little pinch will seal it back together again.

Some cooks recommend coconut oil for baking and pastry but while it has similar properties to butter, it has a strong and distinctive flavour that can mar the taste and texture of the dish, making the pastry extremely rich. Also, although coconut oil has a reputation for being healthy, it's still a fat and has no fibre and is definitely not a whole food, unlike whole coconut flesh, which is delicious and full of healthy fibre.

Eggs

Eggs have two roles in baking; first, they help bind the mix together and second, they act as a raising agent. So how do you manage without them?

Baking powder and bicarbonate of soda are two raising agents you can use to get a good rise in cakes. Even if a recipe calls for self-raising flour you should still add a raising agent to act as a rise-booster.

However, I rarely use bicarb in baking as it has a strong smell of ammonia, which is reminiscent of wee – and that'll spoil the taste of a delicious-looking cake in seconds! Baking powder can also add an unpleasant flavour, so take care how much you use. The other problem with using too much baking powder is that it can lead to an excessive amount of air bubbles in the cake. The result is a big rise in the middle of the cake while it's baking, but it goes flat once the cake is out of the oven, so you end up with a sunken middle – and a big disappointment.

I always advise people to read any recipe carefully and to get to know their baking powder. This may sound like an odd piece of advice, but each brand is slightly different, plus the age of the product might make it less effective. If your raising agent has been in the cupboard for as long as you can remember, and your cakes are always flat, it might well be worth investing in a new tub to get the lift you desire.

In the last few years, a new way of adding lift in a cake was discovered. The magic product was aquafaba or chickpea brine. Yes, the fluid from the tin of chickpeas (unsalted, of course) can be very useful, so don't just throw it away. Some clever scientists from a US university discovered that the protein content in chickpea brine is similar to egg white – that's why it's thick, cloudy and gloopy. When whisked, the brine expands the same way as egg white does – it even gets white and glossy. This is particularly useful for roulades and whisked sponge cakes and makes a like-for-like replacement for eggs. If you've not come across aquafaba, it's worth learning about, so check out the Online Resources and Article References section for aquafaba at the end of the book (*see page 306*).

When it comes to finding binding alternatives, there are a surprising number of innovative options, many of which add flavour, texture and even nutrients so you could claim cake is a health food. The type of binding agent you choose depends on the type of cake you're baking.

- Nothing – some cakes, like a sponge cake, don't need anything. However, if you're using gluten-free flour, make sure there is a gluten replacement like xanthan gum in the mix, otherwise it will all fall apart. Work quickly and don't over mix the cake batter.
- Buttermilk or dairy-free yoghurt – as seen in the 'milk' section, adding a teaspoon of cider vinegar or lemon juice to your dairy-free milk will curdle it slightly, which means it'll act as a good binder for light sponges and cupcakes. Soya milk works best for this. Dairy-free yoghurt acts in a similar way but can be heavier so it's best reserved for muffins or tray bakes where lift and lightness isn't so important. Soya yoghurt works best because nut yoghurts have the same weight problems as nut milk, and you may find it hard to get a good lift.
- Ground flaxseed or chia seeds – when mixed with water, ground flaxseed forms a thick, gloopy mix, similar to whisked egg. One tablespoon of ground flaxseed with three tablespoons of water is equivalent to one medium egg. Just mix the two together then leave to sit for five minutes or so to thicken. Flaxseed is packed with fibre and healthy omega three fatty acids, so another source of extra nutrients that makes it healthy. Use golden flaxseed rather than brown as it can be seen in the batter and can discolour a vanilla sponge, although that's not a problem for chocolate or fruit cake. Ground chia seeds work in the same way, but again their dark colour is not ideal for a light-coloured sponge and they're also less cost effective.
- Fruit or vegetable purée – apple, pear, banana, sweet potato or pumpkin all work well to bind loaf cakes, tray bakes and muffins. And they give you another opportunity to add hidden nutrients into your cake.
- Aquafaba – here it is again! Due to its viscosity, aquafaba can act as a binding agent as well as a raising agent, but you don't need to whisk it if you're using other raising agents. Three tablespoons of aquafaba is equivalent to one medium egg and you just need to stir it in with the rest of the wet ingredients.
- Bought egg-replacement products – there are a number of brands available to buy, each frequently made up of a collection of highly-refined starches that thicken and go gloopy when mixed with water. Personally, I avoid them as there are so many other unrefined options, but it's there if you want to try it.

Flour

It's wholemeal only when following a whole-food, plant-based diet – no highly refined flour here, even when it comes to cake. The downside is that wholemeal is heavier than white flour and so can make the rise a little more challenging. It's possible to buy wholemeal flours that have been designed specifically for baking, so look out for them. And make sure the packet states wholemeal or wholegrain rather than brown – some brands use a colouring agent for brown flour, fooling you into thinking it's the better option when it's not.

If you follow a gluten-free plan, there are a number of brands available that work with reasonable results. The texture can be grainy at times, so you may need to add a little more fluid to ensure your cake is moist and crumbly. The other alternative is to create your own blend by combining different flours together, but make sure you add xanthan gum or a similar binding agent or the cake will collapse once baked. There are some great gluten-free baking books that suggest flour blends you can try (see the Reading List on page 306 in the Online Resources and Article References for more information).

Sugar

With the dairy issue dealt with, the next biggest problem about being a lover of cake is the refined sugar content. This, of course, is why we love cake, as a good slice will tingle the dopamine receptors and infuse you with pleasure so you want more! So how do you make cake that still tastes great but gives you less of a sugar rush?

The simplest solution is to either use less sugar or use a sugar-replacement product that is healthier. Though if you do, you need to be aware that although these sugar alternatives are useful, they can't be used as direct replacements, so follow a recipe until you learn how to use them.

Using less sugar may seem to break all the rules of baking, but in plant-based baking the rules are different anyway so it doesn't matter. Another option is to use a less refined sweetener that takes a little longer to break down in the body, so there's a slower delivery of sugar to the system. Coconut sugar or molasses are both good options for this. However, they have an intense flavour and are dark so they change the colour of the cake. They're also more expensive than refined white sugar, so I tend to use less of them than I do the refined white stuff.

As well as giving texture and flavour, dried and fresh fruit also add sweetness to a cake. So it's no coincidence that most of my cakes contain a fruity element. Dates are particularly sweet and can be used as the main sugar-replacement in cakes, much like the *Sweet Potato Chocolate Brownies* (*see page 276*). The high fibre content of dates also means they release sugar more slowly, putting less strain on the body's metabolism.

Syrups can also be used as sugar alternatives, although some are better than others. Agave for example is marketed as a healthy option with a low GI and used to be recommended to diabetics. The reason for the low GI rating is that it's not digested and absorbed into the bloodstream in the same way as glucose. Instead it goes straight to the liver. If your body doesn't need any glucose at the point when you eat the agave, it gets converted into fat and stored. In fact, any more than a tiny dose of agave is just as bad for the body as high-fructose corn syrup, a manufactured product that's frequently used as a cheap sweetener in processed food products and which has been identified as one of the biggest contributors to weight gain and fatty liver disease.

Maple syrup, while still not ideal, is useful in small amounts. Although it doesn't contain any fibre it's a more natural product than agave. There are fruit syrups, stevia and xylitol on the market too. These are all very sweet and marketed in a way that makes them appear healthy, but they're not. Always question where the sweetener comes from and how close it is to the original plant used to make it. Also, syrups burn more easily than sugar, so you need to make sure you don't use high temperatures when you cook with them.

In reality, the only way to reduce the impact of sugar is to eat less of it. It takes a while to get used to the flavour of cakes that are less sweet, but once your taste-buds have adapted, you'll find that bakes containing refined sugar are just too cloying.

The Whole-food Baking 'Rules'

Now you have the low-down on alternative ingredients, you need to know the basic, but essential rules to follow when baking the whole-food way.

1. Be prepared. Have the ingredients ready, baking tins prepared and the oven heated to the right temperature.
2. Don't go overboard with the baking powder – too much will make your cakes sag once they're out of the oven. Find your favourite brand and be careful with the measurements.
3. When making cakes, you'll need two bowls. One for the wet ingredients, the other for the dry. Make sure you have everything you

need in each before combining. Always mix the wet into the dry.

4. Work quickly – the raising agent starts to work as soon as the wet ingredients hit it. If you take too long or leave the mix too long before putting it in the over, the bubbly energy fizzes out and there's nothing left to make the cake rise while it's in the oven. This is why food mixers lead to disappointing, flat cakes – the air gets knocked out of the mix by the blades. But it's so quick to knock a plant-based cake together, a mixer just adds more time anyway.
5. Tap – to stop the raising agents getting over excited before the mix hits the oven, tap the mixing bowl on the worktop to knock the bubbles back into the mix. When the mix is in the tins tap them just before they go in the oven as well.
6. Be patient – once your cake is cooked, remove it from the oven and leave it to rest in the tin for a while before transferring to a cooling rack. Some tray bakes need to stay in the tin until completely cool, so check your recipe. Don't try to decorate your cake while it's still warm or you'll be sadly disappointed with the result.
7. Enjoy your cake and the surprise expressed by others when they realise both what is and is not in it (or just don't tell them).

Useful Equipment

There are a wide variety of kitchen gadgets and gizmos you can buy to make plant-based cooking easier. Below is a list of my favourites. You don't need to have this equipment before you can make whole-food, plant-based recipes, but they're helpful and can save a lot of time.

Food processor

While it's not essential, if you're planning on making raw desserts or energy balls then a food processor is your best option. When I changed to a plant-based diet, I relied on my trusty old Kenwood food processor that I'd been given as a wedding present almost 20 years earlier. Considering its age, it did a mighty fine job until one day the engine burnt out after a hefty cooking session. If you have a food processor hiding in your kitchen cupboard, start with that before deciding to buy a new one as it might do the job perfectly adequately.

The key benefit of having a food processor is that it saves time. Most have a selection of blades that can chop, slice or grate with minimal input from you.

In fact, the only thing that takes time is cleaning it afterwards, and even that's quick and easy.

If you're buying a new food processor, do some research so you get the right model for your needs. They vary in size, engine capacity, function and price, though a machine that's expensive isn't necessarily the best or right for you. I had a super-cheap food processor in India but it was strong, reliable and had more functions than the expensive Magimix I now own. One feature it's useful to have on a machine is the ability to vary the mixing speed, especially if you're planning to make nut butter. Many models just pulse or have only one speed so check the specifications. Read online reviews and ask your friends for recommendations. Buying a food processor is a big investment, so make sure you get it right.

High-speed blender

If kitchen space is at a premium or you need something small that you can pack in a case, then a high-speed blender such as a Nutribullet or Nutriblend is well worth the investment. There are lots of options on the market these days so look for a robust model with a high-powered motor that won't burn out when a mix is too thick or contains hard seeds.

As well as making smoothies, nut milks, creams and sauces, high-speed blenders can grind whole products like oats or buckwheat into flour. They can also break flaxseed into a powder within seconds. However, they're not so good for making a caramel from soaked dates or turning nuts into a fine meal. In fact, the high-speed blades rapidly turn nuts into nut butter. At the other end of the scale, if the mix is too dry, the blades tend to seize up. So, before you use a piece of equipment, think about what you want it for and remember what it's best suited to doing.

Hand blender with small grinding pot

I probably use my hand blender more than any other gadget in the kitchen. As I'm impatient, most of my soups are puréed with a hand blender rather than being cooled and processed in a large blender. Using a hand blender means you can more easily control the texture of the food you're blending too. The other advantage is that it's small and agile, so you can use it in a jug to make creams and sauces as well as smoothies.

My hand blender comes with a small grinding pot attachment. I find it indispensable for making pesto and hummus, especially if I only want to make a small amount or can't be doing with cleaning up the bigger food processor. These are also great for kids to use as it's easier for them to handle compared to a bigger appliance. They're also cheap to buy, which means you can get started with simple recipes without having to make a big investment.

Steamer

Steaming is always the healthiest option when it comes to cooking vegetables. There are all sorts of gadgets you can buy to make steaming easy. They range from simple flower-like steaming baskets that sit in a saucepan to electrical gadgets with timers that sit on your work-top. If you're working all day, having an electrical gadget can make a big difference to the amount of time it takes to cook an evening meal. I have two steamers – a small one for everyday use and a larger double-storied pan which is useful when I'm cooking for larger parties. I use them both all the time, but neither cost a lot to buy.

Sharp knives

It's an undeniable fact that whole-food, plant-based cooking requires lots of chopping, so a good-quality knife that you can sharpen easily is an absolute must. The higher the price, the better the quality so it's worth shopping around – or maybe ask for it as a gift. Having said that, I've had some cheaper knives that were my favourites for a long time. A good knife will feel right in your hand, so handle a knife before you buy it, if possible. Keeping your knife in tip-top condition is important, so it's helpful to learn how to sharpen it using a steel. If that's too difficult, you can buy gadgets that seem to work just as well. If you care about your knives, hide them from other people in the house or you may find they don't stay at their best for long.

Non-stick and stainless-steel pans

As you're going to be cooking without oil, you'll need good-quality pans that food won't easily stick to. You also want them to be easy to clean. I find good-quality stainless steel pans are the best choice. The only problem is that they're expensive. That said, don't feel you need to rush out and invest in a whole set at once. Assess your selection of pans and start to work out which of them is worth keeping and which to let go because they create a cooking disaster. Then look for the size you'll use most frequently and build up your collection from there.

Non-stick frying pans are a great help, but always take care not to damage the coating. If you have a pan that's scratched then it's best to invest in a new one, otherwise the coating could end up in your food, which is not ideal. Some people advise staying away from non-stick pans altogether, but if you take care of them, non-stick pans will make cooking without oil much easier.

Storage jars

While these are not essential, they're certainly nice to have. I like to keep my dry ingredients in glass jars with good tight seals. Not only do they look good in the cupboard or on the window sill, but it's easier to identify what you've got and saves you having to rummage around looking for a badly sealed packet. If you have a local shop where you can buy dry ingredients loose, then you can take your jar along and fill it with what you need. We have a great local mobile service called Charlotte's Cupboard where you can fill up jars with nuts, seeds, dried beans and pulses, spices and even washing-up liquid. So, having storage jars that look good and are sensitive to the environment as well is a win-win in my eyes.

CHAPTER SIX

MAKING IT WORK FOR YOU

Change; some people love it, others hate it, most people are ambivalent about it. While change can be exciting and stimulating, offering the opportunity to discover something better than before, it can also be frightening, full of uncertainty and potentially dangerous. Change can also be hard and challenging creating waves of uncertainty and disharmony; it's much easier not to change and stay static and in your comfort zone. Ultimately, though, change is always there, whether we like it or not and choosing to change can be empowering and liberating.

When it comes to food, there are all sorts of barriers to making a positive change. It has a pivotal role in all areas of life and is influenced by family, culture, religion, education and finances. Then there's the wider influences of government, national economy, politics and increasingly, the media. We're consistently bombarded with conflicting information, criticisms and opinions; even this book, which is written with my honest desire and passion to help is based on my beliefs and knowledge so could add to this maelstrom.

Some changes occur more rapidly than others. Fortunately, consuming a plant-based diet is becoming more mainstream. In 2006, 150,000 vegans lived in the UK. In 2018 up to 3.5 million people identified themselves as vegan or following a mainly plant-based lifestyle.

Many people have been influenced by awareness campaigns like Veganuary and independent documentaries. But veganism does not necessarily lead to health and the increase in vegan fast food reflects this. It's easy to fall into the trap of believing that anything free from animal products is also healthy. Hopefully what you've read in this book so far has helped you understand the difference and that truly healthy food is:

- Unprocessed
- Natural
- Packed full of amazing nutrients
- Born of the land, not in a factory

As the journalist Michael Pollen says, 'if it's made from a plant, eat it. If it's made in a plant, don't.'

Modern life is demanding in terms of time. Being time-poor is a major reason why people have fallen into the trap of eating fast or convenience food. There's also a whole generation out there who don't really know how to cook.

Starting something as radically different as eating a whole-food, plant-based diet that involves dealing with raw ingredients and cooking from scratch may just seem too hard and too demanding. But it needn't be.

The previous chapter, with its practical techniques and advice, has hopefully helped you gain more confidence in how to make simple and effective changes. This last chapter of Part 1 looks at easier ways of making positive choices, as well as dealing with your own mind-set and some of the external obstacles you might come across.

Once you've made these changes your own, you may well develop your own unique ways of making life simpler for yourself.

Getting Started with a Whole-food, Plant-based Diet

Hopefully, by now, you're ready to start making changes to the way you eat. But you might still feel unsure about where to start. It's all very well knowing *why* you need to make the change, but now you need to know *how* to do it too.

Before you start, it's important to remember that we're all different and will have different reactions to changes in our diet. That's why I can't tell you how you're going to feel as a result of eating a whole-food, plant-based diet or how your body will react to the change. The only way to find out is to try it and see what works best for you.

If you're an all-or-nothing person you might want to throw yourself into it 100 per cent right from the start. If you're not good at going cold-turkey, you might want to take smaller steps and make changes more slowly. Or perhaps you're somewhere in between. The key is not to worry about what everyone else is doing, just do what works for you. This is *your* journey, no one else's.

Equally important, if you slip, don't declare yourself a failure and throw in the towel. Observe how you got there, how you feel as a result and just start again. This is especially important if you're dealing with a health problem. Remember, it isn't the end of the world if you don't keep to your own high standards – the most critical judgement usually comes from within.

That's not to say that others may hold back in declaring their own, often uninformed opinions. Be careful about sharing your journey on social media because you're more likely to come up against many judgemental individuals whose opinions are neither positive nor helpful. It's far better to surround yourself with a small, encouraging group of people or join a dedicated support group. I run one that's nurturing and non-judgemental where the only agenda is the joy of eating great plant-based food.

Above all, remember this is your journey, so follow the path that's right for you – and don't worry if you go on a detour. Follow the simple steps below to get up and running and use my top tips for an easy life so you can keep the transition to whole-food, plant-based eating as smooth as possible.

Step 1: Eat real food

It sounds simple and obvious, but if you want to change the way you eat, you need to take a moment to consider the food in your hand before it goes in your mouth. So much of the 'food' we eat is food-like but not food. It's either highly refined or made more from chemicals than from nature. For example, are you eating a strawberry or a strawberry flavouring? Has your meal come from a packet or from fresh produce? Is the main ingredient real or manufactured? Clever marketing can make an item sound natural and super-healthy until you question where it comes from. Empowerment from making positive choices begins with mindful awareness.

Step 2: Eat more fresh fruit and veg

Even if this is the only change you feel you can make, do it! Once you start getting more of the body-beneficial nutrients available in fresh produce, your body will change and start wanting more. You'll get more vitamins and minerals, multiple phytonutrients and loads of fibre.

Step 3: Go brown, go whole

By this, I mean choose whole grains rather than refined, i.e. whole-grain rice, wholemeal pasta, and wholemeal bread or crackers. If you haven't tried many other types of grains and cereals before, now's the time. In the recipe section, you'll see there are lots of options to help you start exploring. If you combine this with Step 2 you'll automatically be upping both the amount and the variety of fibre you consume. That will make your microbiome very happy.

Step 4: Eat a rainbow every day

Earlier, you discovered how phytonutrients help support the body from tip to toe. They're hidden in the many colours found in plant produce and the best way to gain the full benefit of nutrients available is to eat a wide range of colours. That doesn't mean you have to check them off a list every day (unless you want to!). Instead, simply make an effort to eat food of as many different colours as possible at some point in the day.

Step 5: Minimise processing

Try to eat food that's as close to the real, whole food as possible. This keeps the big nutrients connected with the fibre, meaning you consume the food in the right balance. Remember, once you break a piece of fresh produce down in a blender, the fibre starts releasing the nutrients and you jump a step in the digestion process. Plus, once something is blended, you tend to eat more of it than you would if it was in its original form.

I try to think in degrees of separation from the whole product. Let's take sesame seeds as an example. You can eat sesame seeds whole and they're particularly tasty when toasted. Or you could make them into tahini, a sesame seed paste, by blending them in a food processor until the natural oils are released. It transforms the seeds from hard little dots to a soft spreadable paste. The whole nutrients, like fat and protein, are still connected to the fibre, but it's missed a stage of digestion. Plus you might eat much more of it than the plain seeds.

Making the seeds into sesame oil takes it yet another step away from its original form because the seeds are refined to separate the oil from the fibre and other nutrients, leaving only a delicate, volatile oil. Delicious, but a long way from the original product. So, try to stick to minimal degrees of separation as often as possible.

Step 6: Find good recipes

Using simple, easy-to-follow recipes that work is a must when making changes to the way you eat. You have over 100 of them here in this very book! The internet has a wealth of options too, so browse and be inspired. Once you've found recipes you love, they'll quickly become your new favourites.

Step 7: Find good plant-based swaps

Cutting out animal-based foods like meat and dairy may be easy for you, so you might want to do that straight off. Alternatively, you may decide to gradually decrease your meat intake. Either way, find your favourite alternatives to meat and dairy early on. This will feed your confidence as well as your belly. Use lentils or beans as meat-product alternatives, test all the dairy-free milk options and practice making your favourite cakes with plant-based alternatives.

Step 8: Cut out meat and dairy

If you're going to eat a plant-based diet, you need to get on with it. If you follow all the points above, your transition will be a little smoother – and tastier too.

Step 9: Shopping

Changing to a whole-food, plant-based diet doesn't have to be an expensive process, in fact there's little investment required to start with, apart from your time. As you get more adept at the preparation and understand the processes (even learning short cuts), everything becomes quicker and easier. There are some stock items that need to be bought, like nuts, seeds and pulses, but these may already be in your cupboard.

Step 10: Clear your cupboards

If possible, clear out any processed foods, so you're not tempted to indulge when your will weakens. We all have our challenges – mine was butter shortbread biscuits. If I'd had a packet of those in the cupboard, I would have been irresistibly drawn to them. I wouldn't have been able to leave them alone until they were all gone.

Clearing out is easier to do if you live alone or have a partner who is bravely making the change with you. This, however, is not usually the case so willpower comes into play. If you weaken, don't give yourself a hard time or give up, just start again. Once you begin to experience what 'well' feels like, it becomes easier to resist these temptations because the side effects of giving in are just not worth it.

Step 11: Start chopping

There is no getting away from the fact that cooking a whole-food, plant-based diet involves a lot of peeling, chopping, grating and blending. Fortunately, there are many labour-saving devices that can make life much easier, but you don't need to splash out on expensive items right away (unless you want to, of course!). Hopefully Chapter 5 has already helped give you some handy cooking tips and techniques. And the more experience you get, the quicker and easier it all becomes.

Step 12: Feel the effects

If you want to go for it straight away. Following a programme like Veganuary can help guide you through. But be aware that unless you have a super-healthy gut, it may not be plain sailing. A sudden increase in fibre can result in a mega increase in wind. You'll also find yourself having your bowels open more frequently; this is a very good thing as long as it's not too frequent or loose. You may also find you catch a cold or feel a bit unwell for a few days. This is normal and a sign that your body is adjusting, so just go with it.

For many people, however, the only side-effects are beneficial. They have more energy, a feeling of satiation without being over-full, great hair and skin, and a feeling of simply being well. If you've been feeling poorly for some time, suffering from headaches, bad skin or stomach cramps, it feels wonderful when that goes away. It's at this point that the power of plants hits you and makes the effort you've made feel worthwhile. When I started to feel well, I soon realised that I didn't want to return to that unpleasant world of headaches and fogginess.

Hopefully your curiosity has been piqued and you're ready to learn more.

Top Tips For an Easy Life

1: Know your Why

The fact that you're reading this book and have got this far into it suggests that you're up for making positive changes in the way you eat and believe that a whole-food, plant-based diet is worth a try.

As you have seen so far, I made my changes because of food intolerances. My desire to feel well and to be able to drink wine again gave me the incentive I needed to overhaul my eating habits. That was my Why – to be well – because I wanted so much to be rid of the terrible migraines that were making my life miserable. Proof, through experience, gave me the evidence I needed to persevere on the days when all I wanted to do was face-plant a delicious dairy-filled cream cake, chomp down on a cheese-loaded pizza or knock back a glass of crisp sauvignon blanc. Once I was diagnosed with multiple sclerosis, my Why became even more important – to minimise neurological damage and enable me to be a hands-on granny when the time comes.

Your Why is your purpose in making changes. It could be deep and meaningful, incredibly superficial or a mixture of both. You may want to transform your health or perhaps you want to prevent or manage a chronic or potentially life-threatening condition. You may have been struggling with your weight and have found it hard to diet because traditional diets just weren't working for you. If you have an end goal such as to fit in a wedding dress or climb a mountain then that's even better.

It could be that you feel passionate about animal welfare and no longer want to contribute towards their suffering. Or maybe you're in love with our beautiful planet and want to reduce your impact on the environment. It might be that you've watched a documentary about commercial food production and farming practices and want to resist being manipulated by big business. Or you might simply want to be different to your parents and make a break with what's gone before. It could be that you just like to eat lots of food and that eating plant-based means you can eat more! Or that you're bored with tradition and want to try something different, perhaps allowing you to discover a new passion that has been lacking in your life.

Whatever it is, own it. You don't have to declare it from the rooftops, tell everyone you meet or have it on your Facebook status. In fact, others will probably prefer it if you don't. Just know yourself why you've made the change and have an idea of what outcome you're looking to achieve. It's worth spending some time getting your Why right because you'll need to revisit it often when the going gets tough – and believe me, it will. I'm not writing this to put you off, but to prepare you, because changing to a whole-food plant-based way of life means you're going to be going up against established and ingrained beliefs – your own, your family's and society's as a whole. That may sound grand and rather melodramatic, but it's true.

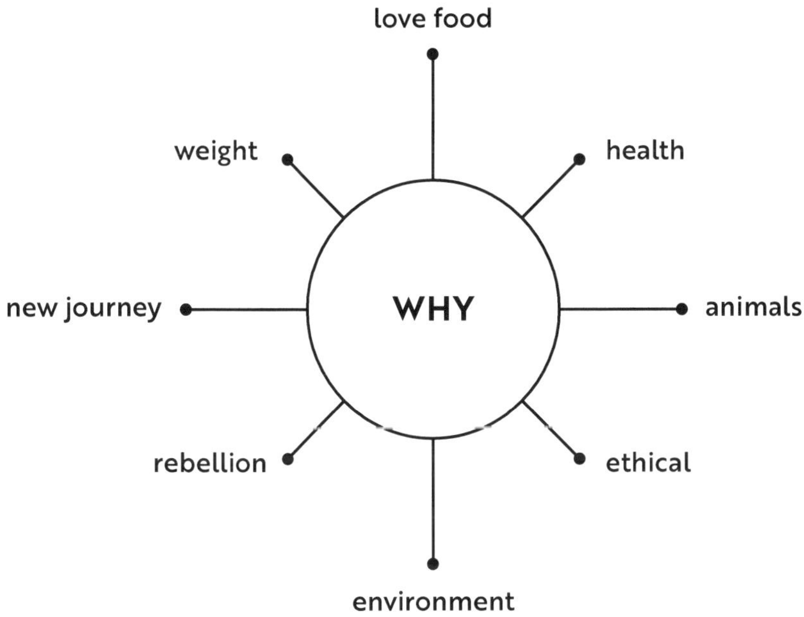

Some of the reasons why you might choose a plant-based diet.

In the Western world, we have been brought up to believe that dairy is good for us, that meat is an essential part of our diet and that not eating it is potentially bad for us. New parents are encouraged to include a 'full range' of foods in their children's diets including animal produce. To bring up a child as a vegetarian or vegan is still frowned upon. I've had friends monitored by their health visitors because they gave their children a vegetarian diet, an act that is deemed potentially harmful.

Most new parents will readily admit that they have no idea what they're doing, so are far more likely to trust a professional opinion and take whatever advice they can get. Now, I'm not knocking my health colleagues, far from it. But the mantra continues to be embedded in our psyche: animal products are essential for health so avoiding them is wrong and potentially dangerous.

Health professionals now promote the five-a-day message as well – five portions of fresh fruit or vegetables a day – but that message is taking much longer to embed into our psyche. Many still see fruit and veg as an add-on rather than a necessity. But as we have seen so far, those five portions are much more of a necessity than anything else we eat.

When I changed the way I ate, I upset a lot of people because I went against the norm. All parents want to give their children the best, so when they reject the way they have been fed, it can seem like a personal affront, especially if that way of eating has resulted in a health problem.

Going against your family's beliefs can cause a wide range of issues and sometimes those reactions can be extreme, like wanting to throw you out of the family home. My husband recounted a conversation he had with a young man who wanted to be vegan but still lived at home. He said his parents would be far more comfortable with him being gay than vegan and had threatened to throw him out if he changed his diet.

Hopefully this is uncommon, but it does illustrate just how deeply passionate some may feel about what you choose to put in your body. Mostly, responses range from mild irritation to disbelief but don't be surprised if those around you're angry, confused, hurt or dismissive. They might feel that you're just trying to create problems for them or that you're an attention-seeker. That's why being able to explain your reasons for making changes (and how you're going to do it) will pave the way to an easier transition. When I made my changes, it did create some friction but nothing too dramatic. But it still helped that I knew my Why and was not going to be deterred.

Family members can present some of the biggest challenges and obstacles to your desire to change the way you eat. Fortunately, as the main cook in the house, I had slightly more control and influence over what I and everyone else ate but if someone else does the cooking, it can be a huge issue and getting them on your side is very important.

I've had concerned parents and frustrated partners come on my Eat Well, Live Well course purely to understand how and what to feed their recently vegan child or partner. Fortunately, once they've completed the course, they feel empowered with the knowledge they need to be able to feed their loved one. It often leads to great changes for themselves too.

However, a course like mine may not be available to the cook in the household and even if it is, they may not be willing or able to do it. This is when knowing your Why is so important because you need to clearly and calmly communicate it to them. Begin by telling them that you appreciate the effort they make in preparing your food – it's rare the cook gets the praise so this will help them feel you understand what they do for you. Next, reassure them that you're not rejecting them and all they do for you but want to talk to them about why you want – or need – to make the change and eat differently.

Challenges to changing your diet can come from many directions.

You may have to negotiate so you can get in the kitchen and do some of the cooking yourself. If you can't cook then this might seem too big a challenge for you, but rest assured that the recipes in this book have been designed to be easy to follow and simple to make. If possible, find a local whole-food, plant-based cookery class or explore YouTube for videos that show you what to do.

Be prepared to answer questions like, 'Where will you get your protein or calcium from?' or 'What's wrong with drinking milk?' Or defensive statements like 'Well, we've eaten that way all our life and we're perfectly fine.' The people who make these comments may be the same people who survive on a concoction of pills and potions due to chronic health problems, so you'd be wise to make mindful and well thought out responses rather than criticise them. But more on that later.

The slow but gradually rising awareness of the connection between what we eat and our health – the food-health connection – is making it easier to transition to a whole-food, plant-based way of eating. But this brings its own potential issues, including accusations of jumping on the bandwagon. But it's a great wagon to be on, so feel happy that you're on board!

Ultimately, your loved ones just want to know you're doing the right thing and that not going to cause yourself harm. Don't dismiss this concern – it comes from a place of love after all – and instead do your best to reassure them. The most effective way to do that is to be healthy. Consume a wide range of whole, plant-based foods and flood your body with marvellous nutrients so you reap the benefits of energy, vitality, improved health, weight loss or whatever your reason for eating this way. Because looking good and feeling great is the best way to allay any loved ones' concerns about your diet.

As well as helping to bring them round to your way of thinking it might even help them address their own dietary challenges. I can hear snorts of derision as I write this because of the number of times people have said to me 'My partner/child/mother/in-law/significant other will never change' only to find somewhere down the line their attitude actually *has* changed. They may not go completely plant-based, but even little changes like cutting down on dairy and meat or eating more vegetables will have a positive impact. Sometimes they shift so much that they go from being your biggest critics to your biggest supporters.

After family, it's your friends and work colleagues who are likely to be the next group to challenge your food choices. So, make sure you're clear on your Why when you find yourself in social situations. If you've been invited out to dinner at someone's home, make sure the host knows what you can eat. If that puts them in a spin, offer to take something along so they don't have to make a separate meal. If you don't share your needs with the host, it can make the occasion hard-going as not eating a meal that has been prepared for you or expecting the host to cater for you without warning can seem rude.

To avoid inconveniencing others, we tend to go out for dinner with friends as it's easier to eat from a menu that suits everyone. That said, I do have some wonderful friends who are up for the challenge of cooking the whole-food way and always provide amazing meals. It turns out they like to experiment on me as much as I do on them!

Social events at work can often be the most awkward for the whole-food eater, especially if you're part of team that has a few judgemental individuals in it or people who feel the need to loudly verbalise their opinions. However, loud objections are often easier to deal with than the furtive encouragement to join in and conform. It's human nature to want to be part of a group, so it can be hard to find yourself on the periphery. Knowing your Why is important as it'll make it easier for you to hold your ground and resist what could feel like constant badgering to join in.

Ironically, this is where having a health problem is an advantage. I found that once my colleagues were aware of the effect my food intolerances had on my health, they launched into protective mode so it became acceptable for me to eat differently to everyone else. However, a colleague who went plant-based to lose weight and negate his familial tendency towards heart disease had a much harder time. He was often pushed into joining in with eating whatever cake or sugary snack had been brought in to share. His colleagues were almost offended that he'd made a *choice* not to have the food, while mine weren't as they accepted that I *couldn't* have it.

Knowing your Why is important in dealing with one final potential detractor – you! Mind-set is so important when you're making a change, especially when you start. And I have to say that out of all the challengers you'll come across, the most difficult and persistent one is the one in your own mind. It's that little devil on your shoulder, constantly whispering that of course you want to eat that deep-fried chicken on the menu or the last bit of creamy cake in the fridge. The hardest voice to contend with is the internal one that mutters that you're wrong, you don't really feel better or that you're just making a fuss or being difficult because it knows where your weakness lies and can push your buttons. It'll do whatever it can to make you feel uncertain, unsure or ready to cave in, because it wants to keep you safe and that means stopping you from changing.

This negative voice can kick in at any moment because it reacts to what triggers you, usually the desire that challenges you the most. It could happen at the start of your journey when everything is new and seems difficult to work out. You might be fine except when you're suddenly faced with your previously favourite dessert. Perhaps you're having dinner at the in-laws' place and they refuse to accept that you won't be eating a fatty piece of roast meat again. Sometimes you may have to compromise, which is when the negative voice kicks in and tells you you're a failure or you've mucked it all up.

The thing is, none of what your negative voice tells you is true. Knowing this and remembering your Why will help you to drown out your sabotaging voice so you can stick to your choice. And if you compromise – so what? Just move on and get back on the plan again afterwards. If it's hard, so what? Make the most of the situation at that moment, remember your Why and that tomorrow is just another, though hopefully better, day. As I said before, change is hard for everyone; this is your journey and it's up to you whether you derail yourself or not. It gets easier, though it never stops and even now I have to remember my Why and ignore the white noise of the negative voice. It's part of being human. So, put it on the naughty step where it belongs.

2: Don't believe everything you read on the internet

The internet is a wonderful thing. There's so much information available there at the press of a button. But while Google might be an abundant source of knowledge – it's certainly been the moderator in many heated family discussions – it doesn't necessarily dispense wisdom. Information is power, but in a world of conflicting 'facts' and a seemingly infinitesimal variety of opinion, how is it possible to know what's 'true'?

Your negative voice loves things you read on the internet, especially if you read claims that conflict with the path you've chosen. Confusion and doubt are clever marketing tools for those that don't want you to make changes, for example big food companies with profits to protect. Advertising has used our own psychology against us for years, employing subtle suggestions and implications to create desire and convince us of questionable truths.

Faced with that, doubt can sneak in so you start to question the validity of your actions. If that happens, check the source of the information. Even scientific research can be skewed. Here are simple questions you can ask to see how valid it is.

- Is this research sponsored by a special food interest? Would it surprise you to learn that research concluding that eating lots of eggs is good for your health has been commissioned by the egg industry for example rather than an independent body? All academic researchers have to declare any financial interest or sponsorship to highlight any potential bias, but it might be their university that is heavily sponsored rather than an individual researcher.
- How big is the study? Small studies can come up with revolutionary or startling conclusions that are, in fact, no more than anomalies. Large studies covering thousands of people will give a clearer indication of trends and results than a small one.
- How long was the research period? Short-term studies may yield different results to long-term ones. When it comes to health, longevity is critical. A way of eating may elicit short-term benefits like rapid weight loss but create serious, long-term health problems.
- Was the study made with animals or humans? Did they use petri

dishes or real-life people? Many of the ideas you see floating around on the internet have no evidence in real life and are more theory and hypothesis than fact. But somehow, they become a 'truth'.

- Who has translated the study? So often, a headline pops up that grabs our attention but doesn't necessarily reflect the facts. More often than not, we only read the headline and not the article, or the original research is difficult to access so we have no way of checking whether the headline is accurate or not. Unfortunately, the more often the headline pops up, the more we're inclined to believe it.

When considering research, it's advisable to go for reliable sources that have a reputation for conducting high-quality research. If you see something that piques your interest, such as an outrageous headline that seems too good to be true, delve a little deeper and check its credibility, because although not everything you read on the internet is true, some of it is and there are some fascinating new things to learn every day.

Also, be aware of clever marketing and sales techniques both online and through traditional media. Marketing can be insidious and slip into our unconscious mind or get represented as 'fact' when it's probably more like fiction.

This is particularly important when it comes to identifying the difference between a plant-based product and a whole-food product. Marketing can be so clever that it's hard to spot the difference between food that's manufactured rather than real and between what's ultra-process and what's natural. The growing vegan movement is big business, and articles like '10 accidental vegan treats' which included Oreo cookies, a brand of instant chicken noodles and party rings can create confusion for anyone looking to eat whole plant food for health or weight-loss. Highly processed, factory-made food is still junk food whether it's vegan or not. It's better for the animals for sure, but not the humans eating it. So be aware and question everything – without getting paranoid of course.

3: Don't force your changes on others

When you've made a major discovery in your life, it can be hard to keep your enthusiasm under wraps. Bursting with excitement and a new-found passion, you naturally want to share it with others so you can help them see the light too. You want them to experience the same great feeling as you. But whether it's religion, politics, exercise, food or even the latest TV sensation, not everyone will get it. Some will become irritated, irate and even explosively angry if they feel judged or criticised. Even if that's not your intention, you need to take care because you don't know how others will receive your enthusiastic take on whole-food, plant-based eating.

Not that I'm telling you not to share your new adventures with food with others (I know you will as it's new and exciting), just be mindful to whom you're talking, how you're talking to them and your relationship with them. So, if you're a young person reading this, please don't go and lecture your mum about how she's been feeding you the wrong way all your life. It won't go down well, trust me! Instead, tell her what you're doing, or want to do, and why, especially if she's the one doing most of the cooking.

The same goes if you're not the one who does most of the food preparation in your house. If your partner is the main cook, take time to explain your reasons for changing and how you want to eat in the future. But take care, as this can be taken as a form of rejection or create barriers in a relationship. If possible, gently guide them so you can bring them along with you rather than forcing them into anything.

Remember, it's your journey, not theirs, so you may well need to step up and take over your own food preparation. This is an empowering process, though, as it means you'll start to take responsibility for your own health. It's good to break the pattern of relying on someone else to feed you. But be sensitive about it. Over the last few years, I've found that The Sensitive Foodie Kitchen is about more than just food sensitivities and health awareness. It's also about being sensitivite to other people, whether they're directly and indirectly involved in your day-to-day life. Being mindful of where they are in their own food journey will help to soothe the potentially choppy waters of change.

Which is why getting on your soap box and preaching the ins and outs of eating plant-based food is rarely a good idea. Firstly, you can give the wrong impression about yourself and your new-found beliefs and second, it rarely encourages others to be receptive to your message. This is one of the problems faced by the vegan movement and can put people off rather than bring them on board. Passion and belief are important but how to translate that effectively isn't straightforward. Everyone is different, so find the way that works best for you and go with it.

Social occasions can be particularly difficult to manage, especially if drunkenness is involved. I've ended up having some heated discussions with people who have had too much to drink and have misinterpreted my explanations about plant-based eating as judgement or criticism of what they choose to eat. Debate is good, but not if it gets personal. And who enjoys the company of a bore who goes on and on about the same subject and doesn't know when to shut up?

If you do find yourself up on your soap-box, just remember to keep it short and sweet. The harsh reality is that most people just aren't that interested in the detail and switch off after a very short period of time. Keep it smart and brief and your message will come over much more effectively – and without boring the pants off the people you talk to.

I believe the best way of sharing the amazing benefits of eating a whole-food, plant-based diet is to *show* it rather than *say* it. Because once you start experiencing the wonderfully positive 'side effects' of eating nutrient-packed food, it shows. People will start commenting on your weight loss, new energy levels, glowing skin or whatever it is that's changed. Or it might be that they're fascinated by the gorgeous lunch you're taking into work and want to try it. That's the moment when positive conversations can happen; you are the evidence that it's really quite safe and normal.

4: Go at your own pace

One of the wonderful things about being human is that we have so much in common and yet we're all so different. It can be hard to remember this if we compare our achievements with those of other people, particularly when it comes to making a change or starting a new programme. When it comes to making simple or profound changes to the way you eat, it's important to go at your own pace and remember that what works for someone else may not work for you.

The current rise in awareness and the increase in demand for vegan food has been created through online programmes like Veganuary. This programme offers 31 days of new food ideas, recipes, encouragement and information that helps to grow your awareness. It's followed up with ongoing support to help you sustain your new way of eating. Programmes like this work well for some, particularly those who tend to be 'all or nothing' in their approach. A swift overnight change and you're off on a new trajectory.

However, issues can arise if your body is not ready for it; a sudden change from a low-fibre, low-veg, high-meat diet to a fully plant-based one can create a few problems, including stomach cramps, headaches, sudden infections and a general feeling of yuck. These issues tend to arise if your microbiome is struggling, which is a common problem. Hopefully, this will be temporary, but it can be off-putting and could result in you deciding that a plant-based diet isn't for you.

A sudden change or a brief 31-day programme can result in a short-term perspective, similar to what you'd experience if you followed a weight-loss plan. The fact that it is limited by an end-date subconsciously conveys the idea that once the programme is finished, you can go back to the way you ate before. But a profound change to the way you eat, whether because of food intolerances, health issues or animal/environmental beliefs, needs a long-term approach so it might take more time to adjust than you think.

The other issue about sudden change is that it can result in negativity, both from your own self-talk and others who feel they have a right to judge. What happens when you fall off the waggon? Have you failed? Is there no point in trying? It can illicit feelings of guilt and despondency, especially if it looks as if everyone else is doing fine (even though, in reality, they might not).

This can be doubly difficult if you're part of a large online group where you don't have a personal relationship with the other participants. These groups are often where the zealots and mean people hang out. They seem to think it's perfectly okay to write things they would never say to someone's face. With social media (and the media as a whole) you could easily walk into a quagmire of nastiness if you're not careful. No one truly knows what's happening in someone else's life, but you know your own truth and that's what matters. So, look for those who offer encouragement and avoid those who just hand out condemnation. Supporting and encouraging others is great, comparing yourself to their progress, isn't helpful. Be you. It's the best way.

Gradual change is fine. You don't have to go all out and turn everything upside down overnight – unless you want to, of course. After all, a meandering journey is far more colourful and much less stressful. It took me three years to switch completely to a whole-food, plant-based diet, and I'm still developing and learning now.

One of the great things about following your own path is that it gives you the freedom to choose a path that works for you, and that's empowering. A gentler process of change is less stressful for you and helps the body heal so you feel well much faster. It's about being kind and sensitive to yourself, something most of us find hard to do.

5: Become a planning wizard

As any good Boy Scout or Girl Guide knows, it's important to Be Prepared. Eating a whole-food, plant-based diet is *not* about spending hours and hours slaving over pots of boiling beans and shredded vegetables. It's about eating great food and not feeling deprived or left out and the best way to achieve that is to think ahead and plan.

Planning does not mean regimental, unless that's what works for you. Some people who have completed my Eat Well Live Well course find writing detailed weekly menus and shopping lists the best way for them. I'm always envious of those who can be quite so strict and organised. My planning is more fluid than that, as it's tucked up in my head rather than written out on a piece of paper. Here are some suggestions and ideas that can help you make a plan that works.

- Identify how you want to shop so you can create a routine that works with your lifestyle and gets you into a rhythm. For example, a weekly online shop or a couple of smaller shops with a big monthly top up. Or maybe something else.
- Think about the week ahead and the routine for each day. Include work, school runs, evening activities and clubs. Identify the days where the evenings are more relaxed and those that are packed full until bedtime. Time balances itself out so once you get into a routine it's easy to eat a variety of delicious dishes throughout the week.
- Create a rough plan of what you might like to eat during the week that fits with the time available to you. On evenings where you have a little more time, choose a meal that takes more time and plan quick and easy meals for the evenings where time is limited. For example, on an evening that's more relaxed you could make the Quick Roasted Squash Chilli (*see page 225*). If you cook some extra rice or quinoa to go with it, you can use the leftovers in a quick stir fry the following night.
- Have a stock of tinned beans and lentils as well as nuts and dried goods so there's always something to turn to. Dried spices and herbs will spark up the plainest of meals as well as add a medicinal kick. It's amazing how creative you can be with very little.
- When you have more time to cook, make more than you need and freeze the rest for another day. This way, you build up a stock for those busy days and always have something in reserve. Remember

to clear out your freezer every now and then though, and label everything, unless you enjoy the mystery excitement of 'Dinner Roulette'. Most of the recipes in this book freeze well.

- Use time-saving techniques. For example, if you're having rice with your evening meal, soak it in water before you leave for work in the morning so it cooks faster. Mix up oat and chia seed-based breakfasts just before going to bed so they're quick to eat in the morning. They also make an amazing energy-boosting snack.
- When you're out and about, make sure you have something to snack on so you don't get caught short. This is one of the most common problems I come across: not being able to find a good snack away from home. I always have some nuts, dried fruit or an apple in my bag just in case. Dried fruit bars, such as Nakd bars, or a small bag of energy balls (*see page 269*) are also great snack options. Remember eating a whole-food, plant-based diet is not about deprivation or hunger. We all need a snack sometimes.
- If your week includes eating out, then it's a good idea to plan this as well, if you have time. This doesn't remove spontaneity, as Google makes it easy to find nearby restaurants and cafes that provide plant-based options on their menus. However, not everywhere is up to speed, so if you want a relaxing night out, research the menu before you go. If you're still not sure if they have what you want, contact the restaurant and ask. This gives them the opportunity to say whether they can cater for you and gives you the information you need to decide whether to go there. In my experience, most places are willing to adapt dishes to meet individual needs, although be prepared for a few hiccups. Sometimes, no matter how well you think you've communicated, the end experience doesn't always meet expectations. If that happens, don't be afraid to politely express your dissatisfaction. My husband and I have had some quite hilarious experiences – and a few free bottles of wine as compensation – when things haven't quite gone to plan.
- Plan to have fun and enjoy yourself. Your food choices don't have to make eating a dull, austere experience. If you embrace this change as a new, exciting adventure, it can be as colourful and pleasing as you wish it to be. I love eating this way and never get bored as there's so much to learn and explore.

6: Keep learning

Even the biggest brains in the land can't know everything, which means there's always something to learn. As a naturally inquisitive human being, you'll thrive if you keep learning and developing. After all, boredom kills the spirit. We're meant to have fun, even with our food.

Make a promise to yourself to keep an open mind and keep learning about the food you eat every day. There's so much we don't know about the human body and the way it works that there's always something fascinating to find out about it. Perhaps you could try a new cooking technique to keep your interest up. Why not eat something different – even if you disliked it the last time you tried it, it's worth tasting again as your taste-buds might have altered.

Become an intuitive cook. Teach yourself how to combine and meld flavours and textures. Experimenting in the kitchen is fun, so get the kids involved too, if you have them. Talk to other whole-food, plant-basted eaters, join groups, read magazines and newspaper articles and search websites, blogs and YouTube channels to find great food ideas.

If the internet is not your thing, check out new cookery books. You don't have to buy them all as your local library might stock them. Even my small local library has a great selection or will bring some in from another branch if I ask. You could also take a trip to a large city library and browse a wider selection.

Look out for workshops and courses that pique your interest and go along to a few. You could also check out one of the large food events like Vegfest or Plant-based Live. There's usually only a nominal entry fee and these events have numerous expert speakers and workshops you can attend as well as products to try or buy.

Connect with like-minded people either online or in person. Depending on where you live, you could have access to a wide range of different groups with a plant-based theme. Get together and inspire each other – it really helps. Life-long learning is fun and refreshing. It helps to keep both your body and mind healthy and will become a key part of your plant-based journey.

So, here we are at the end of the first half of this book. I hope you can now see how closely the food you eat and your health are connected. I also hope you feel amazed at the way your body is constantly working to keep you well and that eating a whole-food plant-based diet can have a positive effect on the world around you too.

Are you feeling inspired and ready to give this way of eating a go? If so, it's time to dive into the exciting part – the recipes! Here, you can road-test new flavours and ideas and start your own journey to wellness.

Have fun learning to eat yourself well!

PART TWO
The Recipes

RECIPE CONTENTS

INTRODUCTION TO THE RECIPES

Now for the fun part of the book – the recipes. Each one is fully tried, tested and packed full of nutrients that your body will love. Have a flick through and hopefully you'll see that there's absolutely no chance you'll be missing out on great food. These recipes may be different from what you're used to but I'm confident that they'll quickly become your new normal. And if you like photos to go with the recipes check out the book link page of the website: www.thesensitivefoodiekitchen.com/book-links

For ease of use, I've split the recipes into five main sections:

1. Start the Day Well
2. Lighter Recipes to Mix and Match
3. The Main Attraction
4. Sauces, Dressings and Creams
5. Sweet Treats (my favourite!)

There are plenty of options to choose from in each section. Some are simple, others more complicated, but none of them requires expert cooking skills. After all, I designed them and I'm no chef!

As this is a new way of cooking for you, there may be a few ingredients that are unfamiliar to you. That's why I've created a handy list at the end of the book for you to refer to (*see page 295*).

One of my main aims as The Sensitive Foodie is to avoid being prescriptive. You have a choice about what you eat and it's up to you to decide what works for you. The same goes for the recipes – just because something is listed in the Start the Day section, doesn't mean you can't have it for lunch or dinner. If this is a new way of eating for you, make it your own. Shake things up a bit and, most importantly, enjoy it to the max.

People often ask me what I eat and these recipes answer that question. This is what we eat as a family, along with some fruit or veggie additions like a simple salad or roast potatoes. Normal stuff.

I am also asked how I plan meals over the week. Well, as you can probably imagine, that depends on the week – who is at home, how busy we are and what season it is. When I map out our meals, I think about the week ahead and make a rough plan of what I'm going to cook. But I don't plan every meal. I've been cooking this way for a while now, so sometimes I just open the fridge and cook whatever's in it. That's not so easy to do if you're a novice, which means you'll have to plan more carefully to begin with. To get you started, I've created an outline you can follow until you get more experienced.

Below is a weekly planner that covers the main meals in each day. It doesn't include snacks or sweet treats so add those yourself, whether it's some fruit, nuts or one of the dips with crackers. Again, adapt this to suit you.

Sample Menu Plan

Day	Breakfast	Lunch	Dinner
Sunday	Oat and Banana Pancakes (Make double and keep in fridge)	Smoky Lentil and Tomato Soup, and Moroccan Spiced Dip with Seedy Crackers	Roasted Squash Tart, Beetroot, Carrot and Kale Salad with Garlicky Greens
Monday	Chia Bowl with Fruit	Beetroot, Carrot and Kale Salad, Witches' Brew Soup and Superfood Bread	Whole-wheat or Rice Pasta with Creamy Pesto Sauce and Green Salad
Tuesday	Oat and Banana Pancakes (Left over from Sunday)	Moroccan Spiced Dip with Seedy Crackers or Toasted Wholemeal and Lemony Millet Salad	Smoky Lentil and Tomato Soup, Savoury Chickpea Pancake, Lemony Rainbow Coleslaw and Roasted Garlic Cashew Cream Dressing
Wednesday	Granola with Seasonal Fruit and Dairy-free Yoghurt	Witches' Brew Soup, Soda Bread with Walnuts and Beetroot Hummus	Mixed Bean and Veggie Burgers (serve in roll or wrap if desired), Lemony Millet Salad and Carrot and Spinach Salad with Tahini Dressing
Thursday	Overnight Oats	Carrot and Spinach Salad with Tahini, Farinata, Beetroot Hummus and Seedy Crackers	Proper Dal with Indian Cabbage and Wholegrain Rice
Friday	Dressed Up Avocado Toast	Leftover Dal (made into a soup), Soda Bread with Walnuts and Asian Salad	Cannelloni Bean and Kale Stew with Wholegrain Rice or Quinoa and Watercress, Pomegranate and Labneh Salad
Saturday	'Bacon and Eggs' with Soda Bread	Butterbean, Roasted Garlic and Rosemary Soup, Beetroot, Carrot and Millet Bites and Asian Salad	Stuffed Pumpkin Wedge with Celariac and Potato Gratin, and Comforting Red Cabbage

If you'd like to create your own plan, go for it, but if you prefer to wing it, that's fine too. Get creative and have fun. It's super-easy as long as you follow the basic guidelines set out below.

Each Day

- Eat a soup, a salad and a portion of cooked vegetables.
- Eat a rainbow.
- Eat 2–3 portions of fruit.
- Eat at least 2 portions of wholegrains.
- Include legumes and pulses in at least 2 meals.
- Spread out your intakes of nuts and seeds through the day.
- Enjoy yourself!

7 Top Tips for Using the Recipes

1. Use Sunday as your planning and prep day, especially if you have a busy week ahead.
2. Think about what you're making – could you make more than one batch and freeze it? What would be easy to make fresh in minimal time?
3. Plan quick and simple meals for the manically busy days.
4. Think about variety so you don't get stuck eating the same foods every day or the same recipes every week.
5. Factor in exercise days as you may want to eat more on these days.
6. Make sure you've got onions, garlic and some form of greens in your fridge so you've always got something to fall back on.
7. Keep a store of tinned pulses, legumes, nuts and seeds that you can turn to if you have limited fresh produce in the fridge.

Entertaining the Plant-based Way

Entertaining can be the other challenge when eating the whole-food, plant-based way. What do you cook if you've got friends or relatives coming round for a meal? After all, you'll want to be able to showcase your new way of eating without scaring them off.

Deliciousness is the main priority in this situation; fortunately, these recipes are all super-tasty so there's plenty to choose from. How well will they be received? Well that depends on your guests!

Below are two suggested menus to help you plan when having guests. The first is for a lunchtime get-together, the second for an evening dinner party. There's something for everyone here.

Lunch or Brunch Buffet Menu

Beetroot Hummus

Moroccan Spiced Pumpkin Dip

Seedy Crackers

*

Farinata (whichever flavour you choose)

Smoky Baked Tofu Slices

Easy Veggie Cakes with Creamy Avocado Mayo

*

Lentil and Sun-dried Tomato Salad

Watercress, Pomegranate and Labneh Salad

*

Sweet Potato Chocolate Brownies

Apple and Date Squares

Evening Dinner Party Menu

Pre-dinner nibbles (*optional*)

Tapenade, Green Dip and Seedy Crackers

*

Slow Roasted Tomato and Asparagus Salad

Or

Courgette and Cumin Soup

*

Smoky Tofu Balls in Spicy Tomato Sauce

Celeriac and Potato Gratin

Garlicky Greens with Cashew and Tahini Drizzle

*

Raw Banoffee Pie

1: START THE DAY WELL

It used to be thought that breakfast was the most important meal of the day and that skipping it was a bad thing. Recently, the message has altered because it seems that it's what you eat when you break your fast that is more important than when you eat it.

Not all of us like eating at the same time of day or eating the same amount at particular meals. Perhaps eating breakfast has always been a struggle for you, making your daily routine and demands on your time a huge challenge when it comes to when and what to eat.

Organising your kids, managing a long commute, handling a demanding job or unsocial working hours can leave you with a limited amount of time to eat a decent breakfast. If you're not hungry early on, time constraints can lead you to eating when you neither want nor need to eat, resulting in you grabbing a highly refined snack mid-morning as you can't last until lunchtime.

I do believe that breakfast is important, but I don't see anything wrong with eating it when you're ready. One of the benefits of working for yourself and from home is that you can choose your own mealtimes. When I used to work 12-hour days at the hospital it was a completely different matter. I would force down a bowl of cereal at 6.30am purely because I never knew when or if I would get a break on a busy shift.

Even if your mornings are a mad rush, try to be mindful of the nutrient quality of any food you eat on the go. Highly processed cereals, white bread, pastries and cereal bars won't do you much good, and neither will the heaps of processed fats and animal protein in a fry-up. The only thing these breakfasts will give you will be empty calories and not the power-giving energy sources your body needs and deserves at the start of the day.

This section offers you a variety of super-tasty and nurturing breakfast recipes, from quick grab-and-go options to lazy weekend feasts. There are even recipes for making your own dairy-free 'milk'. So, have a play with different ideas and treat your body to the best possible start every day.

Make Your Own 'Milk'

If the thought of making your own plant-based milk seems daunting, I am here to assure you it isn't. In fact, it's super-easy, only takes a little planning ahead and rewards you with an amazing taste and lots of extra nutrients. It also has the benefit of being free from additives and cheaper than cows' or goats' milk. If you want to be kind to the planet, an added bonus is that there's no Tetra-Pak carton to dispose of either. Perfect!

Nut Milk

Most types of nuts can be used to make nut milk, so you'll always have a wide range to choose from. Just as each nut has its own flavour, so does the milk, and like the nuts, some are stronger than others. For general use, you need a milk with a neutral flavour, so almonds, macadamias and cashews are a good choice for this. For something nuttier and more unusual, try hazelnut or even walnut. Both are perfect for a recipe where a more intense flavour would work or for making a flavoured coffee. And even though it's not officially a nut, you could even use peanuts – the unsalted variety, of course.

Almond is the most commonly used nut for making milk. Readily available in the shops, they produce a rich, creamy milk. I always use almonds with their skins on, rather than blanched or peeled, because many of the wonderful nutrients are found just under the skin.

Making nut milk is a simple three-step process. Step one requires some forward planning, but after that it's super-quick.

Step 1 – Soaking

Apart from coconut, which requires no soaking, and cashew nuts, that only need to soak for 2 hours, nuts should be soaked for at least 8 hours before being turned into milk. A good soaking achieves three key objectives.

1. Soaking ensures that the water gets through to soften the nut flesh, which makes blending easier and produces a creamier texture.
2. It reduces levels of phytic acid. This naturally occurring chemical is designed to keep the nut dormant until it's in the ideal environment to sprout and grow. This also keeps the nutrients under lock and key. Soaking reduces phytic acid levels and releases the nutrients so they're ready to be absorbed.

3. When nuts are soaked, it activates other enzymes that help make nuts a nutrient powerhouse.

Cashews require less soaking time as they are softer than other nuts and have already been partly processed. Even 10 minutes in boiling water will be enough, so this is worth bearing in mind if you've had a disaster and completely forgotten to soak your nuts.

One other essential thing to remember is that you must discard the soaking water and use fresh for the milk. Don't be tempted to use it as it'll be full of the anti-nutrients and other waste products you're trying to remove.

Step 2 – Blending

You will need a blender or food processor to blitz the nuts and water. This doesn't have to be fancy and expensive, though bear in mind that more powerful motors will be quicker and produce a finer and creamier milk. Just throw the nuts and fresh water into the blender and blitz for anywhere between 20–60 seconds.

Step 3 – Straining

Unless you have used a highly powered blender that has obliterated the fibre, you will need to strain the milk to remove any lumpy bits. Specially made nut milk bags are available to buy. These are useful and result in a smoother product but are not essential; a fine-meshed sieve or muslin cloth will work just as well. When I first started making almond milk, I used a tea towel placed over a sieve and it did a marvellous job.

Place your straining system of choice over a bowl or jug and just pour in the milky fibre mix. Don't go too fast, though, or you'll lose more to the kitchen worktop than you get in the bowl. Let the fluid drain through. Once it slows down, twist the top and give it a good squeeze to extract the last bit of nutty, milky loveliness. You will be left with a flaky pulp in the bag and a separate jug of creamy goodness to use.

That's it, your milk is ready to use – unless you want to add a little flavouring, which you might do, depending on which type of nut you've used.

Flavourings

Dairy milk is both a little sweet and a little salty, so you may find you need to add this to your nut milk, depending on what your milk is made from. It all depends on your taste-buds and what you plan to use your milk for. Personally, I like my milk all natural but if it's needed, I use a pinch of Himalayan salt and a dash of maple syrup. This is your plant-based adventure, so play around and see what works best for you.

Storage

Freshly made nut milks can be stored in the fridge for up to four days. Just remember to give them a good shake before pouring as the fats will have separated from the water. To keep a constant supply, get into the habit of soaking some nuts overnight every two or three days (or daily if the whole family is on-board) so they're ready for blitzing in the morning. If time is just too tight during the week, use shop-bought milk to make life easier. You can make your own at the weekends. Do whatever works best for you, after all, that's the key to making a smooth transition to plant-based eating.

Pulp

As well as fabulous fibre, the nut pulp will contain lots of lovely nutrients, so don't throw it away. It can be used in other things like flapjacks, muesli or crumble toppings. Alternatively, it can be used in veggie burgers, nut cheese or even as a facial scrub. You might come up with other ideas.

Almond Milk

Serves 6–8

Ingredients

140g / 1 cup soaked almonds, drained
1 litre / 4 cups filtered water
A pinch of Himalayan salt (optional)
1 teaspoon maple syrup or agave (optional)

Method

1. Place the nuts and water into a blender or food processor and blitz until well broken down.
2. Pour out through a nut bag or sieve into a bowl (*see page 157*).
3. Add salt and maple syrup to flavour, if required.

Oat Milk

Nut milk is not for everyone. Allergy, taste preference or budget limitations could all mean that nuts are not on the menu. Whatever the reason, oat milk is a delicious, creamy, economical alternative. It may sound obvious, but in the same way that nut milk tastes like its constituent nut, oat milk tastes really oaty! Unless it's destined for a use in a cake, I would strongly suggest adding some salt and maple syrup. You can skip the soaking if you're in a rush, but be prepared to get covered in oat slime when squeezing the nut bag!

If you're planning on soaking the oats overnight, I recommend using larger rolled oats, as smaller ones disintegrate easily and may get washed away when rinsed. Gluten-free oats can be used if necessary. These tend to be more finely processed and so require less soaking.

The leftover oat pulp is great for the skin and is especially useful if you or your child suffer from dry skin or eczema. Just grab a clean tea towel or muslin cloth and place the oat pulp in the middle. Tie up securely with an elastic band to make a small bag. Run a warm bath and add the oat bag. A creamy fluid that contains moisturising fats and anti-inflammatory properties will seep into the water and soothe irritated skin. This used to work wonders for my son, although he did tell everyone I made him bathe in porridge!

Serves 4–6

Ingredients

100g / 1 cup rolled oats
750ml / 3 cups filtered water
A pinch of Himalayan salt
1 teaspoon maple syrup (or agave)

Method

1. Place the oats in a bowl and cover with water. Leave to soak for at least 30 minutes.
2. Drain and rinse the oats under a cold running tap for a minute or so.
3. Tip the oats into a food processor or blender along with the fresh water, salt and syrup. Blend for 20 seconds or until the oats are broken down.
4. Line a sieve with a straining cloth of your choice and place over a clean bowl. Pour in the mixture and drain the milk through. Squeeze the bag to extract all the fluid then taste. Add more flavouring if needed.
5. Store in the fridge for up to four days, shaking well before use.

Overnight Oats

The fibre in oats is amazing. It has many positive effects, including lowering harmful LDL cholesterol (the inflammatory type), promoting healthy and happy gut bacteria and reducing constipation.

When it comes to healthy breakfasts, it's hard to beat porridge made with oats. I love a big steamy bowl topped with fruit or a large spoon of maple syrup. But it's not always the right season for porridge and you might not always have time to make it.

This is where Overnight Oats come in. Assuming you remember to plan ahead, the Overnight Oats recipe takes no time at all to make and provides an awesome, portable breakfast. I used to take a portion of these oats to work when I worked night shifts. They were great in the early hours when I was beginning to flag. A bowl perked me right up and kept me going until the day shift appeared.

If you have a gluten allergy or intolerance, you may need to choose oats marked gluten-free. Avenin is a gluten-like protein found in oats that some people are sensitive to and as oats are processed in factories with other gluten-containing products there is an additional risk of cross-contamination. Unfortunately, this can make them more expensive and the oats lose some of their whole-food status, but it's always best to be sure when it comes to food sensitivities.

Soaking dried fruit with the oats makes them all plump and tasty. This recipe uses raisins and cranberries, but a tropical combination tastes amazing too. Or you could go all super-food and try acai, goji or blueberries.

Serves 1

Ingredients

50g / ½ cup oats (gluten-free if needed)
250ml / 1 cup dairy-free milk of choice
1 tablespoon chia seeds (optional) *
2 tablespoons raisins
1 tablespoon dried cranberries
¼ teaspoon ground cinnamon or ground ginger

Method

1. Before going to bed, place the oats in a bowl (or suitable container if you're taking them out with you) with the chia seeds, dried fruit and spices.

2. Pour over the milk, stir to combine and leave in the fridge overnight or for at least 4 hours when they'll be super-soft and ready to eat.

** If you don't have chia seeds, add a tablespoon of ground flaxseed for extra fibre and a shot of omega 3.*

Breakfast Chia Bowl

Chia seeds make an amazing addition to a plant-based diet. These tiny seeds are packed full of fantastic nutrients and healthy anti-inflammatory omega 3 fatty acids.

This breakfast is perfect for busy mornings. All you need to do is grab it from the fridge – as long as you remember to make it the night before, of course! As well as omega 3, you get a belly full of protein and fibre as well as a host of other nutrients that will kick-start your day and keep you full until lunchtime.

The internet is littered with glamourous photos of chia seed concoctions. Some are easy to create, others, not so much. These are my favourites; both are simple, fresh and seriously tasty.

Serves 1

Simple and Straightforward

Ingredients

1 small banana
3 tablespoons chia seeds
¼ teaspoon ground cinnamon
¼ teaspoon vanilla essence
150ml / ⅔ cup dairy-free milk of choice
2 tablespoons cooked apple
1 tablespoon raisins or sultanas

Method

1. The night before, mash the banana in a bowl and mix in the chia seeds.
2. Sprinkle over the ground cinnamon and vanilla essence, then pour in the dairy-free milk. Mix everything together and place in the fridge overnight.
3. In the morning, the mixture will be thick and gloopy. Just spoon over the cooked apple and raisins and enjoy.

Berry Tasty Breakfast Bowl

Serves 2

Ingredients

150ml / ⅔ cup dairy-free milk of choice
3 tablespoons chia seeds
¼ teaspoon vanilla extract
A handful of raspberries
A handful of blueberries
A handful of strawberries

Method

1. The night before, pour the dairy-free milk, chia seeds and vanilla extract into a bowl and mix well. Leave in the fridge to thicken.
2. In the morning, roughly chop the berries and drop and scatter over the top of the chia mix.
3. Eat straight away or take with you as a portable breakfast.

Dressed Up Avocado Toast

Avocado toast is my go-to quick but tasty breakfast option. I first discovered them in the late 1980s when I left home. They seemed so exotic!

When you have a slightly more relaxed morning, the extra toppings are not only delicious but also add some additional nutrient treats.

Serves 2

Ingredients

100g chestnut mushrooms, sliced
4 slices of bread of choice (Superfood Bread on page 213 works well)
1 ripe avocado, cut in half
2 handfuls of rocket or spinach
1 teaspoon lemon juice
Salt and pepper, to taste
A drizzle of flaxseed oil (optional)

Method

1. Place a small non-stick frying pan over a medium heat and sauté the mushrooms until they soften slightly and just start to ooze out their water.
2. Pop the bread in the toaster, then place the slices on two plates.
3. Meanwhile, mash the avocado, then spread over the toast.
4. Sprinkle over a little lemon juice then add the mushrooms and top with the leaves.
5. Season with salt and pepper and finish with a drizzle of flaxseed oil.

Chickpea Omelette

I've put this in the breakfast section as it's fantastically filling and makes a perfect start to a busy day. But it works just as well for lunch or a super-quick supper. Fill it with anything savoury that you fancy. *Cashew and Tahini Dressing* (page 262) complements it perfectly.

Chickpea/gram flour can be quite stubbornly lumpy, so either sieve the flour into a bowl or whizz the whole mix together in a high-speed blender for a few seconds to make sure it's smooth. It isn't good if you get an unexpected lumpy mouthful!

Makes 1 very big portion or 2 moderate ones

Ingredients

50g / ½ cup chickpea/gram flour
1 tablespoon ground flaxseed
½ teaspoon baking powder
½ teaspoon garlic powder
⅛ teaspoon ground turmeric
180ml / ¾ cup water
A pinch of salt and white pepper

Filling options – *cooked mushrooms, tomatoes, spinach, rocket, dairy-free cheese (or anything else savoury that takes your fancy)*

Method

1. Mix all the dry ingredients together to combine.
2. Add the water to form a batter. It needs to have the consistency of single cream.
3. Grab a 20cm wide non-stick frying pan with a lid. Warm the pan on a medium heat, then pour in the mix. Cover the pan with the lid and leave it for 4 minutes. It's best

to walk away if you're tempted to peak or fiddle. It needs to set properly, otherwise it'll break when you try to turn it.

4. Using a fish slice, lift the omelette and check that the underside is firm. Carefully flip it over and cook the other side, placing your filling ingredients on the top side to warm through. Cook for another 3 minutes.
5. Gently fold over as you would an omelette and slide out onto a serving plate. Eat straight away.

Quinoa Porridge with Apple

Quinoa is more commonly associated with a savoury lunch or dinner, but it makes a wonderful porridge too. This is a great way to use up leftover quinoa – as long as it hasn't been cooked in vegetable stock, of course! This recipe works just as well with brown rice, millet or buckwheat. They all give a different underlying flavour but are equally filling and delicious.

Serves 4

Ingredients

2–3 apples
2 tablespoons water
2 teaspoons ground cinnamon
100g / 1 cup quinoa
500ml / 2 cups dairy-free milk of choice
1 tablespoon coconut sugar
1 teaspoon vanilla extract

Method

1. Peel, core and chop the apples and place in a small pan with the water. Bring to the boil, then reduce the heat and simmer for 10 minutes or until fully cooked and soft. Stir in 1 teaspoon of the ground cinnamon and leave to cool. (This can be done the day before to save time in the morning.)
2. Rinse the quinoa in a sieve under a running tap, then tip into a saucepan. Add the dairy-free milk, coconut sugar, the second teaspoon of ground cinnamon and the vanilla extract. Stir well.
3. Place the lid on the pan, then bring to the boil. When steam comes out of the top of the pan, reduce the heat and simmer gently for 15 minutes or so until the quinoa is soft and fluffy and the dairy-free milk has been absorbed. You may need to add a little more milk to get a porridge-like consistency.

4. Once ready, stir in a little cold dairy-free milk. Serve in bowls with the apple compote as a delicious gut-friendly topping.

'Bacon and Eggs'

I've always been a bit partial to a rasher of bacon or two, even though I think it's one of those foods that rarely tastes as great as it smells. Bacon was one of the foods I really missed when I first went plant-based. Whilst you can buy highly processed fake bacon, I prefer this healthier option.

Carrot 'bacon' has a minimal number of ingredients, is relatively unprocessed and has a surprisingly bacon-like taste. The combination of smoked paprika and liquid smoke creates a truly delicious flavour. If you can't get hold of the liquid smoke, just add more smoked paprika. The flavour won't be as intense, but it's still pretty good.

Bacon and eggs have always been traditional breakfast fare in the UK but pairing the carrot 'bacon' with scrambled tofu 'eggs' makes a fabulous and super-healthy plant-based alternative. I often add some sautéed mushrooms and a few slices of avocado to create a gorgeously tasty and filling rainbow breakfast. Perfect for a laid-back start to the weekend.

Carrot 'Bacon'

Makes 12 slices

Ingredients

2 large, fat carrots
1 tablespoon olive oil
2 tablespoons tamari or 1 tablespoon coconut amines (see glossary on page 297)
¼ teaspoon liquid smoke
½–¾ teaspoon smoked paprika
Black pepper (optional)

Method

1. Pre-heat the oven to 180ºC/350ºF/Gas Mark 4. Line a medium baking tray with non-stick baking paper.
2. Peel the carrots and cut away the rounded edges to give the carrot straight sides. Using a very sharp knife or a mandolin, cut the carrot into very thin strips to make 12 bacon-like slices.
3. Mix together the olive oil, tamari, liquid smoke, smoked paprika and black pepper in a bowl.

4. Pour the mixture into an oval-shaped dish, then dunk in the carrot slices, ensuring both sides are coated. Transfer each coated slice onto the baking tray and repeat until all the slices are covered.
5. Place in the oven for 10 minutes before turning and cooking for a further 10 minutes or until the edges have started to brown. If you like your carrot bacon soft, remove the carrot slices from the oven now. If you prefer them crispy, return to the oven for up to 5 minutes more, keeping a close eye on them so they don't burn.
6. Serve the with the scrambled tofu on the side.

Scrambled Tofu

Serves 3–4

Ingredients

300g / 2 cups firm tofu, drained
1 small or ½ medium white onion, finely chopped
1 teaspoon ground turmeric
1 tablespoon tamari
2 tablespoons chopped fresh parsley
Salt and pepper, to taste
Chopped spinach, courgette, red peppers, chives (optional)

Method

1. Heat a small amount of water in the bottom of a saucepan and add the onion. Sauté for 5 minutes or so on a medium heat until it starts to soften. Do not let it burn – add more water if needed.
2. Crumble in the tofu and stir to combine with the onion.
3. Add the turmeric, tamari and seasoning and simmer for a couple of minutes.
4. *If you're adding extra veggies*, put them in the pan now. Continue to simmer until all the ingredients are cooked through, then stir in the parsley and serve.
5. *If you're not adding extra veggies*, simply stir in the parsley and serve.

Mushroom, Spinach and Potato Rosti

I think everyone has a favourite bit of food in a cooked breakfast. Mine is a hash brown. Crispy on the outside, crunchy on the inside and perfect with a dollop of tomato ketchup. Unfortunately, they're either deep-fried and dripping with oil or they contain dairy. Definitely not on a whole-food, plant-based diet!

For that reason, I had to create these simple hash brown alternatives. Potato rosti may not be quite the same but they still taste delicious and have a satisfactory crunch too.

I must confess that, until recently, I struggled to cook a good rosti because the mix would always fall apart when I turned it in the pan. One evening I saw a TV cookery programme where the chef gave a master class on how to cook rosti. At last, I realised where I'd been going wrong.

Impatience had been my downfall because apparently, the key to cooking great rosti is not to touch them for at least the first 5 minutes after you've added the mix to the pan. I was turning them too early and before the mix had had a chance to bind together. Once cooked and golden brown underneath they don't stick to the pan. At that point, you can loosen them with a fish slice so they're ready for turning.

However, I also discovered that turning them the traditional way didn't work either. The chef advised tossing the rosti like pancakes. You need to keep your nerve and develop a good wrist action, but it works and now I make lovely, crisp rosti.

Of course, rosti are not just for breakfast, so I've added some alternative ingredients to give them bit more pizzazz if you want to eat them later in the day. They can be topped with anything; these veggies are my favourites at breakfast time.

Serves 4

Ingredients

4 medium potatoes scrubbed and peeled (if necessary)
¼ teaspoon salt
1 heaped tablespoon chickpea/gram flour
Ground black or white pepper, to taste

Optional additions for the mix

½ teaspoon garlic powder and/or
1 teaspoon Italian herbs and/or
2 tablespoons nutritional yeast and/or
½ teaspoon chilli flakes

Veggie toppings

250g chestnut or button mushrooms sliced
150g spinach leaves, roughly chopped if large
2 medium fresh tomatoes, sliced or 8 cherry tomatoes (optional)

Method

For the potato rosti

1. Grate the potatoes and place in a large bowl with the salt and pepper. Leave to stand for a couple of minutes. If the potato is very wet, dry it off just a little with a paper towel but leave enough moisture to soak up the dry ingredients. Stir in the chickpea flour and add any of the optional seasonings you wish.
2. Pre-heat a medium non-stick frying pan until it's nice and hot. Pick up a quarter of the potato mix with your hands and drop it into the centre of the pan. Spread it out using your fingers or a fork to form a large, flat pancake-sized rosti. Reduce the heat slightly and leave it to cook for about 5 minutes. Do not fiddle with it!
3. Loosen the edges of the rosti with a fish slice or spatula. It should be lightly browned and easily come away from the pan. Once the whole rosti has cooked underneath, it will loosen from the bottom of the pan. Gently tip the pan to check it's moving freely, then toss it onto the other side, like a pancake. Cook for a further 5 minutes or until it's golden and crispy underneath.
4. Slide the rosti onto a warmed serving plate and keep hot in the oven. Repeat the process until all the rosti are cooked.

For the toppings

1. Heat a couple of tablespoons of water in a large non-stick frying pan. Once the water is bubbling, add the tomatoes and cook until soft and juicy, turning as needed. Transfer to a warm dish and keep hot in the oven.
2. Tip the mushrooms into the same pan and sauté for a couple of minutes until soft and the juices start to run. Add the spinach and let it wilt into the mushrooms for a couple of minutes. Turn off the heat and pop a lid on the pan to keep the mixture warm until all the rosti are ready.
3. Place a rosti in the middle of a plate, spoon over some of the mushroom and spinach mixture and top with the tomatoes. Season to taste.

Oat and Banana Pancakes

When we lived in India, our children had a number of friends who'd grown up in The Netherlands or the USA and they all seemed to have pancakes for breakfast. So, of course, our kids wanted them too. The problem was, I wasn't very good at making them. They always seemed to flop or fold over themselves, and just didn't taste good. And then there was the ingredients – not very whole-food!

Over time, my daughter and I created these simple but delicious versions of fluffy American-style pancakes. Packed with healthy fats and sugars, they really are a weekend or school holiday treat, and they always turn out well. Make sure the pancake pan is fully pre-heated and that you cook the pancakes over a medium heat. And be patient with them – once the top is covered in bubbles, it's time to flip. But if you do it too soon, all you'll get is a sticky heap in the pan – the ghost of pancakes past.

Makes 8–12 pancakes, depending on size

Ingredients

100g / 1 cup oats (use gluten-free if you need to)
1 tablespoon ground flaxseed
350ml / 1½ cups dairy-free milk of choice (oat or rice milk are good)
1 medium ripe banana
1 teaspoon ground cinnamon
1 teaspoon baking powder
A pinch of salt
A little olive oil, for greasing

For the toppings

Anything you fancy, but my daughter prefers berries, maple syrup and a dollop of peanut butter

Method

1. Place the oats and ground flaxseed into a high-speed blender and blitz for a couple of seconds to until they resemble a fine flour. Add the dairy-free milk, banana, cinnamon, baking powder and salt, then blend until smooth.
2. Heat a small non-stick frying pan over a medium heat. Put a little olive oil on some kitchen paper and wipe it over the surface of the pan so it's lightly greased. Carefully pour half a ladleful of the pancake batter into the pan and cook for a few minutes. When the bubbles appear on the surface of the pancake, flip it over and cook for a few minutes on the other side until lightly browned.
3. Transfer the pancake to a warmed plate, cover with a tea towel and repeat the process until all the mix is used up. Serve with toppings as desired.

Beans on Toast

These beans may seem like a lot of effort to go to for breakfast, but trust me, they're worth it. This recipe is traditionally made with flageolet beans but it works equally well with aduki or black beans.

Obviously, this is not a dish for your average weekday breakfast, unless you're super-organised and have prepared them in advance. It's also not just a breakfast dish as you can have these beans any time in the day. I just have a bit of a thing for beans on toast in the morning.

For the toast, use whatever works for you, whether it's wholemeal, sourdough or superfood bread. You don't need to add the spinach, but it works really well. My family would be disappointed if I didn't add it as they're convinced I'd add spinach to almost anything!

Serves 4

Ingredients

4 dates
1 small onion or medium shallot
1 bay leaf
2 x 400g tin of flageolet, aduki or black beans, drained or 4 cups of cooked beans
400ml / 1¾ cups passata
1 teaspoon ground garlic
1 teaspoon paprika
½ teaspoon ground cumin (optional)
1 teaspoon cider vinegar or 1 tablespoon lemon juice
1 tablespoon tamari or coconut amines
Salt and pepper, to taste

To serve

Toasted bread of your choice
Fresh spinach leaves
Flaxseed oil

Method

1. First make the date paste. Pop the dates in a small saucepan and add water until they're just covered. Bring to the boil, reduce the heat and simmer for 10 minutes or until the water has been absorbed and the dates are soft and falling apart. Turn off the heat and leave to cool. Mash to form a paste, adding a little extra water to loosen if the mixture's too thick. Set side.

2. Finely dice the onion or shallot. Heat a tablespoon of water in a medium saucepan until it's bubbling. Add the onion and bay leaf and sauté for 5 minutes or so until soft; lower the heat so it doesn't stick to the pan and stir frequently.
3. Add the garlic powder, paprika, passata, beans, date paste, vinegar or lemon juice and tamari. Fill the passata carton with water and add to the pan. Bring to the boil, then reduce the heat and simmer for 30 minutes on a very low heat, stirring from time to time to make sure it doesn't' stick.
4. Check the flavour, season with salt and pepper and add more tamari or spices as needed. Simmer for another 15 minutes to allow the flavours to develop.
5. Serve straight away or leave to cool and keep in the fridge for up to 5 days. Remember to reheat gently.
6. To serve, toast your bread of choice, cover with a handful of spinach and 2–3 spoons of beans. Top with a couple more spinach leaves and a swirl of flaxseed oil, if desired.

Granola with Yoghurt and Raspberries

The next time you buy granola, take a look at the list of ingredients on the packet. Mixed between the nuts, oats and dried fruit, you'll probably find at least one form of refined oil and added sugar, as well as the usual array of preservatives. Making your own granola may seem like a lot of effort, but if you're a sensitive eater or have a challenging health problem, it's worth it even if for no other reason than that you can add just what you want.

The maple syrup and aquafaba mix replaces the oil and processed sugar. Make sure the oven is not too hot, otherwise it will burn – it's important to be vigilant. The outer oats will cook faster than the inner ones and need mixing up to prevent an under/over toasting, so stir it a couple of times while it's cooking.

Granola can be served with any dairy-free milk but I prefer mine with fresh fruit and dairy-free yoghurt. And it's not just for breakfast either, it makes a lovely quick dessert too!

Serves 8–12

Ingredients

250g / 2½ cups rolled oats (gluten-free if needed)

250g / 2½ cups mixed seeds and grains of choice (pumpkin, sunflower, flaxseed, sesame, buckwheat groats etc.)

250g / 2½ cups chopped nuts of your choice (almonds and/or walnuts/and or pecans)

75g / 1 cup dried fruit (raisins, sultanas, cranberries, chopped dates, dried mango, etc.)

100ml / just under ½ cup maple syrup

5 tablespoons aquafaba

1–2 heaped teaspoons ground cinnamon (optional)

Method

1. Pre-heat the oven to 160°C/320°F/Gas Mark 4. Line a large baking tray with greaseproof paper.
2. Place the oats, seeds, nuts and dried fruit in a large bowl and mix together well.
3. In a separate bowl, combine the maple syrup, water and cinnamon (if using) before pouring it over the oat mix. Stir well to make sure everything is lightly coated – use your hands to ensure an even mix. As you combine the ingredients, some of the oats will start to clump together, which is perfect.
4. Tip the oat mix out onto the baking tray, spread out evenly and place in the oven to bake for 18–20 minutes or until lightly toasted. Remember to keep an eye on the mix and stir a couple of times to ensure it toasts evenly. Do not over-bake!
5. Once ready, remove the tray from the oven and leave to cool completely. Transfer to an airtight container and use as needed.

2: LIGHTER RECIPES TO MIX AND MATCH

This selection of recipes provides my answer to the common question, 'So what DO you eat?' It's a collection of gorgeous soups, salads, crackers, dips and other savoury delights that you can mix and match as you please.

I also hope this wide assortment of recipes also answers another commonly asked question, 'Don't you get bored?' As you'll see, there's an endless number of combinations you can play with here – enough to keep everyone happy – while also using a huge variety of ingredients that will make your gut bacteria dance for joy. Boredom doesn't get a look in.

One easy and enjoyable way of increasing your intake of plant foods is to eat a soup, a salad and a portion of cooked vegetables every day. So, we'll start there.

SOUPS

Who doesn't like soup? I believe that even the most anti-healthy food person can be won over with a piping hot and tasty bowl of soup. And for anyone with food intolerances or who's following an eating plan as a way of managing a health issue, it's an effortless way to up their veg intake.

When the kids were little and learning the power of 'no' with their food, I started getting imaginative with soup. Simple was always best, even better if it had a name. So, pea soup became Witches' Brew, tomato and lentil turned into Holiday Soup. They still have those names today.

I make soup at least three times a week and we have it nearly every day, even in the summer. Filling, tasty and packed with amazing nutrients, these recipes are my favourites. I hope you enjoy them too.

'Creamy' Celery Soup

This is an awesome soup for many reasons: it's super-simple, full of flavour, packed with nutrients and extraordinarily, the children love it – even though they hate celery. Rather randomly, if you add a little extra celery salt, it tastes like chicken soup and offers the same comfort, but without the chicken.

As well as providing protein and healthy fats, the nuts give this soup its wonderfully creamy, rich texture. If you eat nut-free, just add extra potato. It's not quite as rich but still delicious.

A word about seasoning

Add a little celery salt and pepper to begin with, then taste when the soup is cooked and add more if you need it. Celery salt is salty, so take care not to over-season. However, if you want the 'chicken soup' experience, then be bold and add more than a sprinkle of celery salt but include less ordinary salt to balance it out.

Serves 4–6

Ingredients

1 medium onion, chopped
1 medium potato, chopped
2 heads of celery including leaves, chopped
75g / ½ heaped cup cashew nuts
750ml / 3 cups vegetable stock
450ml / 1¾ cups dairy-free milk of choice
A pinch of celery salt
Salt and pepper, to taste

To serve

Chopped fresh parsley
Sliced almonds (optional)

Method

1. Place a large saucepan over a medium heat and add a couple of tablespoons of water. Once the water is bubbling, add the vegetables and sauté for 5 minutes or until they start to soften. Stir frequently so they don't burn and add a little more water if they start to stick.
2. Add the cashew nuts and sauté for a further minute or so, then pour in the stock, scraping up any browned veg from the bottom of the pan. Pour in half the dairy-free milk and season to taste. Bring to the boil, then cover and reduce the heat.

3. Simmer for 20 minutes, or until everything is cooked. Turn off the heat and leave to cool slightly, then blitz with a stick blender or in a blender jug until smooth. Add more milk if the soup is too thick and adjust the seasoning.
4. Reheat and serve with parsley and sliced almonds (if using) scattered on top.

Pumpkin Soup Two Ways

There's something wonderful about the deep orange hue of a pumpkin. It radiates warmth and comfort, perfect for a cold winter's day.

I love pumpkin soup (or squash if there's no pumpkin around). The sweetness hits the tongue first, followed by the heat of the ginger and garlic. And as it's packed full of super-healthy, amazing anti-inflammatory nutrients, that will make both your taste-buds and your body happy.

Pumpkins can be a pain to peel, especially if you have weak wrists, so there are two ways to make this soup.

The first is the peel and cook method where you chop the pumpkin into larger sections before peeling it. You can then chop it into smaller pieces before cooking. The coconut milk in this version gives the soup a rich, Asian flavour.

The second is the roasting method where you cut the whole pumpkin into chunks, roast it in the oven until soft, then peel and cook it in the soup. The second method takes slightly longer but is less effort. It also gives the soup a more intense flavour because the natural sugars have caramelised in the oven.

I couldn't decide which version to include, so you have them both. You can, of course, cook the soup the first way and omit the coconut milk. Just add more stock if you need to.

A word of caution

Pumpkin and squash have a high water content, so take care how much stock you add. If you're using the coconut milk, use less stock in the simmering stage, otherwise your soup will be very runny.

Serves 4–6

The peel and cook method

Ingredients

1 onion, diced
1 medium squash or small pumpkin, peeled and diced
1–2 garlic cloves, crushed
2cm piece fresh ginger, peeled and grated
Up to 500ml / 2 cups vegetable stock
400ml / large tin of coconut milk
Salt and black pepper, to taste

Method

1. Heat 2–3 tablespoons of water in a large saucepan and sauté the onion until it starts to soften. Add the ginger and garlic and continue to cook for 2 minutes, adding a little more water if needed to prevent it burning.
2. Tip in the chopped pumpkin and coat with the onion mix. Pour in enough vegetable stock to almost cover the squash, bring to the boil, put on the lid and cook for 20 minutes or until the pumpkin is soft.
3. Leave to cool slightly, then blend to a smooth consistency with a stick blender, adding in the coconut milk as you go until you get the thickness you desire. Season with salt and pepper and reheat gently before serving.

The roasting method

Ingredients

1 medium squash or pumpkin, cut into large chunks
A splash of olive oil
1 medium onion, diced
1–2 garlic cloves, crushed and diced
2cm piece fresh ginger, peeled and grated
750ml / 3 cups vegetable stock
Salt and black pepper, to taste

Method

1. Pre-heat the oven to 180°C/350°F/Gas Mark 4. Place the pumpkin chunks onto a baking tray, drizzle over a little olive oil and roast in the oven for 20 minutes or until they start to soften and brown. Remove the pumpkin from the oven and leave to cool for a couple of minutes.
2. In the meantime, heat a small amount of water in the bottom of a large saucepan and sauté the onion until it starts to soften. Add the garlic and ginger, and a little

more water if needed. Cook for another couple of minutes, stirring all the time to make sure it doesn't burn.

3. Add 250ml / 1 cup of vegetable stock, bring to the boil, then reduce the heat and simmer.
4. Carefully peel the pumpkin skin off the cooked flesh – it should come away easily in your hands. Add the flesh to the saucepan with enough stock to cover, bring to the boil and cook for another 10 minutes. Blend until smooth and season with salt and pepper.

Courgette and Cumin Soup

This soup always surprises people when I serve it at a workshop or event. People assume that it will be watery and weak. But once tasted, people realise it's definitely not. This soup is thick, sumptuous and absolutely delicious. It's also packed with wonderful anti-inflammatory nutrients and is a tasty way of using up a glut of courgettes in the summer.

As courgettes have a very high water content, you need to take care with the vegetable stock. Add just enough stock to cover the vegetables as they cook. You can add more when you blend the soup if it's too thick. This gives you control over the consistency and avoids watery disappointment.

Sweet potatoes work just as well as white potatoes if you need to substitute. They add extra phytonutrients too, making this soup even more 'souper' healthy!

Serves 4–6

Ingredients

1 teaspoon cumin seeds
1 large onion, chopped
1 large potato, diced
1 large celery stick, diced
3–4 large courgettes, chopped
2 garlic cloves, finely chopped
A sprinkle of celery salt
750ml / 3 cups vegetable stock
Salt and pepper, to taste

To serve

Dairy-free yoghurt
Toasted cumin seeds (optional)

Method

1. Heat a small amount of water in the bottom of a large pan and sauté the onion and cumin seeds for 5 minutes or until the onion starts to soften and the cumin seeds release their aroma. Add the potato and celery, then cook for another 5 minutes, scraping any caramelised bits off the bottom of the pan.
2. Drop in the courgettes and garlic, sauté for another couple of minutes, then pour in the stock to just cover the veggies (see note above). Sprinkle a dash of celery salt into the mix and bring to the boil.
3. Cover with the saucepan lid, reduce the heat and simmer for 15 minutes or until all the veggies are soft and there are gorgeous smells wafting around the kitchen.
4. Turn off the heat and leave to cool for a couple of minutes. Blend until smooth with a stick blender. Add more vegetable stock if needed so you get the consistency you like.
5. Reheat gently, then serve with a dollop of dairy-free yoghurt and more cumin seeds, if desired.

Smoky Lentil and Tomato Soup

Discovering smoked paprika was a Eureka moment for my plant-based cooking. Its warm, rich flavour adds an enticing depth to dishes, making them seem 'meaty' even though there's obviously no meat in them. It's magic!

This soup is seriously satisfying, especially on a cold winter's day. It envelopes you in a soothing hug so you feel warm and satisfied both inside and out. It's super-simple to make and is amazingly tasty, ensuring that this soup pleases even the most doubting plant-based detractors.

Serves 4–6

Ingredients

1 red onion or medium leek
1 large carrot, peeled
2 celery sticks
150g / 1 cup split red lentils
400g / large tin of chopped tomatoes
2 teaspoons smoked paprika
1 teaspoon dried thyme
1 litre / 4 cups vegetable stock
Salt and pepper, to taste

Method

1. Chop the onion or leek, carrot and celery into small dice.
2. Heat a couple of tablespoons of water in the bottom of a large pan and sauté the vegetables for 5 minutes or so until they start to soften. Stir regularly and add more water if needed to prevent the veggies from sticking to the pan.
3. Add the lentils, tinned tomatoes and smoked paprika, stir well and cook for a couple of minutes before adding the thyme and stock. Bring to the boil, then reduce the heat and simmer with the lid on for 25 minutes or so until the lentils are cooked and swollen.
4. Turn off the heat and leave to cool slightly, then blend until smooth with a stick blender. Reheat to serve and season to taste.

Roasted Cauliflower Soup

When you change to a whole-food plant-based way of eating, your taste-buds change too. Flavours are fresher and more intense, and food just tastes more inspiring. But it was still a surprise when I first made this soup and it tasted like cheese.

Not cheese exactly, but it definitely has a cheesy aftertaste. At first, I thought it was just me going mad. I hadn't set out to create a cheese flavour, it was purely accidental.

I first made this soup in a last-minute 'I need something to take to work' panic. A rough recipe had been whirling around in my mind, so I threw it all together, poured it into a flask and rushed out the door. It was only later when I tasted it that the cheesiness hit me. It was a real surprise.

And it wasn't just me. I served it to the family for tea without mentioning the flavour and they all asked if I'd put cheese in it.

A cheesy flavour is hard to replicate in a plant-based diet. Nutritional yeast is commonly used as an alternative, but if you have a yeast intolerance or gut issues or you can't find it in the shops, it might not be an option. This combination of cauliflower, almond and bay leaf creates a great flavour as a natural alternative. If you can't tolerate nuts, use ground sunflower seeds instead; the soup won't taste quite the same but there should still be some 'cheesy' flavour. You can also use this recipe to make a 'cheesy' sauce, just reduce the fluid content and you'll have a thick sauce you can pour on pasta or over a plate of cooked veggies. Result!

Serves 4–6

Ingredients

1 medium cauliflower
Olive oil spray
1 onion, diced
1 garlic clove, crushed
2 bay leaves
2 tablespoons ground almonds or sunflower seeds
1 litre / 4 cups vegetable stock
500ml / 2 cups dairy-free milk of choice
Salt and pepper, to taste

Method

1. Pre-heat the oven to 180°C/350°F/Gas Mark 4.
2. Chop the cauliflower into florets and wash in a colander under a running tap. Shake off some of the water but don't dry them completely as the water droplets will help the cauli to roast. Spray a couple of squirts of olive oil over the florets and spread out on a baking tray. Roast in the oven for 20 minutes, turning a couple of times until the cauli lightly browns and starts to soften. Don't over-roast as it will make the soup a dull brown colour.
3. Whilst the cauli is roasting, heat a couple of tablespoons of water in the bottom of a large pan and sauté the onion over a medium heat with the bay leaves, turning regularly so the onion doesn't burn.
4. Add the garlic with a little of the veg stock and cook for another minute, then stir in the ground almonds or sunflower seeds. Cook for a couple of minutes, then stir in 250ml / 1 cup of the vegetable stock. Bring to the boil, pop on the lid and simmer.
5. Remove the cauliflower from the oven and tip it into the saucepan. Add enough stock to cover, bring to the boil once more, then simmer for another 5 minutes or until the cauliflower is super-soft. Turn off the heat and leave to cool for a few minutes.
6. Fish out the bay leaves, then pour in some of the dairy-free milk. Blitz in a blender or use a stick blender and process until smooth, adding more milk or stock as needed to get the thickness of soup you desire. Season with salt and pepper.

Witches' Brew (or Pea and Lettuce Soup)

This soup is so green, it just has to be the soup that witches eat! Or at least, that's what I told my children one Hallowe'en during one of their more challenging non vegetable-eating times. They were much happier thinking it was special witches' food rather than just Mum trying to get them to eat vegetables.

This soup is so delicious it shouldn't just be for the children, though. Lettuce and pea are an amazing flavour combination – sweet and delightfully moreish – it will please even the most discerning witch or wizard at any time of year, whatever their age.

Serves 4

Ingredients

1 medium onion, diced
1 slender leek, washed, trimmed and shredded
1 medium potato, diced
400g / 4 cups chopped lettuce (Little gem or Cos work well)
400g / 3 cups peas (frozen are fine)
700ml / 3 cups vegetable stock
Salt and pepper, to taste

To serve

Lemon juice
Dairy-free yoghurt (optional)

Method

1. Heat a couple of tablespoons of the vegetable stock in a large saucepan and sauté the onion, leek and potato for 5 minutes, stirring frequently to prevent sticking. Pour in enough stock to cover the vegetables and simmer for 10 minutes or until the potato is cooked.
2. Add the lettuce and a little more stock, but not too much as the lettuce releases lots of fluid as it wilts, which could leave you with a thinner soup than you want.
3. Cook for 5 minutes, then add the peas and enough stock to cover. Cook for another 5 minutes until the peas are soft, then turn off the heat and leave to cool slightly.
4. Blend until smooth, adding more stock to get the consistency you desire. I tend to go for a thicker soup and leave a few peas unblended to make it suitably witch-like, but you may want a slightly more sophisticated, smooth consistency.
5. Season to taste, then serve with a squeeze of lemon juice. This lifts the flavour and helps make the nutrients easier to absorb. Add a swirl of dairy-free yoghurt if you wish.

Butterbean, Roasted Garlic and Rosemary Soup

I couldn't face eating butterbeans for years after being given them as a side vegetable when I was a child. Dull in flavour with a clumpy texture that stuck to the top of my mouth, they definitely landed in the category of 'things I don't need to eat'!

But now, I've come to love them as a wonderful base ingredient. Butterbeans add a thick, creamy texture to dishes, which is ideal for soups, stews or dips. And because they are so bland, they absorb flavours well. Their final accolade is that they are packed full of super-healthy fibre, so both taste-buds and tummy are kept happy.

Roasted garlic and rosemary are strong flavours and both have excellent medicinal properties too. But if a whole bulb of garlic seems too much for you, use less. Although it's worth remembering that roasted garlic has a far more subtle flavour and is much easier on the digestion than garlic cooked in other ways.

Serves 6

Ingredients

1 bulb garlic
2 medium onions, chopped
4 medium celery sticks, chopped
2 x 400g / large tins of butterbeans, drained and rinsed
1 sprig of fresh rosemary, chopped
1 litre / 4 cups vegetable stock
Salt and pepper, to taste

To serve

A couple of handfuls of shredded spinach
A drizzle of flaxseed oil (optional)

Method

1. Pre-heat the oven to 180°C/350°F/Gas Mark 4. Wrap the garlic bulb in tin foil and roast in the oven for 20–25 minutes or until wonderful aromas fill the kitchen and the bulb is soft when squeezed. Remove from the oven and leave to cool (this can be done in advance when the oven is being used for something else, then kept in the fridge if you wish).
2. Heat a couple of tablespoons of the vegetable stock in the bottom of a large pan. Add the chopped onion and celery and sauté for 5 minutes or until they start to soften.

3. Cut open the roasted garlic bulb and separate into cloves as much as possible. Split the skin and squeeze out the soft flesh into the pan.
4. Add the butterbeans, chopped rosemary and enough stock to cover, then stir well. Bring to the boil, cover, then simmer for 10 minutes or until the veggies are cooked and the flavours have developed.
5. Turn off the heat, then blend until smooth, adding more stock as needed to get a creamy but not too thick texture. Season with salt and pepper to taste.
6. Serve with a sprinkle of fresh shredded spinach leaves and a teaspoon of flaxseed oil if desired.

Spicy Chickpea and Lentil Soup

This is the ultimate winter warmer soup. Packed full of nutrients and flavour, with a little spicy heat to take the chill off the iciest weather, this soup is sure to bring some sunshine to the dullest of days.

Despite the number of ingredients, this is quick and easy to make, and if you have any leftovers, it tastes even better the next day.

Serves 4–6

Ingredients

1 onion (red or white)
2 garlic cloves
2cm piece fresh ginger
2 medium carrots, peeled and finely chopped
½ teaspoon ground turmeric
1 teaspoon ground cumin
½–1 teaspoon chilli powder
1 teaspoon ground coriander
400g / large tin of chopped tomatoes
100g / ½ cup split red lentils
200g / 1 cup cooked chickpeas
700ml / 2½ cups vegetable stock
Salt and pepper, to taste

To serve

2–3 tablespoons cooked chickpeas
2 tablespoons chopped coriander
Soya yoghurt (optional)

Method

1. Roughly chop the onion, garlic and ginger and pop into a small hand blender or food processor and blitz to a rough paste. If you don't have a gadget, finely chop by hand.
2. Heat a couple of tablespoons of the stock in the bottom of a large pan and sauté the paste for 5 minutes over a medium heat until it starts to brown and the aromas are released. Don't let it burn.
3. Add the carrot and continue to cook for a couple of minutes. Stir in the spices and the chopped tomatoes and mix together well. Add the lentils and let them cook for a couple of minutes before pouring in the vegetable stock.
4. Bring to the boil, pop on the lid and reduce the heat. Let the soup simmer for 20 minutes or until the lentils are cooked, then add the chickpeas and seasoning. Continue to cook for a further 5 minutes.
5. Turn off the heat and leave to cool for a few minutes, then blend until smooth. Check the seasoning, then serve with a sprinkle of chickpeas, fresh coriander and dairy-free yoghurt if you wish.

SALADS

When I grew up in the 1970s, salad consisted of limp lettuce, a couple of slices of bitter cucumber and an unripe tomato served with lashings of salad cream. Nothing very exciting at all. Fortunately, times have changed and these days, salad can be the dazzling star of a meal or at least have a strong supporting role. There are so many super-tasty plant-based combinations that salad never has to be dull or boring again.

These recipes can all be used as a main dish or as a side. But be warned – they do make large portions for a robust family. So, if it's just you dining on their deliciousness, you might want to halve or even quarter the ingredients. Otherwise you'll be eating it every night for a week!

Roasted Carrot, Spinach and Tahini Salad

The title might not sound enticing, but I can assure you, the taste is delicious. This is one of the recipes I give to my Eat Well Live Well course participants in the first week and it blows them away every time. Roasting carrots intensifies their natural sugars, beautifully complementing the sharp flavour of the dressing. Simple yet effective.

If you can't tolerate sesame seeds and love peanuts, you can replace the tahini with unsalted natural peanut butter. It's equally delicious. If you've no time to roast the carrots, steam chunks of it instead. It won't be quite as sweet, but it still works well with the dressing.

Serves 4

Ingredients

4 large carrots
Olive oil spray
150g / 3 packed cups baby spinach leaves
1–2 tablespoons pumpkin seeds, toasted

For the dressing

2 tablespoons tahini
Juice of 1 lime
2 teaspoons maple syrup
1 garlic clove, crushed
¼ teaspoon ground cumin
Salt and pepper, to taste

Method

1. Pre-heat the oven to 180°C/350°F/Gas Mark 4. Scrub or peel the carrots and chop them into medium chunks. Place in a baking tray and spray with a little olive oil. Roast in the oven for 20 minutes or until soft and lightly browned. Do not overcook.
2. In the meantime, place all the dressing ingredients into the bowl of a small food processor and blitz until combined and creamy. If you don't have a gadget, pop into a lidded jar and shake to combine. If it's too thick, add a little water. Taste the dressing and add a little salt and pepper to season.
3. Once the carrot is ready, remove it from the oven and leave to cool for 5 minutes. Scatter the baby spinach leaves in the bottom of a serving bowl, then add the warm carrot – this will wilt the spinach a little.
4. Drizzle with the dressing, then scatter over the pumpkin seeds.
5. Eat warm or leave it to cool. It tastes fabulous either way.

Asian Salad

I love this salad. The beautiful Eastern flavours settle on the crunchy vegetables, complementing each other in perfect harmony. It's a great rainbow salad and particularly good in winter. You can replace the red pepper with a red chilli pepper instead if you'd like a bit of extra warmth.

Edamame are young soya beans that are harvested early in the growth cycle. You can sometimes find them fresh and still in their pods, but they can be expensive and hard to come by. A more accessible solution is to buy them frozen from the supermarket. If you can't eat soya, then substitute with frozen green peas instead.

If possible, prepare this salad a few hours in advance so the flavours have time to develop. If not, eat straight away as it'll still taste delicious.

Serves 6

Ingredients

For the salad

130g / 1 cup edamame beans, defrosted (if frozen)
2 medium carrots, grated
¼ medium red cabbage, finely shredded
¼ medium green cabbage, finely shredded
1 red pepper, sliced
3 spring onions, sliced on the diagonal

A bunch fresh coriander, roughly chopped
3 tablespoons crushed peanuts or sliced almonds
2 tablespoons sesame seeds

For the dressing

1 small garlic clove, grated
2 teaspoons grated fresh ginger
2 fat limes, juiced
2 tablespoons tamari
1 tablespoon maple syrup
1 teaspoon sesame oil (optional)

Method

1. Blanch the edamame beans in a small pan of boiling water for a couple of minutes. Drain and rinse with cold water. Leave to cool.
2. Combine the dressing ingredients together in a small jar, shaking well to mix.
3. Place the cabbage, carrots, spring onions and red pepper into a large bowl. Scatter over the cooled edamame along with half of the coriander and half of the peanuts.
4. Pour on the dressing and toss well to coat the vegetables. Scatter over the remaining coriander, peanuts and the sesame seeds.

Beetroot, Carrot and Kale Salad

Winter throws up some fabulous options for rainbow eating. These wonderful comforting, earthy flavours are complemented by the sharp, vibrant bite of the passion fruit. Simple but deliciously effective.

Serves 4–6

Ingredients

2 medium raw beetroot, peeled and grated
3–4 medium carrots, peeled and grated
2–3 handfuls of kale, stems removed and finely chopped
2 tablespoons roasted mixed seeds or sesame seeds

For the dressing

2 passion fruit
2 tablespoons cider vinegar or lemon juice
2 tablespoons hempseed or flaxseed oil
Salt and pepper, to taste

Method

1. Cut the passion fruit in half and remove the pulp with a teaspoon.
2. Place the pulp and the rest of the dressing ingredients into a jar, pop on the lid and shake well to combine.
3. Place the chopped kale into a large bowl and pour over half the dressing. Massage the kale with your hands for a few minutes to break down the hard, fibrous walls. This releases the nutrients within and makes it more palatable.
4. Add the beetroot, carrot and remaining dressing to the bowl and mix well with a spoon to combine. Check the flavour and add more salt and pepper if needed.
5. Sprinkle over the seeds just before serving.

Puy Lentil and Sun-dried Tomatoes with Watercress Pesto Salad

This is a great multi-purpose dish. You can serve it cold as a salad or warm as a side dish. And if you have any leftovers, it can be turned into super-tasty patties that bake beautifully in the oven. Three options from one recipe – versatility on a plate.

I prefer to cook the lentils from scratch, but if you're short of time, tinned lentils work just as well. Puy lentils take a little longer to cook and are more expensive but the cheaper green ones are just as good, so experiment with both and see which you prefer.

If you're using dried sun-dried tomatoes, don't forget to soak them in advance. If you use the ones packed in a jar with oil, make sure it's olive oil but still rinse it off as much as possible and dry with some kitchen paper afterwards.

Serves 6

Ingredients

200g / 1 cup Puy or green lentils, uncooked
1 courgette, sliced into strips
3 spring onions, finely sliced
5–6 sun-dried tomatoes, chopped
2 tablespoons chopped fresh parsley
1 tablespoon pumpkin seeds, toasted
80g / 1 cup watercress
2 tablespoons walnuts
2 tablespoons lemon juice

1 garlic clove, grated
A large pinch of Himalayan salt
2 tablespoons flaxseed oil

Method

1. To prepare the lentils, begin by placing them in a sieve and rinsing them well. Pour 625ml / 2½ cups of water into a saucepan and add the rinsed lentils and a bay leaf. Pop on the lid, bring to the boil, then reduce the heat and simmer for 25 minutes or until all the water has been absorbed and the lentils are soft. Turn off the heat and leave to steam for a few minutes, then tip out into a bowl to cool. This ensures the lentils don't get over-cooked and mushy. (You can prepare the lentils earlier in the day or the night before, to save time.)
2. Heat a griddle pan or non-stick frying pan and dry-fry the courgette slices for a few minutes until they start to brown but are still firm to the touch. Turn off the heat and leave to cool, then chop into bite-sized chunks.
3. To make the pesto dressing, pop the watercress, walnuts, lemon juice, garlic and salt into a food processor and blitz for a few seconds until they are broken down. Add the flaxseed oil and a little water and blend again until smooth, adding more water if needed. You want a thick but not solid pesto.
4. Place the lentils, spring onions, courgette, sun-dried tomatoes and half the parsley into a bowl and stir in the pesto to coat. Sprinkle over the remaining parsley and the pumpkin seeds and serve.

Watercress, Pomegranate and Labneh Salad

Flicking through a food magazine one day, I came across a feature on 'superfoods', with the focus on pomegranates, one of my favourite fruits. But it wasn't the gloriously vibrant pink jewels that grabbed my attention – it was labneh.

Thick, white and creamy, labneh is a Middle-Eastern cheese made from strained yoghurt mixed with a little lemon juice and salt. It can be served on a meze platter as a dip for flatbreads or feature as a key salad ingredient. I was fascinated with it for two reasons – first, because I couldn't understand why I hadn't come across it before and second, because I wondered whether I could make it myself, but dairy-free.

It turns out the answer to the first question didn't really matter, whereas the answer to the second did, because it was yes!

There are gadgets you can buy to make your own labneh, but I prefer my home-made method (described below), which costs just pennies. Use a good-quality, unsweetened soya yoghurt and don't spare the lemon then you'll get a creamy 'cheese' that pairs perfectly with pomegranate and watercress. Double the superfood, triple the flavour.

Serves 4

Ingredients

For the labneh

200ml / 1 cup unsweetened soya yoghurt
Juice of ½ lemon (more if you want it tarter)
A pinch of Himalayan salt

For the salad

1 bunch watercress, washed and trimmed
1 avocado, peeled and chopped
1 portion labneh
2–3 tablespoons pomegranate seeds
2 tablespoons mixed seeds, lightly toasted
2 tablespoons chopped fresh parsley
Salt and pepper, to taste

To serve

Lemon juice

Method

1. Make the labneh the day before. Line a sieve with a muslin or a fine-mesh tea towel and place it over a deep bowl. Pour in the yoghurt, then add the lemon juice and salt. Mix gently, then carefully tie up the corners of the fabric to create a bag. Place the bag back in the sieve and balance a heavy object, like a tin of beans, on top. Leave it in the fridge overnight so the excess fluid can drain off. When you are ready to use it the next day, remove the weight, unwrap the material and you will have a firm disc of creamy soft 'cheese'. Carefully tip the labneh onto a plate.
2. To construct the salad, layer up the other ingredients in a large bowl. Create small balls of labneh using a teaspoon, then scatter them across the top. Season with salt and pepper, add some lemon juice, if you like, then serve.

Cauliflower Couscous

Cauliflower has had a make-over recently, and rightly so. Thankfully the days of over-cooked, plain and flavourless lumps are gone. Treated right, cauliflower is full of flavour and blessed with creamy qualities. It's also packed with amazingly healthy nutrients and a special versatility that makes it the chameleon of the vegetable world. There are so many ways of cooking cauliflower that to boil it and eat it plain is almost a travesty, especially as cooking it this way makes it unpalatable to many who shy away from the strong sulphur-like flavour.

This salad is the perfect compromise – the cauli is briefly steamed to soften it slightly but it retains all its nutritional goodies. Mixed with simple yet delicious flavours, this dish is a delight for the tongue. An unassuming superfood salad for sure.

If you can't eat almonds then go for pistachios instead or if you're completely nut-free then toasted pumpkin seeds are a good alternative. If you haven't got all three herbs, just increase the amounts of the ones you do have and the dish will still taste delicious.

Serves 4–6

Ingredients

1 medium cauliflower, cut into florets
2 tablespoons finely chopped fresh mint
2 tablespoons finely chopped fresh parsley
1 tablespoon finely chopped fresh coriander
2 tablespoons flaked almonds
2 tablespoons pomegranate seeds
Salt and pepper, to taste

To serve

A glug of flaxseed oil (optional)

Method

1. Pop the cauliflower florets into a steamer and steam for a couple of minutes. Remove from the heat and tip out into a bowl straight away to cool.
2. Once cold, place the cauliflower into a food processor and blitz a few times so it's broken down into fine pieces. Transfer to a large bowl and stir in the herbs, almonds and pomegranate seeds.
3. Season with salt and pepper. Taste and add more herbs or seasoning as needed. Finish with a glug of flaxseed oil, if you wish, and serve.

Potato, Bean and Cucumber Salad

This salad is a surprisingly tasty store-cupboard mix of flavours and textures and will fill the hungriest of stomachs. I made this originally on one of those evenings when I needed a quick dish but hadn't been shopping. All I had were leftovers to work with, and so I had to get creative – one of my dreaded 'experiments'. Some cold new potatoes leftover from the night before, some odds and ends of herbs and the rest just came together and surprised us all.

Swapping the cold potato for cooled roasted sweet potato alters the flavour as well as the nutritional profile. Chickpeas are still my favourite option, but all sorts of beans work so don't be too tied to the recipe. Fresh, light and crunchy, leftovers never tasted so good!

Serves 4–6

Ingredients

4–5 small salad potatoes, boiled and cooled or 2 medium sweet potatoes chopped, roasted and cooled
½ cucumber, diced
400g / large tin of chickpeas or beans of choice, rinsed and drained
A handful of chopped mint and/or parsley
1 small red chilli, finely sliced (optional, but good)
Juice 1 lemon
Salt and pepper, to taste

Method

1. Chop the cold potatoes into bite-sized pieces then place into a serving bowl with the cucumber and chickpeas.
2. Sprinkle over the herbs, chilli, lemon juice and seasoning and mix well.
3. Add a few extra herbs on top to garnish then serve.

Lemony Rainbow Coleslaw

When I changed to a dairy-free and then fully plant-based way of eating, I was surprised to find one of the things I craved was coleslaw. At first, I wasn't sure why, but then I realised it was connected to a pivotal time in my younger life – leaving home and moving to the bright lights of London to start my nursing training.

Suddenly I was completely responsible for what, and when, I ate. A continental supermarket nearby sold exotic items like hummus, taramasalata and stuffed vine leaves – unheard of at that time in rural Sussex! They also sold pots of thick, creamy coleslaw – not acidic and runny like the ones in the supermarket at home. I loved it – and ate lots of it.

I would pile it in a sandwich with loads of cheese and chow down, enjoying the texture and flavour, but also feeling triumphantly free, striking out on my own culinary path. Although a cheese and coleslaw sandwich was hardly original, it was *my* cheese and coleslaw sandwich, a symbol of freedom and independence.

This version is definitely more than your average slaw. A festival of rainbow colours and gorgeous lemony flavour, it creates a whole new collection of memories.

Serves 6-8

Ingredients

½ green cabbage, finely sliced
¼ red cabbage, finely sliced
1 crisp apple, grated
3–4 medium carrots, grated
1 small red onion, grated
1 portion of Creamy Lemon Mayo (see page 262)
Salt and pepper, to taste

Method

1. Place all the prepared veggies into a large bowl and stir well to combine.
2. Pour in the lemony mayo and stir again. Season with salt and pepper to taste, then serve.

Slow Roasted Tomato and Asparagus Salad

This salad is very simple to make, but posh enough to impress, making it perfect for summer entertaining. It's not a last-minute creation though as the tomatoes need time to roast and reveal their gorgeously rich sweetness, so this salad is all about the planning.

Serves 4–6

Ingredients

For the salad

1 bag of spinach, rocket and watercress leaves
1 bunch asparagus
1 ripe avocado
300g / 1½ cups cherry tomatoes
2 tablespoons sprouted alfalfa or broccoli seeds
A glug of flaxseed oil
1–2 tablespoons grated Dairy-free 'Parmesan' (see page 263)

Method

1. Prepare the tomatoes in advance. Pre-heat the oven to 160°C/320°F/Gas Mark 3. Wash the tomatoes, cut them in half, then spread out cut-side up over a non-stick baking tray. Roast in the oven for 20 minutes until soft and slightly dried out. Remove from the oven and leave to cool.
2. Wash and trim the asparagus to remove any woody parts from the bottom of the stems. Cut off the tips and set aside, then steam the stems for a few minutes or until they start to soften slightly. Add the tips and steam for another minute. Remove from the steamer and lay out on a cold plate to cool. The aim isn't to cook the asparagus, just make is slightly tender.
3. To construct the salad, spread the salad leaves out over the bottom of a large serving dish. Layer the asparagus over the top. Peel and chop the avocado, then scatter it over the asparagus. Next, add the tomatoes. Sprinkle the sprouted seed and 'Parmesan' over the top and finish with a glug of flaxseed oil.

Lemony Millet Salad

If you think that millet is only good as bird-seed then think again. Packed full of plant-based protein and fibre, millet is a surprisingly flavoursome and useful ingredient – and not a grain, but a seed.

Toasting the millet before cooking brings out a lovely nutty aroma that enhances the overall flavour of the dish. Just don't overheat the pan, as the natural oils will become a little irritating to the back of the throat and the flavour will be spoiled. If you can't find black beans, use aduki or even chickpeas – smaller ones are better.

Serves 6–8

Ingredients

100g / ½ cup uncooked millet
375ml / 1½ cups vegetable stock
400g / large tin of black beans, rinsed and drained
150g / 1 cup sweetcorn
1 red pepper, finely chopped
1 small green chilli, finely chopped
Small bunch fresh coriander or parsley, chopped
Zest and juice of an unwaxed lemon
A good glug of flaxseed oil
Salt and pepper, to taste

Method

1. Heat a non-stick frying pan over a moderate heat and toast the millet for about 5 minutes until it releases its nutty aroma and starts to brown slightly.
2. Pour the vegetable stock into a medium saucepan and bring to the boil. Tip the toasted millet into the stock, pop on the lid, reduce the heat and simmer for 15–20 minutes or until all the stock has been absorbed and the millet is soft and fluffy.
3. Turn off the heat and leave to steam for a few minutes. Tip out into a large bowl and leave to cool. This can be done the day before and left in the fridge overnight.
4. Add all the remaining ingredients, mix well and season to taste.

HOT OPTIONS

This section was going to be called 'lunches' but these flexible recipes don't have a set meal time. Some are even great breakfast or brunch options. Most can be frozen so are very useful for when time is short but you don't want to have to resort to ready-meals or take-aways.

My freezer is littered with a mix of leftovers from various meals like these, often just single portions, perfect for when I'm in a hurry and just catering for myself. Having said that, there have been some eclectic family meals when it's time to defrost the freezer, creating a smorgasbord of plant-based bites!

Farinata

Farinata is a traditional Italian dish that is more like a frittata in texture than a pizza base. It's usually made thinner than this, but I like to make mine denser, so it's packed with veggies and herbs, and it uses less oil.

This is best eaten on the day of making, otherwise it becomes a little dry. Leftovers need to be reheated in the oven rather than eaten cold. It can be frozen for up to two months. To use after freezing, defrost thoroughly then reheated in the oven.

There is a little preparation to do but you can do this several hours before. For example, if you want to eat them in the morning, prepare the mix the night before and if you want to eat them in the evening, prep the mix in the morning. Once you've made the batter, the whole dish takes but moments to finish.

With so many flavour combinations, you can mix it up however you like. I've included two options for you to try.

Makes 12 squares

Ingredients

Base Ingredients

250g / 2 cups chickpea/gram flour
½ teaspoon salt
450ml / just under 2 cups warm water
2 tablespoons olive oil
Ground black pepper

Tomato and olive flavouring

2 tomatoes, chopped
½ red onion, diced
3 tablespoons pitted black olives, halved
2 tablespoons chopped fresh rosemary and thyme
¼ teaspoon chilli flakes (optional)

Asparagus and mint flavouring

2 spring onions, chopped
5 asparagus stalks, chopped
3 tablespoons peas, defrosted
2 tablespoons chopped fresh parsley and chives

Method

1. To prepare the farinata base, sift the chickpea flour and salt into a medium bowl to get rid of any lumps. Add the warm water and whisk to combine. Cover with a damp tea-towel and leave to soak for a minimum of 2 hours or up to 8 hours.
2. Prepare the Tomato and Olive or the Asparagus and Mint mix (or use another combination of vegetables, herbs and spices) so it's ready to add to the mix.
3. Pre-heat the oven to 180°C/350°F/Gas Mark 4. Line a 20x20cm baking tin with baking paper.
4. Whisk the olive oil into the chickpea flour mix and season with salt and pepper.
5. Pour the chickpea flour mix into the prepared tin. Sprinkle over the prepared vegetable mix and herbs, and season with a little more salt and pepper.
6. Place the tin in the oven and bake for 10 minutes or until the mix has set and is just beginning to brown on top. Do not overcook as it will become dry.
7. Remove from the oven and leave to set in the tin for 5 minutes. Carefully remove the farinata from the tin and peel off the baking paper.
8. If you are eating straight away, cut into squares and serve. If not, leave to cool then cut and serve.

Sweet Potato Falafels

Falafels are firm favourites in our house. So is sweet potato. Combine them together, and you just can't go wrong.

Falafels are often fried, or worse deep-fried, turning a delicious super-healthy bite into something unhealthy. Baking is the healthiest option, but it can make them a little dry. Adding steamed sweet potato solves that problem, making them moist and seriously moreish.

Serve these with one of the tahini dressings (*see pages* 262–263) and plenty of fresh crisp lettuce for a complementary crunch.

Makes 14–15 pieces

Ingredients

2 small or 1 medium sweet potato
400g / large tin of chickpeas, drained and rinsed
2 tablespoons chopped fresh coriander
2 teaspoons ground cumin
1 teaspoon ground coriander
1 garlic clove, crushed or 1 teaspoon dried garlic powder
1 tablespoon chickpea/gram flour or cornflour (if needed)
Sesame seeds to coat (optional)
Salt and pepper, to taste

Method

1. Peel the sweet potato and chop into small chunks. Steam for 10 minutes until soft, then leave to cool (this can be done the day before if it helps time-wise).
2. Place the cooked sweet potato, chickpeas, herbs, spices, garlic and seasoning into a food processor and pulse a few times to break down the chickpeas and combine everything together. Don't over-pulse as you want some texture, not a purée. If the mix is too wet, add a little chickpea flour or cornflour to thicken.
3. Cover a baking sheet with non-stick baking paper. Take a spoonful of mix and roll it into a walnut-sized ball. Place on the baking sheet and repeat until all the mix has gone. Pop into the fridge for 30 minutes to set.
4. Pre-heat the oven to 180°C/350°F/Gas Mark 4. Remove the falafels from the fridge and sprinkle with the sesame seeds (if using).
5. Bake for 8 minutes, then turn and bake for another 8–10 minutes or until firm and lightly browned. Serve hot or cold.

Beetroot, Carrot and Millet Bites

This is one of the recipes I used to teach in my cooking demos when I first started The Sensitive Foodie Kitchen. They can be made in advance and kept in the fridge or used straight away. Kids love to get involved as the mix becomes all squishy as you bring it all together; it's also an easy way to get them into rainbow eating. Having said that, these tasty bites are not just for kids. Add a sauce on the side and they can be part of a posh dinner party too. I love these with the Creamy Pesto Sauce (*see page 261*).

Makes 12 bites

Ingredients

100g/½ cup millet
375ml / 1½ cups vegetable stock
1 bay leaf
3 medium carrots, grated
1 medium beetroot, grated
1 small red onion, grated
3 garlic cloves, roasted
1 teaspoon Italian herbs
½ teaspoon garlic powder
2 tablespoons finely chopped fresh parsley
3–4 heaped tablespoons chickpea/gram flour
Salt and pepper, to taste

Method

1. To prepare the millet, pour it into a dry frying pan and toast over a medium heat for 5 minutes or until its aromas are released. Turn off the heat and transfer the millet to a small saucepan with a lid.
2. Add the vegetable stock and bay leaf, bring to the boil, then cover, reduce the heat and simmer for 15 minutes until all the stock has been absorbed and the millet is soft and fluffy. Turn off the heat and leave to steam for a couple of minutes before tipping out onto a plate to cool. This will prevent it from continuing to cook and turning mushy. Remove the bay leaf. (You can cook the millet the day before if you wish.)
3. Pre-heat the oven to 180°C/350°F/Gas Mark 4. In a large bowl, combine the cooked millet, carrot, beetroot, onion, garlic, herbs, garlic powder and parsley together. Sprinkle over 3 spoonfuls of chickpea flour and stir well. The mixture should start sticking together when pressed between your fingers. Add more flour if needed and season with salt and pepper.

4. Take a large tablespoon of mixture and press it together firmly to form a golf ball- sized lump. Place on a non-stick baking tray and repeat until all the mixture is used up.
5. Bake in the oven for 20 minutes, then turn bake for a further 15 minutes or until the balls are crunchy on the outside. Serve with a sauce of your choice.

Smoky Baked Tofu Slices

A couple of years ago, my daughter asked for a George Foreman grill for Christmas. We were rather surprised as, being vegan, she didn't have much call for grilling meat. It turned out that she'd grown to love this grill when the ovens at her university accommodation had been removed. She'd borrowed one from a friend so she could use it cook her veggie sausages.

We bought her one and decided to try it out while she was still at home. But when she returned to uni with her new grill, we realised just how useful it had been so we found ourselves popping out to buy one for ourselves.

The grill cooks marinated vegetables and tofu particularly well, including these smoky tofu slices. If you don't have a George Foreman-like grill, don't worry as they cook just as well in the oven, it just takes a little longer.

These smoky tofu slices can be used in many ways, including in toasted wraps, as fillings for pitta, as part of a stir fry, as an accompaniment to roasted vegetables or just on their own with a salad and baked potato. If you can, give the tofu plenty of time to marinade. But if that's not possible, don't worry as these slices will still have some lovely smoky flavours, but just not as deep.

It's important to use a dry, extra-firm tofu. If the tofu is particularly wet, you'll need to press it first to remove the excess liquid. To do this, grab two plates, some kitchen roll and a weight (I use a tin of beans). First tip the tofu in a sieve to drain. Place a few sheets of kitchen roll onto one of the plates, put the tofu in the middle, cover with more kitchen roll and then the other plate. Place the weight on top and leave in the fridge for a few hours or overnight. This forces the excess fluid out of the tofu, making it firmer and easier to cook.

Makes around 10 slices

Ingredients

400g / 1 medium pack extra-firm tofu, cut into 1.5cm thick slices
4 tablespoons tamari or coconut amines
1 heaped teaspoon coconut sugar or maple syrup
1 teaspoon smoked paprika

Method

1. Place the tofu slices in a shallow bowl or deep plate. Mix the marinade ingredients together, then pour over the tofu. Turn the tofu to ensure it's well coated, then leave to marinate for 2 hours, turning half-way through.
2. If you're baking the slices, pre-heat the oven to 180ºC/350ºF/Gas Mark 4. Line a baking sheet with non-stick baking paper and place the marinated tofu on top. Bake for 20 minutes, turning after 10 minutes or when the tofu is firm and slightly browned.
3. Alternatively, pop the tofu slices on the grill and cook for 10 minutes or until firm and hot.

Easy Baked Veggie Cakes

These savoury vegetable cakes are simple to make and very adaptable as you can change the ingredients according to the season or to suit your preferences. For this recipe, I've used fresh, Asian flavours like ginger and coriander, but these cakes work well with chilli or European herbs too. Likewise, you could use red onion, swede and celeriac with some thyme for a more British-flavoured cake.

Be mindful of the amount of fluid that'll seep out of the veggies you use. For example, courgettes have a higher water content and should be dried on some paper towel before adding to the mix, otherwise it'll become water-logged. Parsnips, however, have a much lower water content and can be used as they are.

If you like to batch cook, you can double or even quadruple the amount of ingredients as these lovelies freeze well. They're perfect for a quick lunch or snack. Just pop them in the oven to warm them through.

Makes 12 small cakes

Ingredients

500g / 1lb 2oz parsnips and/or carrots and/or courgettes
4 spring onions, finely chopped
1 garlic clove, grated
2cm piece fresh ginger, grated
2 tablespoons chopped fresh coriander
Salt and pepper, to taste
50g / scant ½ cup chickpea/gram flour

Method

1. Pre-heat the oven to 180ºC/350ºF/Gas Mark 4. Line a baking sheet with a silicon mat or non-stick baking paper.
2. Finely grate the vegetables then place them in a bowl with the garlic, ginger and coriander.
3. Sprinkle over ¼ teaspoon of salt and mix together with a spoon or your hands. The salt will extract water from the vegetables.
4. Sprinkle in the chickpea flour and mix together. Set aside for 5 minutes to allow the mix to thicken.
5. Stir the mix again to make sure everything is combined and coming together. To test it, squeeze a small amount between your fingers. If the mix doesn't stick together, add a little more chickpea flour, stir and leave again.
6. Once the mix is ready, spoon out a tablespoonful of mixture and press together to form a flat cake. Place on the prepared baking sheet and repeat until all the mix has been used.
7. Place in the oven and bake for 20 minutes until the cakes are crispy on the outside and slightly gooey on the inside. Eat warm with a sauce of your choice.

Savoury Chickpea Pancake

This is a super-quick yet super-tasty one-pan meal that all the family will enjoy. Use whatever vegetables people like or what you have in the house. I often make this the day before my veg box is delivered, to use up all the bits and bobs left in the fridge (so it helps reduce food waste too).

This makes a great lunch but is also perfect for a busy weekday evening meal. Top with some fresh rocket or spinach leaves to add a bit more greenery.

Serves 4–6

Ingredients

2 medium leeks, sliced
1 red pepper, chopped
6 mushrooms, chopped
100g / ⅔ cup peas, defrosted
1 tablespoon dried thyme
200g / 1¾ cups chickpea/gram flour
2 tablespoons ground flaxseed
¼ teaspoon ground turmeric
½ teaspoon garlic powder
500ml / 2 cups water
Salt and pepper, to taste

Method

1. Heat a large non-stick frying pan and sauté the leeks and red pepper over a medium heat until they start to soften and brown (about 8 minutes). Add the mushrooms and cook until the juices start to run. Stir in the peas and dried thyme and simmer for a few more minutes.
2. In the meantime, sieve the chickpea flour into a bowl. Add the ground flaxseed, turmeric, garlic powder and seasoning. Gently whisk in the water until everything is well combined.
3. Pre-heat your grill to high.
4. Once the veggies are ready in the pan, carefully pour in the chickpea mix, tipping the pan from side to side to make sure the whole pan is covered. Cook over a medium heat until the mixture starts to solidify and the bottom of the pancake browns. This will take about 10 minutes.
5. Place the pan under the grill, keeping the handle away from the heat. Grill until the pancake has set and the top is lightly browned.
6. Remove from the grill and leave to settle for a couple of minutes, then slice into quarters and serve straight from the pan.

SNACKS AND SIDES

These recipes are a selection of my favourite go-to tasty snacks and side dishes. Each of the dips and vegetable side dishes are vibrant in colour and densely packed with gorgeously healthy, helpful phytonutrients and, most importantly, flavour. The baked goodies are perfect to dunk in the dips or any of the soups to make a satisfying lunch or snack. Mix and match as you like; rainbow eating has never been so easy.

Beetroot Hummus

There's something about homemade hummus that makes it stand out from the shop-bought variety. But when you include the vibrant earthiness of beetroot, it's a complete game-changer. This hummus is so deeply purply-pink you may do a double take before you eat it. But once you do, the gorgeously sweet but rugged beetroot combined with soothing cumin will outweigh any initial reluctance; tuck in with glee.

If you have a pressure cooker, beetroot takes no time at all to cook from raw. Alternatively, they roast well in a tin with some water in the base. However, if cooking from raw is too much trouble, then buy ready-cooked beetroot. Make sure it's only packed in water though, rather than vinegar and other preservatives as these will change the flavour and mean that the beetroot won't be quite as wonderfully healthy as it could be.

If beetroot is not your thing, this works well with steamed sweet potato or roasted red peppers.

Makes 8–10 portions

Ingredients

400g / 2 cups cooked chickpeas
2 medium cooked beetroot
½–1 teaspoon lemon juice
2 tablespoons tahini
1 small garlic clove, crushed
2 teaspoons ground cumin
2 tablespoons flaxseed oil or extra virgin olive oil
Water, as needed
Salt and pepper, to taste

To serve

Chopped fresh parsley or coriander
Ground cumin or toasted cumin seeds (optional)

Method

1. Place the chickpeas, beetroot, lemon juice, tahini, garlic and cumin into a food processor and blend until smooth and combined.
2. Add the oil and blend again. If it's too thick, add a little extra water.
3. Season with salt and pepper, blend again, then taste for flavour. Add more seasoning or ground cumin as needed.
4. Serve garnished with some fresh parsley or coriander and dusted with a little extra ground cumin or toasted cumin seeds.

Moroccan Spiced Pumpkin Dip

When they try this dip, people are always surprised by how a few simple ingredients can create such a delicious flavour. When roasted, the natural sugars in the pumpkin come to the fore and are complemented perfectly by the spices. It makes a seriously tasty and moreish snack. What's even better is that kids love it too. And as it's nut-free, it makes a great healthy lunchbox alternative.

Peeling squash or pumpkin before roasting can be hard work, so if possible, cut it into large chunks and roast it with the skin still on. Once cooked it'll be super-simple to peel. If the skin is thin, you could even leave it on, which not only saves time and energy but leaves less waste too.

If you can't eat sesame seeds, use pumpkin or sunflower seeds instead.

Serves 8–10 portions

Ingredients

1 medium pumpkin or squash
A dash of olive oil
2 tablespoons sesame seeds
1 teaspoon ground cinnamon
1 teaspoon ground coriander
1 teaspoon ground cumin
A handful of fresh coriander
Salt and pepper, to taste

Method

1. Pre-heat the oven to 180ºC/350ºF/Gas Mark 4.
2. Chop the pumpkin into slices ad deseed but leave the skin on. Place on a baking tray and coat lightly with olive oil. Roast in the oven for 30 minutes or until soft and slightly caramelised at the edges. Remove and leave to cool.
3. Put the sesame seeds in a blender and blitz until fine. Remove the skin from the pumpkin and add it to the blender and blitz for a moment to combine with the sesame seeds.
4. Add the remaining ingredients and blitz once more to combine. Taste to check and add more spices or seasoning if needed.

Green Dip

I have a few stock herbs that grow profusely in the garden, but in winter my supply of mint usually ends, which is why I try to freeze some before it dies off, so I always have some to hand.

Full of fresh, clean flavours and packed full of healthy plant protein, this dip is quick and easy to put together and makes the perfect last-minute snack (as long as the freezer is stocked).

Peas, broad beans or edamame beans all make a fabulous base for this dip. Each one gives a slightly different flavour and they are all seriously green. If you want to mix it up a bit, particularly with the edamame beans, swap the lemon juice for lime and add some fresh coriander and a sprinkle of fresh red chilli on the top.

If you are using broad beans, remove the bitter outer shell before blending unless they are very small. It's a bit of a faff, but worth it. Once made, this dip lasts in the fridge for up to 4 days.

Makes 8–10 portions

Ingredients

400g / 3½ cups, peas, broad beans or edamame beans (fresh or frozen)
4 tablespoons dairy-free yoghurt
Juice of 1 lemon or lime
2 tablespoons finely chopped fresh mint, coriander, parsley or chives
Salt and pepper, to taste

To serve

Chopped fresh herbs
Chopped red chilli (optional)

Method

1. Bring a pan of water to the boil. Drop in the peas or beans and cook for 2–3 minutes to blanch, then drain and refresh with cold water.
2. Once cool, place the peas or beans in a food processor with the other ingredients and blend until combined. Blend until you have the consistency you like. This dip works whether it's smooth or textured.
3. Taste and add extra seasoning, herbs or juice as needed.

Tapenade

Tapenade is a paste that originates from the Mediterranean. Each region has its own flavour combination but all traditionally use a combination of black olives, anchovies and capers, plus lashings of olive oil. Wandering around markets in the south of France, you will find all manner of flavour combinations. But, as most contain anchovies, none of them is plant-based.

My version is a simpler, less oily version of tapenade. It still packs a strong punch of flavour and works as a dip, a coating for roasted vegetables or a stuffing for finger food. Add more or less lemon and herbs to suit your taste and, if you want an extra punch, a little fresh red chilli.

Makes 6–8 portions

Ingredients

30g / ½ cup pitted black olives
1 tablespoon capers, rinsed
1 tablespoon chopped fresh flat leaf parsley
1 tablespoon chopped fresh mint leaves
A few chives, chopped
1 small garlic clove, crushed
Juice and zest of 1 lemon
1 red chilli, finely diced (optional)

Method

1. Pop all the tapenade ingredients into a small blender and pulse a few times to break everything down. Take care not to over-blend as you want a little texture, not a black mush.
2. Taste and add more lemon if needed and season with salt and black pepper.

Celeriac and Potato Gratin

This dish is so deliciously rich and creamy it's hard to believe that it's dairy-free. The potato and celeriac enhance the creaminess of the cashews as they cook so you end up with a rich, luxurious side dish that tastes absolutely delicious. It defies any plant-based denier.

Slice the potatoes and celeriac as thinly as possible. A mandolin is good for this, but I always end up slicing my fingers too, so I tend to use the thinnest cutter on my food processor instead. It saves time as well as my finger-tips. A well-greased baking dish is essential. This dish bakes in the oven for a long time and the potato can easily get stuck to the sides if it doesn't have a little help.

Makes 6 large portions

Ingredients

75g / ½ cup cashew nuts, soaked for at least 2 hours
125ml / ½ cup water
1 garlic clove
1 teaspoon French mustard (optional)
Salt and pepper, to taste
500g / 18oz potatoes, scrubbed and thinly sliced
1 medium celeriac, peeled and thinly sliced
2–3 teaspoons dried mixed herbs/thyme

Method

1. Pre-heat the oven to 180°C/350°F/Gas Mark 4. Grease a medium baking dish with olive oil.
2. To prepare the cashew cream, drain and rinse the soaked cashew nuts, then tip them into a high-speed blender with the water, garlic, seasoning and mustard (if using). Blitz until smooth, adding more water if needed. You want the mix to achieve the consistency of pouring cream.
3. Line the bottom of the dish with a layer of potato, overlapping the slices for full coverage. Next, cover with a layer of celeriac. Season with salt and pepper, then

sprinkle over a teaspoon of dried herbs. Repeat until all the potato and celeriac has been used up (about 3 layers), finishing with a layer of potato.

4. Carefully pour over the cashew cream, shaking the dish slightly to makes sure it runs down through the layers.
5. Cover with tin foil and place in the oven to bake for 45 minutes.
6. Remove the tin foil and bake for a further 20 minutes or until the potato is cooked through and the top lightly browned.
7. Remove from the oven and leave to settle for 5 minutes before slicing into squares and serving. Alternatively, leave to cool, then gently reheat when needed.

Comforting Red Cabbage

If I can get a teen to eat red cabbage (or any cabbage), it feels like a win for parents everywhere. Synonymous with soggy school dinners and farty cooking smells, cabbage still has a reputation for being a chore to eat. This recipe, however, could never be a trial. It's purple for a start and who doesn't love the colour purple? The flavours are sweet but savoury and deliciously comforting.

My teens love this dish and are always excited to see it served up. It's not bad for grown-ups either, so make a big batch and earn yourself some superfood brownie points.

Although this takes some time to cook in the oven, it's one of those dishes that can be left to its own devices and needs little attention so you're free to get on and do other things. You can also prepare it in advance and reheat it for added convenience. I use my faithful old le Creuset dish to cook this cabbage and it works brilliantly every time. You could also use a slow cooker on a low setting as you want the cabbage to retain some texture rather than becoming mush.

Serves 6–8

Ingredients

1 large red onion, sliced
1 medium red cabbage, finely shredded
1 large apple, cored and sliced
2 teaspoons dried mixed herbs
2 tablespoons raisins
Salt and pepper, to taste
50ml / ¼ cup vegetable stock

Method

1. Pre-heat the oven to 160°C/320°F/Gas Mark 3. Grab an ovenproof dish with a well-fitting lid and lightly grease the base with a smudge of olive oil.
2. Line the bottom of the dish with a layer of onion, followed by a layer of cabbage then a layer of apple. Sprinkle over some of the herbs and raisins and season with salt and pepper.
3. Repeat these layers at least once more, preferably twice, then pour the vegetable stock over the top. Put on the lid and bake in the oven for 1 hour.
4. Check the dish to make sure the edges aren't burning. Give the cabbage a stir and add a little more stock if necessary – you don't want it wet, but equally you don't want it stuck to the bottom.
5. Return the dish to the oven and cook for a further 30–45 minutes or until all the vegetables are soft and the flavours developed.
6. Remove from the oven and leave to settle for around 15 minutes before serving.

Garlicky Greens with Sesame Seeds

When you start looking for them, you'll soon realise there is an amazing array of seasonal greens available all year round. But it's easy to miss out if you only shop in a mainstream supermarket, as they tend to have to a consistent stock that has little variety and doesn't reflect the seasonality of food.

This is where home-grown produce, markets, veg box schemes and the cheaper, no-frills supermarkets come into their own, as they tend to stock what's abundantly available at that time. As well as the normal green veggies, like cabbage, spinach and kale, look out for chard and seasonal 'greens' such as Brussels sprouts, turnip tops or even beetroot leaves.

Green leaves and other vegetables like cabbage and broccoli also taste amazing when stir-fried as the natural sugars in the leaves caramelise and go really well with fresh, zingy garlic. Add some calcium-dense sesame seeds for a little crunch and this dish becomes a nutritional powerhouse in the guise of a side dish.

Remember to squeeze over a little lemon juice just before serving as this not only lifts the flavour but will help your gut absorb the nutrients more easily.

If you can't tolerate garlic or sesame seeds, it's easy to make tasty substitutions. Replace garlic with cumin or mustard seeds and try toasted pine nuts or sunflower seeds in place of the sesame seeds. They all taste fantastic.

Serves 3–4

Ingredients

250g / 4 cups greens
2 tablespoons sesame seeds
1–2 large garlic cloves
Salt and pepper, to taste
Lemon juice

Method

1. Trim off any woody stems from the greens, then separate the stems from the leaves. Shred both and pop into two different colanders. Rinse under a running tap and leave to drain but do not dry off.
2. Heat a large non-stick frying pan and dry toast the sesame seeds over a medium heat for a few minutes or until they start to brown. Tip out onto a plate to cool.
3. Put the frying pan back on the heat, add a tablespoon of water and sauté the garlic for a minute, stirring all the time. Tip the shredded stems into the pan and stir-fry with the garlic for a couple of minutes or until they start to soften, then add the shredded leaves.
4. Keep stirring all the time to prevent the leaves from sticking or burning. Once the edges of the leaves start to become lightly browned, turn off the heat. Season with salt and pepper and add a squeeze of lemon juice. Sprinkled over the toasted sesame seeds and serve.

SAVOURY BAKES

When I discovered my intolerance to yeast, I had to get used to not eating bread. This was hard as I loved everything about bread, I even made my own every day using my trusty bread maker.

But not being able to eat bread opened a whole new world of bread alternatives. Here are just four of my favourites. Each is packed full of flavour and wonderful nutrients – and they hit the comfort spot too.

Seedy Crackers

Most shop-bought crackers contain some form of refined product and/or yeast, which is no good for me. But I do love a tasty, crunchy cracker to have with dips and salads, so these seedy crackers are the business. They are literally made from seeds and little else and it always surprises me not only how easy they are to make but how well they actually stay together.

As well as tasting amazing, these crackers are packed full of fibre and healthy omega 3 fats. Because of their whole-food credentials, they're very satisfying, so you won't need to eat many before you're full – which is a shame as they're incredibly moreish. They keep for up to three weeks in an airtight container, so make a big batch to keep you going.

If you are intolerant to sesame seeds, replace with extra flax or chia seeds.

Makes 25–30 crackers

Ingredients

90g / 1 cup sunflower seeds
80g / 1 cup pumpkin seeds
85g / 1 cup sesame seeds
40g / ½ cup flaxseed or chia seeds
40g / ½ cup ground flaxseed
¼ teaspoon Himalayan salt
½ teaspoon garlic powder
½ teaspoon dried thyme
250ml / 1 cup water

Method

1. Pre-heat oven to 150°C/300°F/Gas Mark 3. Line the base of a large baking tray with non-stick baking paper.
2. Place all the seeds and seasoning in a bowl and mix well. Pour in the water, mix well again and leave for 5 minutes to allow the seeds to absorb the water.

3. Spoon the mixture onto the baking paper and spread out evenly into two rectangles using the back of a large metal spoon. Ideally, it needs to be ½cm thick with no gaps or holes.
4. Sprinkle over a little more salt and lightly mark out the shape of the crackers with the tip of a knife. They can be square, rectanglular, diamond-shaped, etc.
5. Bake in the oven for 25 minutes, then remove and gently turn over the crackers so you can cook the other side. Carefully peel off the baking paper carefully, put the crackers back on the baking tray and return them to the oven. Bake for a further 20 minutes or until golden brown and firm.
6. Remove from the oven and leave to cool for 10 minutes then transfer to a cooling rack and leave to cool completely. Carefully cut the crackers into the shape you marked out and store in an airtight tin.

Superfood Bread

This bread is the alter-ego of white, nutrient-devoid bread. It's dense, being packed full of fibre, protein and healthy fats. It's also very filling so you can only manage a small amount at a time. Even better, it tastes fantastic toasted and is especially good when topped with freshly made hummus.

This recipe works well whether you use almonds or oats, so it's perfect for anyone who is nut and/or gluten intolerant.

If wrapped in non-stick baking paper, it keeps in the fridge for up to 4 days. It also freezes well, so get ahead of the game and double the quantities to make two loaves. That way, you can eat one fresh and slice the other to put in the freezer. You can then take out a couple of slices at a time when you're in need of some superfood comfort.

Makes 10 slices

Ingredients

120g / 1½ cups pumpkin seeds
150g / 1 cup almonds or 100g / 1 cup oats (gluten-free if needed)
140g1 cup buckwheat flour
45g / ½ cup sunflower seeds
2 tablespoons chia seeds
3 tablespoons psyllium husks
1 teaspoon Himalayan salt
500ml / 2 cups water
1–2 tablespoons mixed seeds (for the top)

Method

1. Place 80g / 1 cup of the pumpkin seeds in the jug of a high-speed blender and blitz to a fine meal then tip out into a bowl. Repeat with the almonds or oats then add these to the ground pumpkin seeds.
2. Add the remaining whole pumpkin seeds, sunflower seeds, buckwheat flour, chia seeds, psyllium husk and salt to the bowl. Mix together well, then stir in the water. Keep mixing until everything is well combined. The 'dough' will be thick, gloopy and a little grey looking.
3. Cover with a slightly damp tea towel and leave to rest for at least 1 hour or until all the water has been absorbed and the mix is very solid with no sign of the water.
4. Pre-heat the oven to 180ºC/350ºF/Gas Mark 4. Lightly grease a 900g/2lb loaf tin with olive oil.
5. Spoon the mix into the prepared loaf tin, pressing it down firmly to get rid of any air pockets. The mix does not spread as it cooks, so make sure it's level and equally spread in the tin. Sprinkle over the additional mixed seeds, pressing them down lightly to make sure they're stuck on.
6. Place in the centre of the oven and bake for 40 minutes. Check to see if the bread is cooked by inserting a long cocktail stick into the loaf – it should come away clean. The sides should also be pulling away from the edge of the tin. Return it to the oven for few more minutes if necessary.
7. Once done, remove from the oven and leave the bread to cool in the tin before tipping it out onto a cooling rack. The outside of the loaf should be crispy while the inside is solid but soft.

Rosemary Oatcakes

Oatcakes were my go-to alternative once I stopped eating bread. They're crunchy, versatile and very filling. Unfortunately, most shop-bought versions include palm oil, something that's excluded from the Overcoming MS programme.

Fortunately, oatcakes are very easy to make at home. And, as with anything homemade, you can control what goes in them. They store well in an airtight container and you can add other flavours to suit your tastes.

I love the powerful aroma of rosemary and adding just a teaspoon of this wonderful herb creates a more deeply-flavoured oatcake that is a joy to eat.

Makes 14 x 6cm round oatcakes

Ingredients

150g / 1½ cups oats
2 teaspoons finely chopped fresh rosemary
½ teaspoon salt
Up to 125ml / ½ cup warm water
2 tablespoons olive oil

Method

1. Pre-heat the oven to 200°C/400°F/Gas Mark 6.
2. Place the oats into a blender or food processor and pulse a couple of times to make a rough flour. Make sure it retains a little texture.
3. Tip the oats into a bowl with the rosemary and salt. Mix well.
4. Pour in the olive oil and stir together, then add most of the water. Bring together into a stiff dough. If the mix is too dry add a little more water, but not too much as it will make the mix sticky.
5. Roll the dough out onto a silicon mat or sheet of non-stick baking paper until it's ½cm thick. Using a 6cm cookie cutter, cut out more rounds. You should be able to get 14 cakes out of the dough.
6. Transfer the tray to the oven and bake for 10 minutes, then turn the oatcakes over and bake for another 5 minutes or until the tops are firm and lightly browned.
7. Remove from the oven and transfer to a cooling tray. Store in an airtight tin for up to 3 weeks.

Soda Bread with Walnuts and Rosemary

The first time I had proper Irish soda bread was when we attended a friend's wedding in Dundalk in Ireland. Huge chunks of it were served still warm from the oven and I fell in love with it there and then.

Soda bread uses bicarbonate of soda instead of yeast as the raising agent. However, traditional and shop-bought versions use buttermilk, so it's not dairy-free. Fortunately, dairy-free soda bread is super-quick and easy to make at home. It freezes well too, so you can have a lovely fresh loaf to hand with none of the hassle but all of the taste.

Soda bread should be crusty on the outside, soft and delicate on the inside. The crust is formed from steam in the oven during baking. To create the steam, just place a small bowl of water in the oven while the loaf is baking.

You can, of course, make plain and simple soda bread but the addition of walnuts and herbs makes it extra special and perfect for dipping in soups and stews. The recipe makes one small loaf but if you want a larger one, just double the quantities and bake for an extra 5 minutes or so.

Makes 8–10 slices

Ingredients

375g / 2 ⅓ cups spelt flour
1 teaspoon bicarbonate of soda
1 teaspoon Himalayan salt
30g / ¼ cup walnuts, chopped
1 tablespoon finely chopped fresh rosemary
200ml / ¾ cup soya milk
1 teaspoon vinegar or lemon juice

Method

1. Pre-heat the oven to 200°C/400°F/Gas Mark 6 and line a medium baking tray with baking paper. Place a small bowl of water in the bottom of the oven.
2. Sift the flour, bicarb and salt into a large bowl. Add the chopped walnuts and rosemary, then stir well to combine.
3. Make the buttermilk by combining the soya milk with the vinegar or lemon juice. Leave it for a minute so it curdles to form a non-dairy 'buttermilk'.
4. Pour the buttermilk into the flour mix and quickly stir to form a soft dough.
5. Knead the dough for 1 minute to make sure everything is well combined then form it into a round and place on the baking tray. Cut a cross into the top of the dough using a knife then place the loaf in the middle of the oven and bake for 20 minutes.
6. Remove the loaf from the oven. The top should be firm and crusty. Pick up the loaf carefully with oven gloves and tap the bottom – it should be firm to the touch and sound hollow. If it's still a bit soft, return it to the oven for a few more minutes. Once cooked, remove from the oven and transfer to a cooling rack.

3: THE MAIN ATTRACTION

People often ask me whether I get bored 'just eating vegetables'. Of course not! For a start, there's a lot more than just veggies on the menu. There's also tons of variety, taste and general rainbow awesomeness. This selection of main meal options should give you enough variety to ensure you're never bored or stuck for something delicious to eat.

This section is split into three areas for ease of use – Quick Dinners when time is short, India Inspired as I love to share some of the amazing dishes I discovered in my time there and Posh Dinners so you can really showcase how wonderful and delicious plant-based eating can be when you have guests.

QUICK DINNERS

These recipes are perfect for those busy weekday nights when there's not much time to throw a good meal together. Once you get familiar with them, most of these recipes only take 30 minutes to make. The ones that take a little longer freeze well, so it's worth making bigger batches so you have something to hand when there isn't time to cook from scratch – much faster, tastier and healthier than a ready-meal!

Vegetable Fajitas and Refried Beans

One of the regular features of our weekday evening meals, fajitas are always a hit. Quick and tasty they're easy to adapt to accommodate intolerances, dislikes and seasonal produce. It's also the easiest meal to make rainbow compliant as it includes a gorgeous array of colourful vegetables.

I strongly suggest you make a batch of fajita seasoning mix rather than buying it in the shops. Once you start being a vigilant label-reader, you'll soon realise there are often unwanted additives going into the mix. It's easy to make a batch and you can keep it in a jar so you always have some on hand when you need it.

I used not to like refried beans. For me, they always tasted too acrid from the chilli or had a nasty gloopy texture. It's easy to avoid these pitfalls when you make your own. My daughter was the one who persuaded me they were good and now I love them! You can adjust the flavour and texture to suit your own preferences.

Serving the beans alongside the fajitas means this is a nutrient-packed and filling meal. Using large lettuce leaves instead of wraps or flatbreads makes it slightly lighter for those with a less hearty appetite.

Serves 4–6

Ingredients

For the fajita seasoning

1–2 teaspoons red chilli powder
2 teaspoons ground cumin
½ teaspoon garlic powder
½ teaspoon salt
1 teaspoon smoked paprika
½ teaspoon cayenne pepper

For the refried beans

1 small onion, diced
1 teaspoon ground cumin
½ teaspoon paprika
½–1 teaspoon red chilli powder
400g / large tin of pinto beans, rinsed
4–5 jalapeno peppers rinsed and chopped

For the fajitas

4 carrots, peeled and thinly sliced lengthways
1 green pepper, sliced
1 yellow pepper, sliced
1 red pepper, sliced
½ head of broccoli florets
2 small courgettes, sliced lengthways
2 medium red or white onions, sliced
2–3 teaspoons fajita seasoning
8 large lettuce leaves (like cos) or 8 wholemeal wraps

Method

1. First, make the fajita mix by combining all the spices together. Store in an airtight jar and use as needed.
2. To make the refried beans, heat a small amount of water in a small saucepan and sauté the onion for a few minutes until it softens.
3. Stir in the spices and cook for further 2–3 minutes before adding the beans and 80ml / ⅓ cup of water. Bring to the boil then add the chopped jalapenos. Reduce the heat and simmer for 5 minutes until everything is warmed through.
4. Turn off the heat and mash, adding more water if the texture is a bit dry. Keep warm until ready to serve.
5. Finally, make the fajitas. Heat a small amount of water in a large frying pan or wok then add the vegetables and stir fry until they start to soften, stirring all the time. Add more water to prevent the vegetables from sticking to the pan.
6. Sprinkle on the fajita mix and stir well to coat. Lower the heat and let the veggies simmer for a couple of minutes.
7. Pile the fajita mix into the lettuce leaves or wholemeal wraps. Add some mashed avocado and/or soya yoghurt if required and serve accompanied by the warm refried beans.

Lentil Ragu

Ragu is one of those dishes where the flavour develops over time so it's worth making it the day before. Then all you have to do is reheat the sauce and cook some pasta, making it perfect for one of those frantic family weekday nights.

If you're short on time, use a couple of tins of pre-cooked lentils and add them half-way through the cooking time rather than at the beginning otherwise they'll become over-cooked and mushy. Use the wine if you can as it really contributes towards the deep, rich and satisfying flavour. But don't worry if you can't as this ragu is still delicious without it.

You can eat the ragu with pasta or as part of a lasagne or aubergine bake. It freezes well, so make a double portion and keep one ready for another day.

Serves 4

Ingredients

1 medium onion, finely chopped
1 large celery stick, finely chopped
1 large carrot, finely chopped
2 garlic cloves, finely chopped
½ bunch flat leaf parsley, stems and leaves separated, finely chopped
2 bay leaves
100g / 1 cup uncooked green or brown lentils or 2 x 400 g / large tins ofcooked lentils, drained
125ml / ½ cup vegan red wine (optional)
1 teaspoon dried oregano
1 teaspoon dried thyme
1 teaspoon paprika, plain or smoked
400ml / 1½ cups passata
300ml / 1¼ cups vegetable stock (if using uncooked lentils)
Salt and pepper, to taste

Method

1. Heat a little water in a large pan and sauté the onion, carrot and celery on a low heat with the lid on for 10 minutes or until the veggies are all soft. Stir from time to time to make sure they don't stick. Add a little more water if necessary. Add the garlic, chopped parsley stems and bay leaves and cook for a further 2 minutes.
2. If you're using dried lentils, rinse them well under a running tap, then add them to the pan along with the dried herbs.
3. Stir well, simmer for a minute, then pour in the wine. Let it bubble for a minute or two, then add the passata, vegetable stock and paprika. Stir well, bring to the boil, then reduce the heat and simmer with the lid on for 30 minutes or until the lentils are well cooked and the sauce is thick.
4. If you're using tinned cooked lentils, add to the pan half-way through the cooking time (after about 15 minutes).
5. Season with salt and pepper. Don't forget to remove the bay leaves before serving.

Mixed Bean and Veggie Burger

Burgers must be one of the easiest go-to items when encouraging your family to eat more of a plant-based diet. They can be disguised or dressed up so no-one can tell that they're good for you.

These burgers are super-healthy as they feature the rainbow power of carrots and sweet potato. But more important than that, they taste amazing and are quick and easy to prepare. They also freeze well, so make a big batch and pop some away for another day when time is short and hungry mouths want feeding.

Serve them up as they are or in whatever wrapping you desire – they work equally well in anything from a wholemeal bun to a crisp, crunchy lettuce leaf. And don't forget your toppings. I particularly like fresh tomato slices and avocado mayo but experiment to find your own favourites.

Makes 8 small burgers

Ingredients

2 medium carrots
¼ kohlrabi or celeriac
1 medium sweet potato
½ red or white onion
400g / large tin of mixed beans, drained and well rinsed
1 teaspoon dried garlic powder
1 teaspoon Italian herbs
Salt and pepper, to taste
2–3 tablespoons chickpea flour

Method

1. Line a large baking sheet with a silicon mat or non-stick baking paper.
2. Grate the carrots, kohlrabi or celeriac and sweet potato and finely slice the onion.
3. Place the beans in a large bowl and roughly mash. Add all the veg, herbs and seasoning, then mix together. The best way to do this is to get your hands in there and massage the mix.
4. Sprinkle the chickpea flour over the top and stir in. Leave to rest for 5 minutes.
5. The mix should now be sticky – if not, massage it a little more to get everything combined. Take a tablespoon of the mix and form into a burger, using your hands or a cooker cutter (place the round cutter on the baking tray, add the mix and press down; when you remove the cutter, you'll have a perfect shape). Repeat until all the mix has been used up. If you have time, chill in the fridge for 20 minutes to set.
6. Pre-heat the oven to 180ºC/350ºF/Gas Mark 4. Place in the middle of the oven and bake for 25–30 minutes, turning half-way through the cooking time. When done, the burgers should be brown and crispy on both sides.

No-meat Balls

These no-meat balls are surprisingly filling and make a great plant-based alternative to the animal kind. Packed full of plant protein and fibre, they're quick to make, so ideal for a busy weekday night. It's also a great recipe to make with the kids, perfect for something to do on a wet day in the holidays.

Because of the smoked paprika and cumin, these no-meat balls have a warm, smoky flavour. If that's too strong, swap the smoked for normal paprika and halve the amount you use, replacing it with dried mixed herbs. And if you're intolerant to garlic and/or onion, then add a couple of pinches of asafoetida into the mix so you get the flavour without the indigestion.

I've chosen black beans for these balls because of their size and colour, but if you can't get hold of them, replace with kidney or brown aduki beans. If you fancy a fiery kick, replace the red pepper with a red chilli.

Serve with The Perfect Roasted Tomato Sauce (*see page 254*) and whole-wheat or brown rice spaghetti.

Serves 4 (makes 24 balls)

Ingredients

1 medium red onion, diced
1 fat garlic clove, finely diced
4 tablespoons tamari sauce
2 x 400g / large tins of black beans, drained and rinsed well
70g / ¾ cup oats
1–2 tablespoons water (if needed)
2 teaspoons smoked paprika
2 teaspoons ground cumin
1 teaspoon garlic powder
Freshly ground black pepper

Method

1. Heat 2–3 tablespoons of water in a small pan and sauté the onion for 5 minutes or until it starts to soften. Add the garlic and the tamari sauce and simmer for a few more minutes. Turn off the heat and leave to cool slightly.
2. Place the beans, onion mix, oats and spices into a food processor and pulse a few times until the everything has broken down and is well-combined but the mixture still has some texture – you want it partly puréed with some lumps. Add a little water if it's too dry. The mix should be soft and malleable but not wet and sticky.
3. Pre-heat the oven to 180°C/350°F/Gas Mark 4 and line a large baking tray with

a silicon mat or non-stick baking paper. Take a tablespoonful of mixture and roll into a ball. Place onto the baking tray and repeat until all of the mixture has been used up.

4. Pop the balls in the oven and bake for 10 minutes. Once the mix starts to firm up, turn the balls over and bake for a further 15 minutes until brown and firm.

Beany Shepherd's Pie

This is the ultimate in plant-based winter comfort food. It's warming and full of flavour. It's also incredibly filling and can satisfy the hungriest of stomachs.

This is a favourite recipe with attendees of my Eat Well Live Well course, especially those with families to feed: even the carnivores enjoy it. I felt particularly honoured when I discovered a friend's son chose this as his 'last supper' before moving to Japan for a year because it was a dish he was going to miss.

Feel free to mix the veggies up a bit – sweet potato and celeriac make delicious mash alternatives – and make sure you season well as it makes all the difference.

Serves 4–6

Ingredients

1 small onion, finely chopped
1 small leek, trimmed and finely chopped
2 medium carrots, diced
1 medium celery stick, diced
400g / large tin of aduki, black or black-eyed beans, rinsed and drained
400g / large tin of chopped tomatoes
2 teaspoons mixed herbs
1 tablespoon tamari sauce
130g / 1 cup frozen peas
Salt and pepper, to taste

For the mash

3 medium potatoes, peeled and chopped
3 medium parsnips, peeled and chopped
1 tablespoon flaxseed oil
Salt and pepper, to taste

Method

1. Heat a couple of tablespoons of water in an ovenproof pan or medium saucepan and sauté the onion, leek, carrot and celery for 5 minutes or until they start to soften. If needed, add more water to prevent sticking.
2. Stir in the mixed herbs, beans and tomatoes. Bring to the boil, then pop on the lid, reduce the heat and simmer for 10 minutes.
3. Meanwhile, place the potatoes and parsnips into a large pan of boiling water and cook for 15–20 minutes or until soft and mashable. Drain, then mash with the flaxseed oil and season well. Keep warm.
4. Stir the beany mix in the pan and add the tamari and peas. Season to taste then turn off the heat. The peas will continue cooking in the hot mix. If you have cooked the mix in a saucepan, transfer it to an ovenproof dish.
5. Pre-heat the grill to high. Spread the mash over the bean mix, fluffing up the surface with a fork so you get some crispy bits. Pop it under the grill for a couple of minutes until it's lightly browned. Serve with green vegetables and a satisfied smile.

Chickpea Tagine

Traditionally, a tagine cooks slowly, so the deep, rich flavours have time to develop. But in the everyday hustle and bustle, time is a valuable commodity so this tagine is quick to make, but still very tasty. If possible, make it the day before so the flavours come out to play when you re-heat it or make a double batch and freeze one for another day.

If you're intolerant of any of the listed vegetables, just substitute with more of the others or add some green beans or sweet potato. Play around until you get the perfect combo that suits everyone.

Serves 4

Ingredients

1 medium onion, diced
1 red or green pepper, chopped
1 medium aubergine, chopped
1 medium courgette, chopped
1 large garlic clove, finely chopped
400g / large tin of chopped tomatoes
1 tablespoon ground cumin
½ tablespoon ground coriander

½ tablespoon ground cinnamon
400g / large tin of chickpeas, drained
75g / 1 cup dried apricots, roughly chopped
1 teaspoon harissa (optional)
½ bunch fresh coriander, roughly chopped
Salt and pepper, to taste

Method

1. Heat a couple of tablespoons of water in a large saucepan or ovenproof dish (I like to use a Le Creuset dish). Add the onion and sauté for a couple of minutes to soften, then add the pepper, aubergine and courgette. Stir well, lower the heat a bit and pop on the lid.
2. Leave to sauté for 5 minutes, stirring a couple of times to make sure the veggies don't stick to the bottom of the pan. If they do, add a little more water and lower the heat.
3. Add the garlic to the pan then cook for another couple of minutes.
4. Add the spices, a pinch of salt and mix well, making sure all the veggies are coated.
5. Pour in the tomatoes, bring to the boil, then reduce the heat and simmer with the lid on for 20 minutes or until everything is soft and the flavours of the spices have developed. Add a little water if there is not much sauce.
6. Stir in the chickpeas, apricots and harissa, if using, and simmer for another 10 minutes. Season with salt and pepper to taste. If you are eating straight away, garnish with the fresh coriander and serve over steamed rice or couscous. If not, leave to cool and keep in the fridge until you're ready. Reheat gently, garnish with coriander when piping hot and serve.

Quick Roasted Squash Chilli

Chilli is a weekday regular for us. Adding roasted sweet potato gives a new dimension to the texture and flavour of the chilli. Best of all, the sweet potato can be roasted while the chilli is bubbling away, so it doesn't add to the overall cooking time.

As with most spicy recipes, the flavour continues to develop, which means it tastes even better the next day making it perfect for lunches and leftovers. It also freezes well, so make double the amount and keep half for one of those nights when there's no time to cook.

Serve with cooked wholegrain rice or buckwheat. Alternatively use as a baked potato topping or to stuff a wholewheat wrap.

Serves 4

Ingredients

1 medium butternut squash
1 medium onion, cut into 8 segments
1 small red chilli, deseeded and quartered
1–2 garlic cloves, roughly chopped
1 small bunch fresh coriander, leaves and stems separated
2 bell peppers of any colour, chopped
400g / large tin of chickpeas, rinsed and drained
400g / large tin of red kidney beans, rinsed and drained
2 x 400g / large tins of chopped tomatoes
1–2 teaspoons smoked paprika
1–2 teaspoon ground cumin
Freshly ground black pepper

Method

1. Pre-heat the oven to 180°C/350°F/Gas Mark 4. Wash the squash but don't peel it. Chop it into 2–3cm chunks and arrange on a large baking tray. Brush or spray with a little olive oil and roast in the oven for 15 minutes or until soft and lightly browned.
2. Place the onion, chilli, garlic and coriander stalks into a small blender and blitz until finely chopped. Add a couple of tablespoons of water and blitz again to make a paste.
3. Place a large saucepan over a medium heat. Add the paste and sauté for a couple of minutes, stirring all the time so it doesn't stick.
4. Add the spices and cook for a further minute, then stir in the chopped peppers, chickpeas, beans and tinned tomatoes. Bring to the boil, then reduce the heat and simmer for 10 minutes.
5. By now, the squash should be starting to caramelise. Remove it from the oven and carefully cut off any tough or thick bits of skin – it's ok to leave thin skin on as it gives extra texture – and stir into the chilli. Cook for another couple of minutes, then turn off the heat.
6. Chopped the coriander leaves and add to the pan with black pepper to taste.

Cannelloni Bean and Kale Stew

This dish came together on one of those nights when I needed to make something quick but hadn't been shopping so had to throw something together with the bits and bobs left in the fridge. In the past, these meals became legendary in our house, creating a sense of dread when the answer to the kids question, 'What's for tea?' came back as 'An experiment'. To be fair, there were only a couple of interesting disasters which, of course, they choose to remember.

As experiments go, this one was a huge success, not only because it was wolfed down with requests for seconds, but it was the first time my son ate kale without complaining.

If you think the amount of garlic is a typing error, it's not. It really needs a good amount to come through to complement the kale and beans. It is the star of the dish, along with good seasoning. Serve over mashed potatoes or rice. You can even turn it into a soup if you wish, just chop the veggies smaller and add more stock. Adaptable recipes are always the best!

Serves 4

Ingredients

1 medium onion, finely chopped
4–6 garlic cloves, finely chopped
150g / 3 cups kale, washed and chopped
1–2 courgettes, cut into 1–2 cm pieces
400g / large tin of cannelloni beans, drained and rinsed
2 large fresh tomatoes sliced into 8 segments
1–2 teaspoons dried Italian herbs
500ml / 2 cups vegetable stock
1 tablespoon lemon juice
Salt and pepper, to taste

Method

1. Heat 2 tablespoons of water in a large saucepan and sauté the onion on a medium heat for 5 minutes or until soft. Add the garlic and cook for a further minute.
2. Stir in the courgettes and add the kale along with a little more water. Sauté for 2–3 minutes or until the courgettes start to soften and the kale starts to wilt.
3. Add 250g of the cannelloni beans, the tomatoes, herbs and seasoning. Stir well, then pour in enough stock to cover, pop on the lid and simmer for 5 minutes.
4. Place the remaining cannelloni beans in a small blender along with a little stock then blitz to form a smooth cream. Stir into the simmering pan to make the sauce slightly creamy. Cook for another 15 minutes until the veggies are soft and the air is full of wonderful aromas.
5. Turn off the heat, stir in the lemon juice and season to taste.

Creamy Pea and Broad Bean Spaghetti

I disliked broad beans intensely for years. When I was young, my dad went through a 'grow-your-own' phase and produced a huge crop of broad beans. They should have been fresh and sweet, but I recall them being tough and bitter. Being a child, I probably wasn't very kind about them! Years later, I tried them again, this time without the bitter outer layer. To my surprise they were sweet and utterly delicious. Who knew?

It may be a bit of a faff to remove the hard outer skin, but it's worth every second of effort. You can make the job easier by blanching the beans first. Just bring a pan of water to the boil, drop in the beans and simmer for a minute or so. Drain then cool under a running cold tap so you can handle them without scalding your fingers. Then simply pick off the wrinkled outer layer.

This creamy white wine sauce complements peas and broad beans rather wonderfully. It tastes so rich and decadent, it's easy to forget it's all plant-based and good for you too. It may seem like a long list of ingredients, but this recipe is also surprisingly quick, making it perfect for a weekday meal that's also just a little bit special.

Serves 4

Ingredients

1 medium onion, sliced
2 garlic cloves, sliced
100ml / ½ cup vegan white wine
120g / 1 cup peas, fresh or frozen
100g / ½ cup silken tofu
70g / ½ cup cashews, soaked and drained
A pinch of salt
140g / 1 cup broad beans, skins removed
2 handfuls of fresh herbs, such as oregano, chives, parsley
½ teaspoon garlic powder (optional)
400ml / 1¾ cups water
Salt and pepper, to taste
Extra virgin olive oil
Whole-wheat or brown rice spaghetti
Dairy-free 'Parmesan' (see page 263)

Method

1. Bring a large pan of water to the boil and add the spaghetti. Follow the instructions on the packet, then leave it to cook while you make the sauce.
2. Heat 2 tablespoons of water in a pan and sauté the onion for 2–3 minutes until it starts to soften. Add the garlic and cook for a further minute.
3. Pour in the wine, allow the liquid to come to the boil then turn down the heat and let it simmer for 10 minutes.
4. Add the peas and simmer for a 2–3 minutes.
5. Make the cream sauce by placing the tofu, cashews and salt into a high-speed blender and cover with water. Blitz until smooth, adding more water if necessary.
6. Pour the cream sauce over the vegetables, add the broad beans and most of the chopped fresh herbs, keeping back a tablespoon to garnish.
7. Place over a low heat for 2–3 minutes to warm through. Add more water if the sauce becomes too thick as it needs to be quite loose to coat the pasta. Season with salt and pepper.
8. Drain the spaghetti and return it to the pan. Add the sauce and stir to ensure the pasta is coated.
9. Serve with a scattering of fresh herbs, a good glug of extra virgin olive oil and a spoonful of dairy-free 'Parmesan' (*see page 265*).

INDIA-INSPIRED RECIPES

Our time in India had a huge impact on my life in so many areas. Food-wise, I discovered deliciously simple dishes that tasted amazing, the best of which were those eaten at our friends' homes. Here, I have included the homely dishes that were deemed too simple for a restaurant, but to me were the most tantalising and enjoyable. The accompaniments were as wonderful as the dish itself, so I've included a small range to tickle your taste-buds.

The level of heat you go for is up to you. These recipes are made to my palate – tasty without having a harsh chilli burn, but you can use more or less depending on your own preferences.

Proper Dal

Out of all the recipes I brought home from India, this is The One. It's perfect every time and it tastes much better than any dal I've eaten in a UK curry house. Fresh tomato and curry leaves are the two key ingredients as they make a big difference to the base flavour. Adding the spices, or the tempering, at the end keeps the flavours fresh and delicious.

If you've not come across the term 'tempering' before, it's all to do with releasing amazing flavours. Whole spices are toasted at a high heat so they release their aromas. They're then added to the dal near the end of the cooking time. Traditionally, spices are cooked over a high heat using oil or ghee, here they're dry toasted but they still taste wonderful.

My top tip is to place the pan over a high heat for a few minutes until it's very hot. Add the seeds then immediately reduce the heat to low while giving the pan a good shake to prevent the spices from burning. After a couple of minutes, your nose will tingle with the spicy aromatics, which is the sign that they're ready for use.

Serves 4

Ingredients

750ml / 3 cups water
1 medium onion, finely chopped
¼ teaspoon salt
2 medium juicy tomatoes, chopped
2 garlic cloves, minced
½ teaspoon ground turmeric
150g / 1 cup split red lentils
2 sprigs of curry leaves

For the tempering

1 teaspoon cumin seeds

1 teaspoon black mustard seeds

2cm piece fresh ginger, cut into julienne slices or chopped

4 dried red chillies

4 fresh green chillies (optional)

Juice of ½ lemon

½ bunch fresh coriander, roughly chopped

Method

1. Place a heavy-based saucepan over a medium heat, add 2 tablespoons of water and wait for it to start bubbling. Lower the heat slightly and add the onion and salt. Sauté for a few minutes until it starts to soften, stirring all the time so it doesn't burn.
2. Add the tomatoes and garlic and cook for another 2 minutes. Next, add the turmeric and lentils. Stir well to ensure the lentils are completely coated with the sauce, then add the curry leaves and water.
3. Put the lid on the pan, bring to the boil, then reduce the heat to a simmer. Cook for 25 minutes until the lentils are very soft and most of the water has been absorbed.
4. Heat a small pan and add the cumin and black mustard seeds. Once the aromas are released and the seeds start to pop, reduce the heat and add the ginger and chillies. Sauté for a couple of minutes, then tip into the pan of lentils.
5. Cook for 5 more minutes until everything is combined. Stir in the lemon juice, then sprinkle over the fresh coriander.
6. Remove the chillies, if you wish, and serve with chapattis or steamed brown rice.

Matar Paneer or 'Cheesy Peas'

My children were reluctant to try Indian food when they were little. Fortunately, they had overcome this resistance by the time we moved to India. 'Cheesy peas' was the first dish they tried and they've enjoyed various versions of it ever since. They taste great with warm chapattis.

Of course, traditionally, this dish is made with paneer, a firm Indian cheese. This version uses extra-firm tofu instead. Do your best to ensure the tofu is very dry by draining off any excess water. If it's still soft to the touch, place some kitchen roll either side of the tofu and press it between two plates to force out any remaining liquid. A tin of bean acts as a good weight for the top plate, if needed.

Fresh chillies are best for this recipe, but if you don't have any to hand, chilli powder will work too.

Serves 4

Ingredients

1 medium onion
5cm piece fresh ginger, grated
1–2 fresh red chillies or 1–2 teaspoons chilli powder
300g / 10½ oz pack extra firm tofu, drained and pressed
A pinch of salt
1 teaspoon ground coriander
1 teaspoon garam masala
200g / 1¼ cups peas, fresh or frozen
2 tablespoons dairy-free yoghurt (optional)

To serve

Fresh coriander, chopped

Method

1. Roughly chop the onion, ginger and chilli (if using). Place in a small blender and blitz to a paste, adding a little water if necessary.
2. Cut the pressed tofu into bite-sized chunks. Heat a non-stick frying pan over a medium heat and carefully dry-fry the tofu, turning regularly so it browns on all sides. Tip into a bowl and set aside.
3. Put the frying pan back on the heat, add the onion-ginger-chilli paste and sauté over a medium heat for 5 minutes or until soft and starting to brown. Add a pinch of salt and the ground coriander and garam masala. Cook for another 2 minutes but don't let it burn – you may need to add a little water so it retains its paste-like consistency.
4. Add the peas and another 2 or 3 tablespoons of water, then simmer for 3 minutes. Add the browned tofu and stir well to combine so it heats through.
5. Finally, stir in the dairy-free yoghurt (if using) and sprinkle over the fresh coriander before serving.

Malabar Curry

Infused with warming spices like cinnamon and cloves, this gorgeous dish will transport you to tropical sunshine even on the dullest winter day. Although it's possible to buy a Malabar spice mix from specialist supermarkets, I prefer to make my own. The freshly ground spices provide a deeper flavour and keep more of their medicinal properties too.

If you can't eat coconut, replace the coconut milk with a cashew cream flavoured with a drop of coconut essence. It's not quite the same, but it still tastes gorgeous.

Don't be put off by the number of ingredients in this recipe; it's easier to make than it looks. Serve with wholegrain brown or red rice or wholemeal chapatti with a little cucumber salad on the side.

Serves 4

Ingredients

For the spice mix

2 teaspoons ground cinnamon
3 cloves
4 cardamom pods

For the curry

½ teaspoon black mustard seeds
A sprig of curry leaves (approx 10–12 leaves)
A pinch of asafoetida
½ teaspoon ground turmeric
1 teaspoon red chilli powder
1 tablespoon freshly grated ginger
2 onions, chopped
2 medium tomatoes, blitzed to a pulp
3 carrots, chopped
150g / 2 cups green beans or broccoli
100g / 1 cup frozen peas or sweetcorn
300ml / 1¼ cups coconut milk
250ml / 1 cup warm water
Salt and pepper, to taste

To serve

Chopped fresh coriander

Method

1. Begin by making the spice mix. Pop the cardamom pods into a pestle and mortar and crush to release the seeds inside. Discard the outer casings, add the cloves and pound until ground down to a rough powder.
2. Add the ground cinnamon to the mix and set aside.
3. Next, make the curry. Heat 2–3 tablespoons of water in a large pan until bubbling. Add the mustard seeds, asafoetida and curry leaves. Cook for 2 minutes or until the seeds start to splutter and pop.
4. Add the onion and ginger. Cook over a medium heat until soft, stirring constantly so the mixture doesn't stick to the bottom of the pan. Add the tomatoes and a pinch of salt then reduce the heat to low and simmer for 10 minutes.
5. Stir in the chilli powder, turmeric, spice mix and vegetables. Pour in the water, put on the lid and reduce the heat. Simmer until the vegetables are cooked.
6. Stir in the coconut milk, heat through on a low heat but do not boil. Check the seasoning and add salt and pepper to taste. Garnish with coriander, then serve.

Sweet Potato, Chickpea and Spinach Curry

This dish is my version of Sag Aloo – spinach and potato curry. Traditionally used as a vegetable accompaniment, my version is pumped up with every plant-based eater's go-to protein: chickpeas. It's sweet and savoury at the same time and packed with so many nutrients it will have you zinging with energy and vitality.

Serves 4

Ingredients

A pinch of asafoetida
1 red onion, chopped
2 garlic cloves, finely chopped
1 red chilli, finely chopped
2cm piece fresh ginger, grated
3 medium sweet potatoes, peeled and chopped into bite-sized chunks
½ teaspoon ground turmeric
400g / large tin of chickpeas, rinsed and drained
400g / large tin of chopped tomatoes
200g / 4 cups spinach leaves, washed and roughly chopped
Salt and pepper, to taste

Method

1. Heat a medium saucepan over a medium heat and sprinkle in a little asafoetida. Let it cook for a minute or until its sulphurous aromas have been released. Add the chopped onion and a little water and stir into the asafoetida. Sauté for a 2–3 minutes or until the onion starts to soften.
2. Tip in the garlic, chilli and ginger and continue to cook over a medium heat for another 2 minutes. If necessary, add a little extra water to make a thick paste. Stir to ensure the paste doesn't stick or burn.
3. Add the chopped sweet potato and a little salt. Pop on the lid and reduce the heat then leave the veggies to sweat for 5 minutes.
4. Sprinkle in the turmeric then add the tinned tomatoes and chickpeas. Stir well to combine, then simmer for a further 15 minutes or until the sweet potato is soft and starting to fall apart.
5. Add the spinach a few handfuls at a time, letting it wilt into the sauce. Season with salt and pepper to taste, then serve.

Indian Cabbage

This is one of my favourite veggie side dishes. In Karnataka, this cabbage dish is called Poiryral, but it probably has other names in different states. What sets this dish apart is the combination of mustard seeds and sweet toasted coconut. It's a great way to get your family to eat cabbage. Fresh or frozen coconut flesh is better than desiccated, if you can find it in the shops.

Serves 4

Ingredients

1 medium green cabbage, finely sliced
1 teaspoon black mustard seeds
1 teaspoon urad dal or split lentils
A pinch of asafoetida
¼ teaspoon ground turmeric
1 red chilli, deseeded and finely chopped
5 curry leaves
2 tablespoons grated coconut (fresh, frozen or desiccated)
Salt, to taste
2 tablespoons chopped fresh coriander

Method

1. Place the prepared cabbage into a steamer basket and steam for 5 minutes or until it's *al dente* (cooked but firm to the bite).
2. While the cabbage is cooking, heat a small pan over a medium heat and add the mustard seeds to toast. Once they start to pop, add the urad dal, asafoetida and turmeric. Stir well.
3. After 2–3 minutes, when the kitchen is filled with the gorgeous aromas of the spices, add the chilli and curry leaves. Stir well then turn off the heat.
4. Transfer the steamed cabbage to a serving bowl and sprinkle over the toasted spices, coconut and salt. Garnish with the chopped fresh coriander and serve straight away.

Spiced Rice

Wholegrain rice takes a little longer to cook than refined white rice. But don't let this put you off using it as it's packed with nutritional goodies. Plan ahead instead and soak it in advance. Not only will this reduce the cooking time, it'll also help to activate enzymes and release the nutrients.

If you plan to have rice in the evening but are out all day, get it ready before you go. It takes just 2 minutes to weigh it out, rinse it and pop it in a pan with the water.

Serves 3–4

Ingredients

200g / 1 cup wholegrain rice (brown, black or red)
500ml / 2 cups water

Whole spices

2 cinnamon sticks
6 cloves
3 star anise
6 cardamom pods

Method

1. Pour the rice into a sieve and rinse well. Tip into a large bowl with the water and leave to soak for at least 30 minutes.
2. Heat a large saucepan and add the whole spices. Toast for a minute or so until their delicious aromas are released. Move the pan off the heat for a moment to cool slightly, then pour in the rice and soaking water. Take care as it will spit.

3. Stir to combine the rice and spices, then cover the pan and bring to the boil. When steam starts to escape from under the lid, reduce the heat to low and leave to simmer for 20 minutes or until the rice is cooked and all the water has been absorbed.
4. Turn off the heat and leave to steam for a few minutes before serving.

Spicy Raita

This raita is much more than the standard Westernised version. Packed with health-giving spices, it is often stirred into plain cooked rice and eaten as a form of medicine, especially after a dodgy stomach bug. But you don't need to be poorly to enjoy it as it tastes wonderful however you're feeling.

You can use soya or coconut yoghurt for this. Coconut is thicker and creamier, while soya yoghurt is more of a like-for-like dairy replacement.

Serves 4

Ingredients

1 teaspoon cumin seeds
1 teaspoon mustard seeds
200ml / ¾ cup dairy-free yoghurt
⅓ cucumber, finely diced
¼ red onion (optional)
1 red or green chilli, finely chopped (optional)
10 curry leaves
½ bunch fresh coriander, finely chopped
Salt
Lemon or lime juice

Method

1. Heat a small non-stick frying pan and dry fry the cumin and mustard seeds for 1–2 minutes or until they start to release their aromas. Turn off the heat and tip the seeds onto a cold plate to stop them toasting any further.
2. Pour the dairy-free yoghurt into a medium bowl and stir in the cucumber, onion and chilli (if using), curry leaves and half the chopped fresh coriander. Sprinkle with salt, add a squeeze of lemon juice. Add 1½ teaspoons of the toasted seeds and stir well to combine. Add more seasoning if needed.
3. Finish off with a garnish made up of the remaining coriander and seeds.

Sweet Potato Chapatti

Simple chapattis can be made with just flour and water, but they often have refined fats added. The sweet potato acts as a fat replacement, gives a little extra flexibility and of course adds some extra wonderful fibre and nutrients as a bonus. They take a little time to make, but it's worth the effort. If you have any leftover, keep them covered in the fridge for a few days, or wrap them in greaseproof paper to separate them and pop them in the freezer.

Makes 8 medium chapattis

Ingredients

1 medium sweet potato
100g / scant ⅔ cup whole-wheat/spelt/gluten free flour
A pinch of salt
1 teaspoon cumin seeds (optional)
Water, to bind

Method

1. Peel the sweet potato, cut it into chunks then steam until it's very soft. Set aside to cool, then whizz in a small blender to make a purée.
2. If you're using the cumin seeds, toast in a non-stick pan for 1–2 minutes or until the aromas have been released. Remove from the heat and leave to cool.
3. Sift the flour into a bowl with the salt. Stir in the cumin seeds and the sweet potato purée, bringing everything together with your hands to form a stiff dough. Add some water, a little at a time, until the dough has a pliable but not wet consistency.
4. Lightly knead until all the ingredients are well combined, then pop the dough back in the bowl, cover with a damp tea towel and leave to settle for 30 minutes.
5. Place a silicon mat or piece of non-stick baking paper on the worktop. Take a golf ball-sized amount of dough and roll it into a ball. Place in the middle of the mat or baking paper, flatten slightly with your hand then cover with another piece of baking paper.
6. Roll the ball of dough into a round, about ½cm thick. Heat a medium non-stick frying pan and lightly grease with a dash of olive oil. Peel off the top layer of baking paper, then flip over the chapatti and peel away the silicon mat. Either leave on a floured board and roll out the remaining chapatis now or cook as below and roll out the next one during cooking time.
7. To cook, drop a chapatti into the frying pan and cook for 2–3 minutes until firm and lightly browned. Turn it over cook the other side. Transfer to a warm plate and cover with a tea towel while you repeat the process and cook the remaining chapattis.

Coriander Chutney

One of the things I loved about eating out in India was the amazingly tasty chutneys that accompanied snacks like samosa and pakora or the ultimate king-sized crispy pancake, masala dosa (a family favourite).

This vividly green and tangy coriander chutney is one of my favourites. If you can't handle a chilli kick, be careful how much you add. Nibble a bit of the chilli before you add it to see just how hot it is as heat levels in chillies are incredibly variable. Some chutneys are more like a sauce. This one uses a solid base to help give it more body, but you can leave it out and stick to herbs only if you like. That's the best thing about cooking at home – you can make a dish just how *you* like it!

Serve alongside any of the Indian recipes here. It's particularly good with the sweet potato chapattis.

Serves 4–6

Ingredients

30g / ⅓ cup cashew nuts or fresh coconut or sunflower seeds
80g / ½ cup fresh coriander, roughly chopped
2 tablespoons roughly chopped fresh mint (optional)
1 green chilli, deseeded and roughly chopped
1cm piece fresh ginger, peeled and chopped
¼ teaspoon salt
Juice 1 lemon or lime

Method

1. Place the cashew nuts (or coconut or sunflower seeds) in the bowl of a small food processor and pulse a few times to break down.
2. Add the remaining ingredients and blitz until the mixture becomes a vivid green and slightly chunky paste. Taste and add more seasoning or juice as needed.
3. Spoon into a jar or sealable container and store in the fridge for up to 4 days.

Tamarind Sauce

This sauce is wonderfully versatile so it's worth having some in the fridge. It can be used as a dressing for salad or vegetables, added to stews or veggie bakes and used as the base of a curry sauce. It gives a gorgeously deep sweet and sour flavour. You can keep it in the fridge for up to 15 days or you could make double and freeze it in small batches.

Although you can buy tamarind paste in specialist stores, make sure you check the ingredients first as many contain lots of refined sugar and preservatives. Fortunately, it's quite simple to make at home using a block of tamarind, though it does take a little time. To find out how to do this, go to the website for more information www.thesensitivefoodiekitchen.com/book-links.

Serves 6-8

Ingredients

125ml / ½ cup water
150g / 1 cup pitted dates
2 tablespoons tamarind paste
½ teaspoon chilli powder
¼ teaspoon roasted cumin seeds
A pinch of asafoetida
Salt, to taste

Method

1. Pour the water into a small saucepan then add the dates. Bring to the boil, reduce the heat and simmer for 10 minutes or until the dates are soft, sticky and start to caramelise. Remove from the heat and leave to cool slightly.
2. Transfer the cooked dates to a small blender and blitz to form a paste. Add a little water if it's too thick.
3. Add the remaining ingredients and blitz again to combine.

POSH DINNERS

I started running supper clubs so people could experience just how innovative and delicious a whole-food plant-based way of eating could be. I served a three- or four-course meal, all plant-based and gluten-free, sharing a little information about a particular ingredient or cooking method as I went along.

They were great evenings, all wonderfully hosted by my friend Jane. All sorts of people attended, but most didn't follow a plant-based diet, they were simply interested in great-tasting great food and enjoying a different kind of evening.

It can be hard to find main meals recipes that are suitable for entertaining as they need to be slightly different from the norm but still fancy enough to impress. Below I've included some of the recipes I served at the supper clubs. Although they have a lot of components, none of them is difficult to make and all are worth the effort, especially if you're looking to create something special. Enjoy!

Roasted Squash Tart

Finding a pastry recipe that doesn't need highly refined fats to work has been a hard job. Before I created this one, I had lots of tasteless disasters that collapsed in a heap. It was only when I realised that the base I used for raw desserts could be modified for cooked savoury pastry that the problem was solved. It was so simple and yet so effective.

Walnuts are my nut of choice for this pastry. They contain a variety of healthy fatty acids but also give the pastry a slightly rich and decadent quality that complements the lovely caramelised flavours of the roasted vegetables. If you can't tolerate nuts, then sunflower or even pumpkin seeds work well too. And if you can't eat soya products, leave out the tofu and use an extra 70g / ½ cup of ground pumpkin seeds. Whatever you use to make it, follow the instructions for making the pastry carefully and visit my website at www.thesensitivefoodiekitchen.com/book-links where you can find more information and pictures if you need them.

You can prepare this tart in advance by roasting the veg the day before and keeping it in the fridge overnight. This tart freezes well but make sure it's properly defrosted before you reheat it in the oven.

Serves 6–8

Ingredients

For the pastry

150g / 1½ cups oats (gluten-free, if necessary)
160g / 1½ cups walnuts
¼ teaspoon salt
1½ teaspoons dried thyme
2 tablespoons ground flaxseed
120ml / ½ cup water

For the filling

1 medium red onion
1 small-medium squash or pumpkin
3–4 garlic cloves
70g / ½ cup pumpkin seeds split into two portions of 50g / ⅓ cup and 20g / ⅛ cup
150g / 1 cup firm tofu
Salt and pepper, to taste

Method

1. First, prepare the vegetables. Pre-heat the oven to 180°C/350°F/Gas Mark 4. Peel the onion and chop into quarters. Wash the outside of the squash, deseed and chop into large chunks but don't peel. Leave the garlic cloves whole with their skin on.
2. Place all the veg onto a large baking tray and spray with a little olive oil. Roast in the oven for 20 minutes or until they are soft and starting to caramelise.
3. Remove from the oven and leave to cool, peeling the skin off the squash and garlic when they're cool enough to handle.
4. Next, make the pastry. Place the oats into a high-speed blender and pulse a few times to make a flour. Tip into a large bowl. Repeat this process with the walnuts but take care not to over-process or you'll end up with a rough walnut butter.
5. Tip the ground walnuts into the bowl with the oats then add the thyme and ground flaxseed and season with salt and pepper. Stir well to make sure everything is well distributed.
6. Pour in the water and mix together, first with a spoon, then your hands. Bring together into a ball. It will be a bit sticky at first. Leave for 10 minutes while the water is absorbed. If it's not sticky but dry, add a little more water but take care not to make it too moist.
7. Roll out a silicon baking mat or large piece of non-stick baking paper on the work-top. Place the pastry ball in the middle and cover with a large piece of non-stick baking paper. Press down slightly to flatten.

8. Take a rolling pin and roll the pastry into a round of about 1cm thick so it's large enough to cover the base and sides of a 23cm round loose-bottomed flan tin.
9. Peel the baking paper off the top of the pastry and carefully turn over the silicon mat. Position the pastry over the top of the tin, gently peel away the silicon mat and allow the pastry to drop into the tin. Don't worry if it cracks or breaks, just press it back together again. Trim the edges and use the excess to patch any uneven or broken areas.
10. Scrunch up the baking paper and pop it inside the pastry case. Place the tin onto a baking tray and bake in the oven for 7 minutes. The pastry will start to dry out a little and smell amazing.
11. While the flan base is in the oven, place the 50g / ⅓ cup of pumpkin seeds into a food processor and grind to a powder. Add the roasted vegetables and tofu with some salt and pepper and blend until smooth.
12. Remove the tart base from the oven, pour in the pumpkin mix and spread it evenly over the pastry case. Sprinkle over the remaining whole pumpkin seeds and place back in the oven. Bake for a further 20 minutes or until the mix is firm and the seeds lightly toasted.
13. Remove from the oven and serve warm or leave to cool and reheat gently when desired.

Aubergine Parmigiana

I love soft, juicy slices of roasted aubergine, particularly when combined with crunchy breadcrumbs, a rich tomato sauce and salty cheese. But when I went dairy and yeast-free, Aubergine Parmigiana was off the menu. I used to envy my friends who ordered it in restaurants, but not any more now that I've worked out how to make it plant-based. And it's so easy to make, I can have it any time I want!

Chickpea/gram flour and water makes an easy egg-wash replacement that works for anything that requires a breadcrumb coating; it's particularly helpful here with the aubergine slices.

Serves 4

Ingredients

1 portion basic The Perfect Roasted Tomato Sauce (see page 254)
4 tablespoons chickpea/gram flour
8 tablespoons water
100g / 1 cup breadcrumbs of choice – fresh, dried, panko, rice crumbs, gluten-free
2 large aubergines
Olive oil spray (optional)
Dairy-free 'Parmesan' (see page 265), *to top*

Method

1. Prepare the tomato sauce, then set aside.
2. Sift the chickpea flour into a bowl, add the water and whisk well to combine. Place the breadcrumbs onto a large plate. Pre-heat the oven to 180°C/350°F/Gas Mark 4.
3. Wash the aubergine and slice widthways into 1cm-wide round slices. Dip each slice into the chickpea flour mix, then into the breadcrumbs, coating both sides. Transfer to a baking tray and repeat with all the slices.
4. Spray both sides of the aubergine slices with a little olive oil if you like a darker, crisper bake. Place in the oven for 20 minutes or until the crumbs are golden and the aubergine is soft to the touch.
5. Remove from the oven and transfer to a warmed serving plate. Spoon over the tomato sauce then sprinkle over the dairy-free 'Parmesan'.
6. Serve with a simple green salad and some bread to mop up the juices.

Rainbow Vegetable Layered Risotto Loaf

This was one of the first recipes I served at my supper club. It was a bit of a risk, as there was the potential for it to collapse. But never being one to shy away from a challenge, I went with it as it both looks and tastes fabulous.

Red rice is amazing. It is packed full of nutrients and fibre and has a slightly nutty flavour. It's suitably sticky and glutinous when cooked, so works well as a replacement for Arborio rice.

Serve drizzled with Spinach and Walnut Pesto (*see page 261*), the vibrant green sauce complements the loaf's rainbow colours perfectly.

Serves 4

Ingredients

1 medium onion, finely diced
2 fat garlic cloves, finely chopped
2 medium tomatoes, chopped
1 medium courgette, cut lengthways into slices
Olive oil spray
1 red pepper
1 orange pepper
1 teaspoon fennel seeds
¼ teaspoon ground turmeric
1 tablespoon dried Italian herbs
A sprinkle of chilli flakes (optional)
300g / 1½ cups red rice, soaked for 2 hours then drained
100ml / ½ cup white wine (optional but worth it, make sure it's vegan)
1 litre / 4 cups vegetable stock
1 sweetcorn cob, kernals removed or half 200g / medium tin of sweetcorn
4 tablespoons nutritional yeast (optional)
Salt and pepper, to taste

Method

1. Prepare the vegetables. Pre-heat the oven to 200ºC/400ºF/Gas Mark 6. Place the courgette slices onto a non-stick baking tray, spray with a little olive oil and roast until soft and lightly browned. Remove from the oven and cool. At the same time, pop the whole peppers in the oven on a tray and roast for 20 minutes or until soft and the skin is blackened in places. Remove and leave to cool, then peel off skin. This can be done in advance or whilst the rice is cooking.
2. Heat a small amount of water in the bottom of a heavy-based pan, add the fennel seeds and cook for a minute. Add the onion and cook on a medium heat for 5 minutes until it starts to soften. Add the garlic and chopped tomato and cook for another couple of minutes, then stir in the turmeric, herbs and rice.
3. Cook for a couple of minutes, stirring so it doesn't stick to the bottom of the pan. Add the wine (if using), stir well then add two-thirds of the stock. Mix well to combine everything. Bring to the boil, then reduce the heat and simmer, stirring regularly and adding more stock as needed. Add the sweetcorn about half way through.
4. Once all the fluid has been absorbed and the rice is soft and cooked through, turn off the heat, leave to cool slightly then stir in the nutritional yeast and season to taste.
5. If you haven't just roasted the vegetables, pre-heat the oven to 180ºC/350ºF/Gas Mark 4. Lightly grease a 900g / 2lb loaf tin and spoon half the mix into the bottom,

pressing firmly into all the corners. Arrange the roasted peppers and courgettes over the mix, then spoon the remaining amount on top of that, pressing down carefully to ensure it's packed into the tin.

6. Bake in the oven for 30 minutes until the top is golden. Remove from the oven, leave to cool and firm slightly. Carefully loosen the edges with a knife, then tip out onto a serving plate. Slice and serve drizzled with Spinach and Walnut Pesto Sauce.

Chestnut and Cranberry Roll with Chard Stuffing

A Sunday nut loaf roast is tasty but can become a bit of a bore if you have it too often. So, when it comes to special occasions, like Christmas, it's worth looking for something a little more imaginative and inspiring.

This dish definitely hits the spot. The filling is packed with delicious Christmas flavours, and when paired with red wine gravy (*see page 257*) it hits a wonderfully decadent note. You can make different parts at different times, which is a relief as there's quite a lot to do. However, the recipe all comes together remarkably easily so don't be put off. This recipe makes big portions, so be ready for leftovers on Boxing Day.

Serves 6–8

Ingredients

For the pastry

250g / 1½ cups plain wholemeal, spelt or gluten-free flour, plus extra for dusting
A pinch of salt
6 tablespoons olive oil
7 tablespoons water
Dairsy-free milk of choice

For the filling

50g / ½ cup oats (gluten-free if needed)
50ml / ¼ cup water
4 medium shallots, finely chopped
1 celery stick, finely chopped
1 garlic clove, finely chopped
150g / 2 cups chard, leaves and stems separated, stems chopped
180g / 6oz packet of whole cooked chestnuts, chopped
100ml / ½ cup vegan red wine

1 tablespoon tamari
2 teaspoons dried thyme
40g / ½ cup dried cranberries, soaked in hot water for 15 minutes then drained
Salt and pepper, to taste

For the stuffing

Chard leaves from above, roughly chopped
50g /½ cup walnuts
2 garlic cloves, roasted

Method

1. To make the filling, mix the oats and water togethe, then set aside.
2. Heat 2–3 tablespoons of water in a large non-stick frying pan and sauté the shallots and celery until they start to soften. Add the garlic, chopped chard stems and a little salt. Continue to cook, stirring frequently so it doesn't burn. Add a little more water if needed.
3. Stir in the chopped chestnuts, increase the heat slightly and pour in the wine. Deglaze the pan, scraping up any caramelised bits that have stuck to the bottom as these add extra flavour. Bring to the boil, then reduce the heat to a simmer, stir in the tamari, thyme and salt and pepper, to taste. Cook for 2 more minutes then add the drained cranberries and oats. Stir until all the ingredients are combined and the mixture becomes thick and sticky. Turn off the heat and leave to cool.
4. To make the chard stuffing, bring a small pan of water to the boil then plunge in the chard leaves to blanch. Drain, reserving the cooking water.
5. Pop the walnuts into a small blender bowl with the roasted garlic and blitz until combined. Add the drained chard leaves and blitz again to form a paste. Use a little of the chard water to loosen if it's too thick – you want a paste that's spreadable but not too wet. Season with salt and pepper, then set aside.
6. To make the pastry, place the flour and salt into a bowl and stir to combine.*
7. Pour in the oil and carefully combine with a knife to form a breadcrumb-like mix. Pour in 5 tablespoons of water and mix with your fingertips to form a pastry. Cautiously add a little more water if it's too dry but don't let it get wet and sticky.
8. Tip the dough out onto a lightly floured worktop and knead for a couple of minutes then wrap in baking paper and chill in the fridge for at least 30 minutes.
9. To construct the bake, form the filling mix into a rectangular block of around 18x6x6cm, using your hands to press it together.
10. Remove the pastry from the fridge. Roll it out on a silicon mat or well-floured worktop to form a rectangle of approximately 22 x 16 cm and around ½cm thick.
11. Spread the chard paste from the middle of the pastry, covering a slightly larger area than your block of filling mix. Place the filling block of top of the paste-

covered area and carefully wrap the pastry around it so it's completely covered. Trim any excess pastry from the corners and make a few diagonal slashes across the top.

12. Carefully transfer to a baking tray. The bake can be kept in the fridge like this overnight or cooked straight away.
13. To cook, pre-heat the oven to 180ºC/350ºF/Gas Mark 4. Brush with dairy-free milk and place in the middle of the oven for 30 minutes until the pastry is firm and lightly browned. Remove from the oven and rest for 5 minutes. Trim off the ends, then carefully cut into slices and serve with the red wine jus on the side.

* **Note**: *If you are using gluten free flour, add ½ teaspoon xanthum gum to the flour mix. Make a flaxseed 'egg' by combining 1 tablespoon ground flaxseed with 3 tablespoons of water than add this alongside the oil to help the pastry stay together when rolled out. Use 4 further tablespoons of water instead of 7 or it will be too sticky.*

Stuffed Pumpkin Wedge

If you're looking for vibrant colours to entice others into eating plant-based dishes, anything with the vivid orange of pumpkin or squash is a great place to start. Overall, this recipe takes about two hours from beginning to end. Much of that is cooking time though, so as long as you're prepared in advance, it's not as labour- and time-intensive as it may first look.

Sweet mama squash look like pumpkin on the outside, but the flesh has a deeper colour and the texture is slightly drier. It takes stuffing really well. If you can't find this particular squash, then go for what is available. If you happen to come across some mini squashes or pumpkins, you can serve each diner their own individual pumpkin bowl.

Serves 6

Ingredients

200g / 1 cup red rice, rinsed
500ml / 2 cups warm water
1 bay leaf
1 medium sweet mama squash
1 small red onion
1 small leek
1 celery stick
2 garlic cloves

6 medium mushrooms
1 tablespoon dried thyme
A good splash of coconut amines or tamari
Salt and pepper, to taste

Method

1. To make the rice, first put the rice in a pan with the warm water and leave to soak for 2 hours. Once soaked, add the bay leaf to the pan and put on the lid. Bring to the boil then lower the heat and simmer for about 15–20 minutes or until all the water has been absorbed Turn off the heat and leave to cool, then remove the bay leaf.
2. Slice the sweet mama squash in half and remove the seeds and fibre using a sharp-edged teaspoon. Carve out a little of the flesh to create more stuffing space (don't discard it though – use it as part of the filling). Season the cavity with salt and pepper. Pierce the skin a few times using the tip of a sharp knife or a skewer to allow the steam to escape during cooking.
3. Finely chop the all the vegetables including the squash flesh. Heat a small amount of water in a saucepan. When bubbles form, add the onion, leek and celery. Reduce the heat a little and sauté for about 2 minutes until they start to soften. Add the garlic, mushrooms and thyme along with the chopped squash and the coconut amines or tamari.
4. Continue to cook for a few more minutes until enticing aromas waft in the air. Don't forget to stir regularly as you don't want the garlic to burn. Add a little more water to the pan if needed. This will also help deglaze the pan and keep all the lovely caramelised flavours in the mix.
5. Lower the heat, pop on a lid and continue to simmer for a further 10 minutes or until the vegetables are soft and flavourful.
6. Pre-heat the oven to 180ºC/350ºF/Gas Mark 4. Tear off 2 large pieces of baking foil and place crossways on a large baking sheet. Lightly grease with a drizzle of olive oil.
7. Once the vegetables are soft and luscious, stir in the cooked rice and season well with salt and pepper. Taste and add more seasoning, thyme, coconut amines or tamari as needed. Heat through for a few minutes to make sure all the flavours are well combined.
8. Turn off the heat and spoon the mix into the cavities of the two prepared squash. Press the mix in so it's packed in tightly, then press the two halves together so they're cuddling up tight. Wrap with the prepared foil – not too tight, but not too lose, just enough to allow some heat to circulate on the inside to help it cook.
9. Pop the squash parcel into the oven and bake. It will take between 1–1½ hours, depending on the size of the squash. To see if it's ready, carefully unwrap the foil and give the squash a squeeze. If there is some give and it feels soft, it's ready.

10. To serve, unwrap and cut into wedges. If you're feeling rustic, leave it in the foil and take it to the table as it is, letting everyone dive in and grab their share of this awesome rainbow dish.

Spinach Pancake with Spicy Sweet Potato Stuffing and Tamarind Sauce

These savoury pancakes are delicious. If at first glance they seem like a lot of effort, don't be put off. They're not as time-consuming as they seem, plus both elements can be made in advance and reheated when you want them.

Makes 8 filled pancakes

Ingredients

For the spicy sweet potato

1 small onion
2 garlic cloves
2cm piece fresh ginger
½ bunch fresh coriander - keep a handful to one side
2 large fresh tomatoes, chopped
3 medium sweet potatoes, peeled and cut into small dice
½ teaspoon each of ground turmeric, chilli powder and ground cumin
Salt and pepper, to taste

For the pancakes

140g / 1 cup buckwheat flour
2 tablespoons chickpea/gram flour
1 tablespoon ground flaxseed
¼ teaspoon salt
1 teaspoon garlic powder
60g / 1 cup fresh spinach
350ml / 1½ cups dairy-free milk of choice
100ml / ½ cup water

To serve

2–3 tablespoons Tamarind Sauce (see page 240)

Method

1. First, make the sweet potato filling by roughly chopping the onion, garlic, ginger and fresh coriander. Place in a small food processor and blend to a paste. Add a little water to help bring it together.
2. Heat 2–3 tablespoons of water in a medium pan and cook the paste for 5 minutes,

stirring regularly so it doesn't stick. Add the chopped tomatoes and cook for a further 2 minutes.

3. Add the diced sweet potato, stirring well to coat. Put on the lid and continue to cook for 5 minutes.
4. Add the spices and a pinch of salt along with a little water to make a very thick sauce. Bring to the boil, then reduce the heat and simmer for 20 minutes or until the sweet potato is soft and well cooked. Stir from time to time.
5. Once ready, season with salt and pepper. Finely chop the reserved fresh coriander and sprinkle over the top.
6. While the stuffing is cooking, make the pancake mix. Place all the pancake ingredients in a high-speed blender and blitz until smooth. Leave to stand for 10 minutes to thicken.
7. Smear a little olive oil over a non-stick crepe pan and pre-heat for a couple of minutes on a medium setting. Pour a ladleful of mixture into the middle of the pan and spread it out evenly using the back of the ladle.
8. Cook for a couple of minutes until bubbles appear on the surface and the pancake lifts easily from the side. Flip over with a fish slice and cook the other side until firm. Transfer to a plate to keep warm and repeat until all the mix is used up.
9. To assemble, take one spinach pancake and fill with a couple of spoonsful of spicy sweet potato. Spoon over a little tamarind sauce, fold the pancake in half then drizzle the top with more tamarind sauce, making a zig-zag pattern. Repeat with the remaining pancakes and filling.
10. Serve with a fresh cucumber salad and raita

Smoky Tofu Balls

The most common complaint I hear about tofu is that it's bland but has a slightly strange taste. It's true that without some assistance, tofu can be simply horrid. Its key advantage is that it absorbs flavour rather beautifully, making it adaptable and very useful for the plant-based kitchen.

One way to get extra flavour from tofu is to use one that has been gently smoked over wood chips. If you're brave and have lots of time, you could give that a go yourself. However, most of us have many other things to do so it's worth trying out different brands to find one you like.

Don't be put off by the long list of ingredients for this dish as most of them will be in your fridge or store cupboard. It's fairly quick to make too as the balls can be prepared while the sauce is cooking and it all comes together surprisingly quickly. The flavour of these balls is satisfyingly deep while the texture is surprisingly soft and delicate. Well worth the effort.

Serves 4

Ingredients

For the sauce

1 onion, diced
2 garlic cloves, finely diced
1 teaspoon ground cumin
1 teaspoon paprika
400g / large tin of chopped tomatoes
150g / 1 cup cherry tomatoes, halved
A sprinkle of chilli flakes
200ml / just under 1 cup water
A couple of handfuls of chopped spinach
Salt and pepper, to taste

For the balls

1 small red onion
1 large carrot
1 medium courgette
1 garlic clove, crushed
200g / 7oz pack smoked tofu
1 teaspoon smoked paprika
1 teaspoon ground cumin
1 teaspoon garlic granules
2 tablespoons brown rice or chickpea/gram flour
Olive oil, to grease
Salt and pepper, to taste

Method

1. To make the sauce, heat 2–3 tablespoons of water in a medium pan. Sauté the onion until soft. Add the garlic and spices along with a little salt and continue to cook for 2–3 minutes, stirring often so it doesn't stick or burn. Add a little more water, if needed.
2. Stir in the tinned tomatoes, cherry tomatoes, chilli flakes and water. Bring to the boil, then reduce the heat and simmer with the lid off for about 20 minutes or until the sauce reduces and thickens and the flavours have developed.
3. To make the tofu balls, finely grate the red onion, carrot and courgette (it's important that it's not too chunky) and place in a large bowl with the garlic. Drain off any excess fluid from the smoked tofu and crumble into the vegetables. Add the

spices and salt and pepper. Mix well so everything is thoroughly combined, then stir in the flour.

4. Lightly grease an ovenproof dish. Take a spoonful of mixture and shape it into a ball. If there is a lot of excess fluid in the mix, squeeze it out of the ball as you shape it. Place on the bottom of the prepared dish. Repeat the process until all the mix is used up. There should be enough for 12 balls.
5. Place the balls in the fridge to chill for 30 minutes to 1 hour.
6. Pre-heat the oven to 180°C/350°F/Gas Mark 4. Pop the chilled tofu balls in the oven for 15 minutes.
7. Taste the tomato sauce and adjust the seasoning as needed. Stir in the chopped spinach and cook until it wilts.
8. Remove the balls from the oven and carefully spoon the sauce around them so the whole dish is covered but the balls are not smothered.
9. Return to the oven and bake for a further 10 minutes or until the balls are golden brown and the sauce thick and bubbly.
10. Serve carefully – the balls can be a little fragile, but they taste great.

4: SAUCES, DRESSINGS AND CREAMS

It's easy to turn a dull dinner into something much more exciting by simply adding a vibrant, flavoursome sauce or dressing. These recipes can be used to complement many of the recipes found in the book. They can also be stirred into cooked pulses, vegetables, pasta or rice and drizzled over a simple salad. Use them to create dish after dish packed with fabulous flavours and you'll keep everyone happy.

The Perfect Roasted Tomato Sauce

This sauce is so simple and yet so tasty, you'll want to have it with everything. Well, maybe not quite *everything* but it's such a handy sauce it'll be high on your must-make list. I use this as a pasta sauce, as a sauce with nut or lentil loaves, on roasted or stuffed vegetable ... the list goes on. You can make it as the simple, basic sauce or include some peppers or chillies to add some extra zing. This sauce is perfect to make in bulk, especially when tomatoes are in season and they're cheap and taste amazing. Just separate into portions and freeze in pots.

The redness of tomatoes comes from a variety of phytonutrients which are all beneficial to health. Traditionally, recipes using fresh tomatoes advise discarding the skins and seeds but I prefer to keep them in as they add more fibre and once blitzed you'll never know they were there.

Serves 4–6

Ingredients

500g / 2 ½ cups fresh tomatoes, cut in half
2 garlic cloves, skin on
1 medium onion, cut into quarters
A drizzle of olive oil
1 red pepper, cut in quarters and deseeded (optional)
1 red chilli pepper, cut in half and deseeded (optional)
Salt and pepper, to taste

Method

1. Pre-heat the oven to 180°C/350°F/Gas Mark 4. Spread the tomatoes evenly on a baking tray making sure they're not too crowded together. Dot the onion chunks and garlic cloves (and the red pepper or chilli, if using) between the tomatoes and drizzle with a little olive oil.
2. Place in the oven and roast for 20 minutes or until the tomatoes are cooked and mushy and the onion and garlic soft to the touch.
3. Remove from the oven and leave in the tin to cool. Pick out the roasted garlic and squeeze the soft pulp into the tin, discarding the paper skins. Tip all the veggies into a blender and blitz until smooth.
4. Add salt and pepper to taste and reheat as needed.

Roasted Pumpkin Sauce

Both pumpkin and squash make beautifully flavoursome sauces when roasted and puréed. Butternut squash tends to have the highest water content and therefore makes a looser sauce. By contrast, the sweet mama squash have a deeper colour but less moisture so it makes a thicker and more intense sauce.

Peeling gourds can be a real pain, so just wash the skin and chop them into chunks. The skin comes off with no problem once it's roasted and soft. If the skin is really thin, it can even be left on, adding extra fibre and nutrients, which is always a bonus.

This recipe makes a fantastic sauce for pasta or can be used as a flavouring for risotto.

Serves 4

Ingredients

½ small pumpkin or squash
1 bulb of garlic
Sprigs of fresh thyme or rosemary
Salt and pepper, to taste

Method

1. Pre-heat the oven to 180°C/350°F/Gas Mark 4. De-seed the pumpkin or squash but leave the skin on. Chop into smallish chunks and place on a large non-stick baking tray. Wrap the garlic bulb in tin foil and pop in the middle of the tray.
2. Spray the pumpkin with a little olive oil and scatter over the sprigs of herbs. Place in

the oven and roast for 20–30 minutes (depending on how big the chunks are) until soft and lightly golden. Remove from the oven and leave to cool.

3. Carefully peel the skin off the pumpkin or squash and put the roasted flesh into a food processor. Unwrap the garlic and carefully cut away 3–4 cloves. Keep the rest wrapped up in the fridge for use another time. Cut off one end of each clove and squeeze the soft, roasted garlic into the bowl. Season with salt and pepper, add any roasted herbs that are still soft and blitz until smooth.
4. Taste and add more seasoning if required. Pour into a small saucepan and warm through on a low heat before serving.

Roasted Jerusalem Artichoke Cream

These rough, unassuming tubers are aptly named 'fartychokes' in our house. Containing inulin, a fabulous pre-biotic fibre, Jerusalem artichokes can have a powerfully explosive after-effect, particularly if your microbiota are struggling a bit. Take care how many you eat in one go if these are new to you.

Having said that, it can be hard to resist gobbling down a load in one go as they taste wonderful. Earthy and rich, Jerusalem artichokes create a sublime depth of flavour, livening up the most boring of dishes.

Like the Roasted Pumpkin Sauce (see previous recipe), this cream is fabulous with both pasta and risotto.

Serves 4

Ingredients

300g / about 3 Jerusalem artichokes
A dash of olive oil
Fresh thyme or sage
Salt and pepper, to taste

Method

1. Pre-heat the oven to 180°C/350°F/Gas Mark 4.
2. Prepare the artichokes by scrubbing them under a running tap keeping on as much skin as you can. If possible, scrape off any rough or dark bits rather than peeling them. Once the skin is removed, the flesh oxidises rapidly and turns an unappealing brown colour so if you do need to peel them, put them in a bowl of water and lemon juice until you're ready to use them. Chop into 2cm chunks and transfer to a non-stick baking tray. Spray with a little olive oil, then massage it in with your hands.

3. Place in the oven and roast for 15–20 minutes or until soft and lightly golden. Remove from the oven and leave to cool.
4. Trim off any tough skin or blemishes then transfer the roasted artichoke chunks to a food processor bowl. Adding a little thyme or sage and season to taste, then blend until smooth. Pour back into a small saucepan and warm through before serving.

Red Wine Gravy or *Jus*

Some meals just need a good gravy to finish them off, especially if it's a Sunday roast. Incorporating red wine ensures that this gravy is rich and flavoursome. If you can't tolerate or don't like wine, then leave it out and use extra vegetable stock instead. It won't be quite as luxurious, but it will still taste great.

Serves 4–6

Ingredients

1 large onion, chopped
1 medium carrot, chopped
1 celery stick, chopped
1 garlic clove, chopped
1 bay leaf
2 tablespoons cornflour or arrowroot powder
500ml / 1 cup vegetable stock
250ml / ½ cup vegan red wine
2 tablespoons tamari
A sprig of fresh rosemary (optional)
Salt and pepper, to taste

Method

1. Heat 2–3 tablespoons of water in a medium saucepan and sauté the onion, carrot and celery for a few minutes. Add the garlic and bay leaf and cook for a further 2–3 minutes until the vegetables start to brown slightly.
2. Meanwhile, put the cornflour or arrowroot powder into a small dish and stir in a little of the vegetable stock to make a thick, gloopy mix. Put to one side.
3. Pour the wine into the pan, scraping up any caramelised bits from the bottom of the pan. Add the vegetable stock, tamari and rosemary, then season with salt and pepper. Bring to the boil, then reduce the heat and simmer for 15 minutes.
4. Pour in the flour mix and simmer for another couple of minutes, whisking to stop

any lumps forming. Once thick and glossy, turn off the heat and leave to cool. You now have two options, depending on how posh you're feeling.

To make a thick gravy:
Blitz the mix with a hand-held blender, leaving a few onion strands for texture.

To make a delicate jus:
Place a sieve over a large bowl or wide jug and pour in the mixture, mashing it down to force out as much fluid and flavour as possible. Discard the leftovers and reheat the smooth, delicate jus.

Cashew Cream

Cashews are much softer than other nuts, making them easier to break down in the blender. With the right amount of water, you can create a thick and creamy texture with no need to strain. This has three major bonuses:

- It means the cashews stay whole so none of the lovely fibre is discarded.
- None of the nutrients is wasted.
- It's super-quick to make!

This is one of those times where having a high-speed blender like a NutriBullet come into its own. With this piece of kit, it takes only moments to whizz the nuts into a super-thick cream. But if you don't have one, you can still make the cream using a less powerful device. But you'll need to persevere with the blitzing to avoid the cream having a grainy texture instead of a luxuriously smooth one.

As cashews have a neutral flavour, this cream is amazingly adaptable and can be used for both sweet and savoury dishes.

Basic Cashew Cream

Serves 4–6

Ingredients
150g / 1 cup cashew nuts
125ml / ½ cup water
A pinch of salt

Method

1. Soak the cashews in hot water for 10 minutes or cold water for 2 hours to allow them to soften slightly. Drain and rinse.
2. Place the nuts in a blender and add the salt and enough of the water to just cover. Blitz until smooth and thick and has a pouring consistency. If it's too thick, add a little more water and blitz again for a moment.

Roasted Garlic Cashew Cream

I always keep a bulb of roasted garlic wrapped in foil in the fridge as it can transform the simplest recipe in the blink of an eye. Add a few cloves to the Cashew Cream, stir it into pasta, rice or vegetables and you have a delicious meal in an instant. Roasting garlic brings out the hidden sweetness making it more digestible for those who otherwise find it hard to take. As the flavour is mellower, you need to use more cloves than if it was raw.

Serves 4–6

Ingredients

150g / 1 cup cashew nuts
125ml / ½ cup water
3 roasted garlic cloves
Salt and pepper, to taste

Method

1. Soak the cashews in hot water for 10 minutes or cold water for 2 hours to allow them to soften slightly. Drain and rinse.
2. Place the nuts in a blender. Cut the ends of the garlic cloves and squeeze the roasted flesh into the pot. Add the water and season to taste with salt and pepper.
3. Blend until smooth and thick. Taste and add more garlic or seasoning as needed as well as more water if it's too thick. Blend again to combine.

Tarragon Cashew Cream

The lightly aniseed flavour of tarragon is beautiful in a cream. Used in French cooking with fish or chicken, I love it in a sauce alongside leek and mushroom.

Cashew cream can take a good amount of tarragon without being overpowered, and bakes well in the oven or warmed through as a serving sauce. Use fresh tarragon in the summer months, and dried in winter.

Serves 4–6

Ingredients

150g / 1 cup cashew nuts
125ml / ½ cup water
2 tablespoons chopped fresh tarragon or 1 tablespoon dried
Salt and pepper, to taste

Method

1. Soak the cashews in hot water for 10 minutes or cold water for 2 hours to allow them to soften slightly. Drain and rinse.
2. Place in a blender with the water and blitz until smooth.
3. Finely chop the tarragon, stir into the cream and season with salt and pepper. Taste and add more seasoning if needed.

Sweet Cashew Cream

This makes a sweet cream with a single cream consistency. If you want a thicker version for the Banoffee Pie on page 269, use 80ml / ⅓ cup of water instead. It will take a little longer to blend but should become thick and creamy.

Serves 4–6

Ingredients

150g / 1 cup cashew nuts
125ml / ½ cup water
1 teaspoon vanilla extract
1 tablespoon maple syrup

Method

1. Soak the cashews in hot water for 10 minutes or cold water for 2 hours to allow them to soften slightly. Drain and rinse.
2. Place in a blender with the water, vanilla extract and maple syrup. Blitz until smooth, adding a little extra water if necessary.

Dairy-free pesto

Fortunately, you don't need cheese to make pesto. Here are three different versions to try. They all taste distinctly different and are vibrant and fresh. The first two recipes give two nut-free options as well.

Watercress Pesto

Serves 4

Ingredients

1 bunch watercress

2 tablespoons almonds or sunflower seeds

1 garlic clove, grated or crushed

¼ teaspoon salt

2 tablespoons lemon juice

1 tablespoon flaxseed oil (optional)

A little water, to bind

Method

1. Place the almonds or sunflower seeds into a small food processor and pulse a few times to break down.
2. Add the watercress, garlic, salt, lemon juice and flaxseed oil and blitz again until all the ingredients are mixed together. Add a little water to encourage the mixture to bind if needed.
3. Continue blitzing you have a thick paste. Check the flavour and add more salt or lemon juice as needed.

Creamy Pesto Sauce

Serves 4

Ingredients

80g / 1 bunch fresh basil leaves

1–2 garlic cloves, crushed

½ teaspoon salt

2 tablespoons flaxseed oil

50g / ½ cup cooked white beans, such as cannelloni

1–2 tablespoons lemon juice

A little water, to bind

Method

1. Place all the ingredients in a blender with 2 tablespoons of water and blitz until smooth.
2. Add more oil, water or seasoning as needed.
3. Serve cold as a dressing or warm as a sauce. To heat through, pour the pesto sauce into a small saucepan and warm over a low heat. Do not boil otherwise the fragile oil will be spoilt.

Spinach and Walnut Pesto

Serves 4

Ingredients

100g / 1 cup fresh baby spinach leaves
3 tablespoons walnuts
1–2 garlic cloves, crushed
¼ -½ teaspoon salt
2 tablespoons lemon juice
1 tablespoon extra-virgin olive oil
Ground black pepper

Method

1. Pack the spinach into a small blender with the walnuts, garlic, salt, lemon juice and olive oil.
2. Blitz to form a thick green paste, adding a little water to get the right consistency, if necessary.
3. Add some black pepper and pulse again. Check the taste and add more seasoning as needed.

Tahini Dressings

Tahini is a really useful ingredient to keep in the fridge and can be used for so much more than just hummus. These dressings are quick and easy to make and can be kept in a jar for up to five days in the fridge.

Cashew and Tahini Dressing

Serves 4

Ingredients

50g / ⅓ cup cashew nuts
2 tablespoons tahini
1 teaspoon Dijon mustard (optional, but good)
1 small garlic clove, crushed
A little water
Salt and pepper, to taste

Method

1. Soaked the cashew nuts in warm water for at least 2 hours then drain and place in a high-speed blender along with the tahini, mustard and garlic.

2. Add enough water to just cover and blend until smooth, adding more water if needed. You want a consistency that's thick but spoonable.
3. Season with salt and pepper, blitz again then taste and add more seasoning, as required.

Tahini Dressing 1

Serves 4

Ingredients

3 heaped tablespoons tahini
60ml / ¼ cup water
Juice ½ lemon
1 small garlic clove, crushed
Salt and pepper, to taste

Method

1. Place the tahini, lemon juice, garlic and seasoning into a blender and add three quarters of the water. Whizz together and add more water to get the consistency you like.
2. Check the flavour and add more lemon juice or seasoning as needed. Transfer to a jar or squeezy bottle.

Tahini Dressing 2

Serves 2

Ingredients

1 heaped tablespoon tahini
Juice 1 lime
2 teaspoons maple syrup
1 small garlic clove, crushed
¼ teaspoon ground cumin
Salt and pepper, to taste

Method

1. Place all the ingredients into a small jar and shake well to combine. Add a little warm water if it's too thick.
2. Check the flavour and adjust the seasoning to taste.

Mayo Three Ways

I love mayonnaise. It can liven up the dullest of salads and adds that extra flavour hit and texture to a multitude of dishes. There are a number of vegan versions available to buy which taste great but contain a high percentage of highly processed ingredients.

These mayo recipes use three different alternatives – nuts, tofu or avocado – to create wonderfully tasty and gloriously creamy mayos. None of them takes a long time to make either. A little effort for a big taste.

Creamy Lemon Mayo

Serves 4

Ingredients

70g / ½ cup cashew nuts
125ml / ½ cup water
Juice and grated rind of 1 unwaxed lemon
1 garlic clove, crushed
1 tablespoon flaxseed oil (optional)
Salt and pepper, to taste

Method

1. Soak the cashew nuts in warm water for at least 2 hours, then drain and place in a small food processor or blender. Add the water until the nuts are just covered and blend until smooth, adding more water if it's too thick.
2. Add the lemon juice, rind, garlic and seasoning and blend again until everything is well combined. Add the flaxseed oil if using and blend one more time. Store in the fridge for up to 3 days.

Tofu Mayonnaise

Serves 4

Ingredients

100g / 1 cup silken tofu
Juice of ½ lemon
½ small onion, chopped
1 small garlic clove
A pinch of salt
½ teaspoon mustard or mustard powder
A pinch of sugar
2 tablespoons cold-pressed olive or flaxseed oil (optional)

Method

1. Place all the ingredients in a blender and blitz until smooth.
2. Check the flavour and add more lemon, salt or mustard as needed to suit your taste.

Creamy Avocado Mayo

Serves 4

Ingredients

1 ripe avocado
45g / ½ cup sunflower seeds, soaked in warm water for 1–2 hours, then drained
2 tablespoons extra virgin olive oil or flaxseed oil
½ small white onion, chopped
1 garlic clove, smashed
125ml / ½ cup water
Juice 1 lemon
Salt and pepper, to taste

Method

1. Spoon the avocado flesh out of its skin and pop into a high-speed blender jug with the rest of the ingredients.
2. Blitz until smooth. Check for flavour and add more salt and pepper if needed. Use straight away.

Dairy-free 'Parmesan'

Serves 10–12

Ingredients

75g / ½ cup cashew nuts or sunflower seeds
¼ teaspoon garlic powder
½ teaspoon Himalayan salt
4 tablespoons nutritional yeast (I use Engevita yeast flakes)

Method

1. Place the cashew nuts or sunflower seeds into a high-speed blender and pulse a few times to break down.
2. Add the other ingredients and blitz for a few seconds to combine. Don't over-blend, as you want a little texture.
3. Add more salt, garlic powder or nutritional yeast if you want a stronger flavour.
4. Transfer to a glass jar and keep in the fridge for up to one month.

5: SWEET TREATS

I'm a big fan of desserts, especially when I eat out. In fact, before I changed my diet, I sometimes preferred them over any savoury option. When I switched to a whole-food, plant-based way of eating, desserts were pretty much off the menu when I went to a restaurant, unless I wanted a fruit salad – but that just didn't hit the spot when everyone else was tucking into a gloriously rich chocolate cake.

Fortunately, things are changing, with plant-based desserts beginning to appear on mainstream menus. Despite this, I still find it hard to find a dessert that suits my needs. And I'm not alone; desserts and cakes are the most popular recipes on my blog. It seems that I'm not the only one who wants to have their cake and eat it.

This selection of sweet treats is split into three parts: Raw, Baked and Desserts. Raw desserts are becoming increasingly popular. They score high on whole-food ingredients, are incredibly filling and have intense flavours. The baked section includes my favourite cake recipes (and I do love a good cake). They are lower in refined sugar than other vegan cake recipes and include some form of fruit or vegetable. Finally, the desserts include some of the recipes served at my supper clubs. They take a little longer to make, but are worth the effort, especially if you want to impress a staunch plant-based doubter.

RAW TREATS

This section gives you three energy ball recipes that are quick and easy to make and perfect for snacking, eating on the go and for livening up lunch boxes. Packed full of dried fruit and nuts, they are energy and nutrient dense, as well as satisfying and very tasty. The three raw desserts take longer to make and do not travel well. But they taste amazing and will surprise and delight your family and friends, proving there is no need for boring desserts in a whole-food, plant-based kitchen.

Raw Carrot Cake Balls

My favourite cake is carrot. I fell in love with it while working at a café when I was a teenager. The owner made an amazing carrot cake. Even though I couldn't bake at the time, I was always trying to sneak a peek at the recipe, sadly, without success as it was a well-kept secret. Even though I've now made many carrot cakes, I still wonder what magic ingredient went into that cake to make it so special.

Carrot cake can be delicious but also has a tendency to be a bit dense. In contrast, these raw carrot cake balls are light and absolutely gorgeous. They may not be the original carrot cake I fell in love with, but I enjoy them just as much.

Makes 10–12 bite-sized balls

Ingredients

75g / ½ cup pitted dates
50g / ½ cup raisins
1 medium carrot, peeled and grated
50g / ½ cup oats
1 teaspoon ground cinnamon
A pinch of nutmeg
30g / ¼ cup desiccated coconut

Method

1. Place the dates and the raisins in a food processor and pulse a few times to break down. Add the carrots, oats and spices and blend for 30 seconds or until everything is well-combined. If the carrots make the mix too wet, add a few more oats.
2. Spread the desiccated coconut out onto a plate. Take a teaspoonful of cake mix and roll it into a ball using the palms of your hands. Roll the ball in the coconut until it's completely covered. Repeat the process until all the mix has been used up.
3. Store the balls in the fridge for up to 4 days (although they're unlikely to be around that long!).

Raw Choc 'n Nut Balls

The first time I tasted a raw 'energy' ball it blew me away. Part of that may have been because I had just turned up at someone's farm in an alternative community in the Indian countryside riding double pillion on a rusty old moped. We joined a group who had gathered for a simple veggie meal that included raw chocolate and nut balls. The flavours in the first bite just astounded me because they were so delicious.

Now, you can buy energy balls in the shops – though at a price – but the ones you make at home taste oh so good, it's so worth making the effort. They freeze well too, so you can make a big batch and keep some for another day.

To keep this energy ball completely raw, use cacao powder; cocoa is heated as part of the refining process and is therefore not technically raw. But if you only have cocoa and you don't really mind if it's officially 'raw', then it's perfectly okay to use it.

Makes 10–12 balls

Ingredients

150g / 1 cup of mixed nuts – cashew, almond, walnut, macadamia, pecan, they all work well
75g / ½ cup pitted dates, soaked in hot water if very dry
50g / ½ cup raisins
50g / ½ cup dried cranberries
2 tablespoons orange juice or water
1 tablespoon raw cacao powder or cocoa powder
1 tablespoon ground cinnamon
3 tablespoon desiccated coconut or extra cacao powder

Method

1. Place the nuts in a food processor and pulse a couple of times to break down. Add the dried fruit, cacao or cocoa powder and blend for 1–2 minutes or until everything is crushed. Add 1 tablespoon of the orange juice or water and blitz again to combine all the ingredients.
2. Pinch a little of the mixture together to see if it sticks. If it's not soft enough, add the other tablespoon of fluid and blend again, but only if you really need to. The mix needs to be firm but not too sticky.
3. Mix the ground cinnamon and desiccated coconut or cacao powder together on a plate. Take a heaped teaspoon of the mix and roll into a ball between the palms of slightly wet hands. Then carefully roll the balls in the coconut mix until it's completely coated. Place on a plate or tray and repeat until all the mix is used up.

Gingerbread Energy Balls

These balls may look small and unassuming, but they have quite a ginger whack when you bite into them. Packed full of amazing nutrients as well as flavour, they really hit the satisfaction spot. If you need to avoid almonds, replace them with sunflower seeds to make these nut-free.

The sesame seeds on the outside are there for decoration rather than flavour so if you're intolerant, try rolling the balls in ground sunflower seeds or desiccated coconut instead. It changes the overall taste a little, but only in a good way.

Makes 10–12 balls

Ingredients

100g / 1 cup oats
100g / 1 cup almonds / sunflower seeds
75g / ½ cup dates, soaked in hot water for 10 minutes if a little dry
50g / ½ cup flaxseed
50g / ½ cup raisins
2 teaspoons ground ginger
A pinch of salt
2 tablespoons sesame seeds

Method

1. Place the almonds in a food processor and pulse a couple of times to roughly break down. Add the oats, flaxseed, raisins and ground ginger and blend until everything is well combined, adding a little water if the mix is too dry.
2. Take a teaspoon of mix and roll it into a ball between the palms of slightly wet hands. Roll in the sesame seeds to coat, then pop on a plate whilst you repeat the process until all the mix is used up.

Raw Banoffee Pie

I adored Banoffee pie from the first time I tasted it. It became my dessert of choice whenever we ate out. Packed full of cream and sugar, it hit all my taste-buds and pleasure receptors, but never did my body any good with its high dairy content. Going dairy-free also meant going Banoffee-free. That was until my wonderful husband found a recipe on the internet and made me my first raw Banoffee pie. It was amazing; I knew there was a reason why I love that man!

I've adapted that recipe to make a pie that's slightly less sweet and a bit more whole-food, but it still tastes amazing and delights and surprises anyone who tucks into it for the first time. Don't be put off by the long recipe, it's quicker to make than it looks.

In essence, this is three recipes in one: the base, the caramel and the cream. All can be made separately and then combined. You can do this on the same day or over a few days when you have time. It's well worth the effort and you will be rewarded with that super-tasty creamy caramel-banana combination that makes Banoffee pie simply irresistible. Make sure you remember to put your tin of coconut milk in the fridge the night before you plan to make your Banoffee pie so it's well chilled.

If you need to leave out the coconut, use some Sweet Cashew Cream as an alternative (*see page 260*).

Serves 8–10

Ingredients

For the pie base

100g / 1 cup oats
90g / 1 cup sunflower seeds
150g / 1 cup pitted dates (plus a few extra if needed)
A pinch of salt

For the caramel layer

225g / 1½ cups pitted dates, soaked in hot water if very dry
250ml / 1 cup dairy-free milk of choice
1 teaspoon vanilla extract
A pinch of salt

For the coconut cream

400g / large tin of full fat coconut milk, chilled for at least 12 hours
Vanilla extract
A pinch of salt (optional)

To finish

3–4 bananas
A squeeze of lemon juice
A dusting of cacao powder

Method

To make the pie base

1. Place the oats, seeds and salt in a food processor and blitz until they resemble breadcrumbs. Add the dates and process until you have a sticky dough. You can test it by removing a small amount of the mix and pressing it together with your fingers. If it sticks in a lump, it's ready. If not, you may need to either add more dates (especially if yours are a bit dry) or add a little water and blend again until it sticks.
2. Take the dough out and press it firmly into an 18–20cm loose-bottomed round or square flan tin. You will need to press the dough in firmly to ensure it is spread evenly across the base of the tin.
3. Place in the fridge to set or, if you're in a hurry, pop it in the freezer for 30 minutes while you prepare the next layer

To make the caramel

1. Place the soaked dates, half the dairy-free milk and the vanilla extract in a food processer and blend until smooth. Add the remaining milk and blend again.
2. If you still have a few chewy bits of date that just won't blend, that's fine as they'll add some great texture to the caramel.

To make the whipped coconut cream

1. Remove the tin of coconut milk from the fridge. Open and carefully scrape out all the solidified coconut milk into a bowl. Do not let any watery milk slip through.
2. Add the vanilla extract and gently whip until it's thick and creamy but still spreadable. Put back in fridge until you're ready to use it.

Constructing your Banoffee Pie

1. Remove the pie base from the fridge but keep it in the tin. Spoon the caramel over the base then put it back in fridge while you prepare the coconut cream (if not already done).
2. Remove the coconut cream from the fridge so it has time to soften slightly.
3. Peel and slice the bananas and stir half the bananas into the coconut cream. Sprinkle the remaining bananas with a little lemon juice to prevent discolouration.
4. Ease the pie out of the tin but keep it on the base. Spoon the coconut/banana cream over the caramel then scatter over the remaining banana. Sift a little cacao powder over the top of the pie to decorate. Put back in the fridge and keep until you're ready to serve. It's important that you don't allow the pie to get warm as the coconut cream may start to melt.
5. When you're ready to serve, remove the pie from the fridge and carefully cut it into slices, placing any leftovers back in the fridge straight away.

Raw Salted Caramel Cheesecake

If you look at this recipe and think there's a lot to it, you're right. But don't let that put you off making it. With a little planning and forward thinking, it's not that difficult at all. And anyway, it tastes so divine, it's completely worth the effort!

I first made this for one of my supper clubs and it was a huge success. It's super-sweet and rich, which is why I like to serve it with some sharp berries. It's so decadent that your guests will find it hard to believe it's both whole-food and plant-based!

Serves 4

Ingredients

For the base

140g / 1½ cups oats (gluten free, if needed)
80g / ½ cup ground flaxseed
130g /1 cup desiccated coconut
240g /1½ cups dates (soaked in hot water if dry)
A good pinch of Himalayan salt

For the caramel

180g / 1¼ cups dates (soaked in hot water if dry)
60-80ml / ½-⅓ cup water or dairy-free milk
4 tablespoons almond butter
1 teaspoon vanilla extract
¼ teaspoon Himalayan salt

For the cheesecake layer

260g / 1¾ cups cashew nuts (soaked for at least 2 hours)
80g / ½ cup dates (soaked in hot water if dry)
1 tablespoon vanilla extract
125ml / ½ cup coconut milk (the thick part is best)
A good pinch of Himalayan salt

For the chocolate topping

*1 tablespoon coconut oil **
3-4 tablespoons maple syrup
2–3 tablespoons raw cacao powder

To decorate:

Frozen black or red currants and/or freeze-dried strawberries

Method

1. Prepare the dates for each section of the cheesecake by weighing them out in separate bowls and soaking them in hot water. If you're using expensive but super-soft and sticky Medjool dates, you won't need to do this.

For the base layer

1. Place all the base layer ingredients into the food processor and blitz until combined and sticky. Add a little of the date soaking water if it doesn't come together, but not too much as you don't want it too wet.
2. Take a 23cm spring-form cake tin and, using your hands, press the dough into the base and about 3–4cm up the sides. Try to spread the mixture out evenly and firmly. Place the tin in the fridge to chill while you make the next layers. Remember to clean the processor bowl before moving on.

For the caramel

1. Place all the caramel ingredients into the food processor and blend until they form a thick, creamy caramel. Check the flavour and add a little more salt, if needed (remember this is salted caramel so you need to use more than feels normal). Pour out into a bowl and try not to eat it all whilst you make the next layer.

For the cheesecake

1. Wash the food processor bowl again then add all the cheesecake ingredients. Blend together until thick and creamy. This may take a few minutes, depending on how long the cashew nuts have been soaked. Keep blending until the mix is smooth and not grainy.

To construct the cheesecake

1. Remove the cheesecake base from the fridge. Pour in the caramel so it covers the bottom equally. Cover the caramel with the cheesecake mix.
2. Using a chopstick or the thin handle of a spoon, gently swirl the layers together slightly – you should see a little caramel swirl appear in the cheesecake layer. Place in the fridge to set for at least 6 hours.
3. Alternatively, cover the cheesecake and pop it in the freezer. Take it out 8 hours before you want to add the chocolate layer so it has time to defrost. If you're not sure, take it out the night before and leave it in the fridge until you're ready to decorate it.

For the chocolate topping and decoration

1. Place the coconut oil* in a small pan and gently melt it over a low heat until it becomes liquid.
2. In a separate bowl, mix together the cacao and maple syrup. Add the coconut oil and stir well. If it's too thick or not sweet enough, add more maple syrup. If it's too thin or not chocolatey enough, add more cacao powder.

3. Once you're happy with it, pour the chocolate sauce over the top of the cheesecake, spreading it evenly and up to the edges.
4. Scatter with berries and freeze-dried strawberries to decorate then return to the fridge to set.
5. To serve, release the clip on the side of the cake tin and very carefully push the cheesecake up and away from the sides but leave it on the base of the tin. Cut into slices with a sharp knife and decorate each serving with an extra sprinkle of freeze-dried strawberries or fresh berries.

* *The coconut oil can be omitted but this means the chocolate topping stays very soft so it's a bit messy when serving, though it still tastes great, of course.*

'Bailey's' Cheesecake

I loved having a glass of Bailey's with ice at Christmas and missed it like crazy when I went dairy-free. So one year I decided to make my own and haven't missed out on this delicious pleasure since. Bailey's now comes in a dairy-free variety, but I still prefer my home-made version. It may not taste quite the same, but it's cheaper and I know exactly what's gone into the bottle.

For drinking, I prefer to use oat or almond cream as the foundation of the 'Bailey's'. But if you want to make it to use in this amazing cheesecake, use coconut milk instead as it sets hard in the fridge.

Serves 4

Ingredients

For the Bailey's

400ml / large tin of coconut milk
1 teaspoon vanilla extract
2 tablespoons maple syrup
2 tablespoon cacao powder
100ml / ½ cup Jameson's Irish whiskey

For the cheesecake

80g / ½ cup pitted dates, soaked in hot water for 10 minutes
75g / ½ cup almonds
75g / ½ cup cashew nuts, soaked for at least 2 hours
80ml / ⅓ cup melted coconut oil, at room temperature
1 portion Bailey's (as above)
A dusting of cacao powder, to decorate

Method

For the 'Bailey's'

1. Pour the coconut milk, vanilla extract, maple syrup and cacao powder into a jug and whisk together well until combined. Add the whisky and whisk again. Pour into a clean glass bottle if you're not going to use it straight away and keep in the fridge. Remove from the fridge at least 30 minutes before you use it so it warms to room temperature.

For the base layer

1. Place the almonds in a food processor and pulse a couple of times to break down. Tip into a dish and set aside. Drain the dates, retaining some of the soaking liquid, and place them in the food processor. Pulse a few times to break up.
2. Add the almonds back into the food processor and blend until well combined, adding a little of the soaking water if the mix is too dry. Once the mix is sticking together in a ball, scoop it out and press it into the base of a 20cm diameter, loose-bottomed flan tin. Place in the fridge to set whilst you make the next layer.

For the cheesecake layer

1. Drain the cashew nuts and place them in a clean food processor bowl. Pulse to break down. Pour in the Bailey's mix and coconut oil and blend together. If the mix looks curdled with fat sticking to the sides of the bowl keep blending, scrapping down the sides from time to time. After about 8 minutes, the mix will be smooth and fully combined. Taste and add more vanilla or maple syrup if needed.

To construct the cheesecake

1. Remove the base from the fridge and pour in the cheesecake mix. Dust the top with cacao powder then carefully return to the fridge to set for at least 4 hours.
2. To serve, remove from the fridge and carefully push the cheesecake out of the flan ring but leave it sitting on the base. Cut slices carefully and serve straight away, placing any remaining cheesecake back in the fridge until ready to use again. Keeps for 4 days in the fridge.

BAKED TREATS

The huge success of programmes like The Great British Bake Off shows that I'm not the only one who's in love with baking. Or maybe it's just the cake! For me, baking is a meditative way of channelling my creativity, with delicious results.

Baking without eggs and butter can present a few challenges when it comes to whole-food, plant-based baking, though none are insurmountable. For top tips and trouble-shooting advice, take another look at the baking section in Chapter 5 (*see pages 109–123*). Once you've got used to the new techniques, you'll wonder what all the fuss was about.

All these recipes have been tried and tested many times in my own kitchen and by the attendees of my Eat Well Live Well course. One lady who eats gluten and dairy-free described the Lemon and Blueberry Loaf Cake as the best cake she'd ever eaten. The sweet potato chocolate brownies surprise everyone. I've even shared this at a talk for the Women's Institute, an organisation renowned for their baking talents. Happily, they were impressed.

Sweet Potato Chocolate Brownies

The ultimate in whole plant food baking, these brownies are rich, gooey and super-delicious, so it's not surprising that they never fail to delight and surprise anyone who eats them. The sweet potato provides both sweetness and texture but is subtly disguised by the other ingredients.

The dairy-free chocolate drops are an added bonus, but if chocolate is off the menu due to special diets, just leave them out and finish off with an extra sprinkle of raw cacao powder.

These brownies taste even better the day after they're baked, so make them in advance if you have time. They keep in an airtight tin for up to five days and freeze well too.

Serves 9-12

Ingredients

350g / 3 cups sweet potato, cooked, cooled and peeled
300g / 2 cups pitted dates
500ml / 2 cups warm water, for soaking
250ml / 1 cup dairy-free milk
2 tablespoons maple syrup
1½ teaspoons vanilla extract
125g / ¾ cup whole-wheat or gluten-free self-raising flour

55g / ¾ cup cacao powder
½ teaspoon baking powder
A pinch of salt
100g / ⅔ cup dairy-free chocolate drops (optional)
Cacao powder, to dust (optional)

Method

1. Put the dates in a bowl and cover with the warm water. Set aside to soak for 10 minutes.
2. Meanwhile, pre-heat the oven to 180°C/350°F/Gas Mark 4 and line a 22cm square tin with greaseproof paper.
3. When the dates are ready, place a sieve over a bowl and drain them, reserving the soaking water. Tip the dates into a food processor and pulse a couple of times to break down.
4. Add the sweet potato, maple syrup, vanilla extract and half the dairy-free milk. Blend until smooth and creamy then add the remaining milk and blend again. If there are still a few bits of date that haven't broken down, don't worry as they'll give the brownies a chewy texture.
5. Sift the flour, cacao powder, baking powder and salt into a large bowl. Spoon in the date and sweet potato mix and stir well to combine. The mix should be very thick but moveable. If it's too thick or dry, add a little more of the date water to make it more pliable but take care not to make it too loose. Stir in half the chocolate drops, if using.
6. Pour the batter into the prepared cake tin, gently spreading it out to fill the corners. Flatten the top of the cake and sprinkle with the remaining chocolate drops, lightly pressing them into the mix with the palm of your hand.
7. Bake in the oven for 35 minutes then check whether the brownies are cooked by inserting a skewer or tooth pick in the centre. If it comes out clean, it's done. The brownies may need up to another 20 minutes to bake, depending on the wetness of the batter.
8. Remove from the oven and leave to cool completely in the tin. Lift out of the tin using the greaseproof paper and cut into 9 large squares or 12 smaller rectangles. Sprinkle cacao powder on top to decorate.

Apple Cake

I love the combination of apple and cinnamon in anything, and here they add a wonderful flavour to a light, crumbly cake. Gut bacteria also loves apple, or rather the pectin, that's released when they're cooked. Pectin is a pre-biotic, making it a great food for the friendly bacteria that live in the gut while cinnamon helps with the absorption of sugar into the cells. I wonder if that makes it a health food? Maybe not exactly, but it's extra satisfying to enjoy a sweet treat that helps your body too.

I always use dessert apples for cakes as they're sweeter, which means you don't need to add so much sugar. You don't even need to peel the apples as the skin breaks down when heated. The topping for this cake begins on the bottom as it's an upside-down cake.

If you'd like an alternative to apple and cinnamon, try pear and ground ginger. Follow the instructions below using pears instead of apples and ground ginger instead of cinnamon.

Makes 6–8 slices

Ingredients

250g / 1½ cups whole-wheat or gluten-free self-raising flour
1 teaspoon baking powder
1 teaspoon ground cinnamon
A pinch of salt
70g / ½ cup coconut sugar
85ml / ⅓ cup olive oil
190ml / ⅔ cup soya or oat milk
1 tablespoon lemon juice
1 teaspoon vanilla extract
1 dessert apple, chopped

For the 'topping'

A drop of olive oil, to grease the base of the tin
2 dessert apples, thinly sliced, 1 chopped
1½ teaspoons extra coconut sugar

Method

1. Pre-heat the oven to 180°C/350°F/Gas Mark 4. Grease a loose-bottomed 20cm round cake tin and line the base with non-stick baking paper.
2. To make the 'topping', sprinkle the coconut sugar over the base and arrange the sliced apples on top using a circular pattern, until the base is covered.

3. To make the cake, sift the flour, baking powder, cinnamon and salt into a large bowl then stir in the coconut sugar.
4. In a separate bowl, mix the oil with the milk, lemon juice and vanilla extract. Whisk well to combine.
5. Pour the wet ingredients into the dry and mix swiftly, gently folding in the chopped apple as you go. Take care not to over-mix. If the batter is too thick, add a little extra milk.
6. Pour the batter into the prepared tin, tap on the worktop to remove any air bubbles and rapidly transfer to the pre-heated oven.
7. Bake for 25 minutes. The cake should have risen and the top should be lightly browned. Insert a skewer or tooth pick to check that it's cooked through. If it comes out clean, it's ready. If it's not, return to cake to the oven for another couple of minutes and check again.
8. Leave the cake to cool in the tin for 10 minutes then carefully tip out onto a cooling rack, gently peeling off the baking paper. Take care not to dislodge the apple design on the top.
9. Eat warm with some dairy-free ice cream or leave to cool completely. Store in an airtight container for up to 3 days.

Blueberry and Lemon Loaf

I love lemon cake, and I love blueberries, so this is the perfect cake for me. The lemon cuts through the sweetness whilst the blueberries are soft and just melt in your mouth. It works brilliantly with gluten-free flour as well as wholemeal, something that's not always the case when it comes to baking.

As well as tasting wonderful, this cake is also remarkably easy to make. Once the wet and dry ingredients have been combined, the mix may seem a little runny – don't worry, it still bakes brilliantly, it may just need a few more minutes to cook through. And don't be too eager to eat this as soon as it's out of the oven; leave it to cool completely otherwise you could be in danger of it collapsing all over your plate.

If you really love the sharpness of lemon, you can omit the additional sugar for the drizzle at the end. Just spoon some fresh lemon juice over the top and get ready for your tongue to zing.

Makes 8 slices

Ingredients

250g / 1½ cups whole-wheat or gluten-free self-raising flour
1 teaspoon baking powder
A pinch of salt
100g / ¾ cup coconut sugar
2 tablespoons maple syrup
200ml / ¾ cup soya or oat milk
85ml / ½ cup organic rapeseed oil or olive oil
1 teaspoon vanilla extract
1 unwaxed lemon, zest and juice
100g / 1 cup fresh blueberries

For the drizzle

Juice 1 lemon
2 tablespoons extra coconut sugar

Method

1. Grease and line a 900g / 2lb loaf tin. Pre-heat the oven to 170ºC/338ºF/Gas Mark 3 .
2. Sift the flour, baking powder and salt into a large bowl.
3. In a separate bowl, mix together the sugar, maple syrup, oil, milk, vanilla and lemon juice. Add the lemon zest and stir well again.
4. Pour the wet ingredients into the dry and combine. Gently fold in the blueberries. The batter might be quite runny but that's ok, just pour it into the prepared tin, tap the tin on the worktop to remove any air bubbles and bake in the oven for 35 minutes or until cooked. Insert a skewer or toothpick into the centre of the tin. If it comes out clean, the loaf is ready, if not, put it back in the oven for a little longer. When ready, remove from the oven but leave in the tin.
5. Mix the lemon juice and extra sugar together in a small bowl. Prick lots of holes in the top of the cake and spoon the lemon-sugar mix over the top. Leave in the tin to cool, then remove and serve.

Banana Bread

I made banana bread all the time when we were in India; the bananas were small and deliciously sweet because the heat made them ripen quickly. It seems there were always some that needed to be used up, and no-one ever complained there was too much banana bread.

This recipe is super-simple and never lets me down. The riper and mushier the banana, the better the cake. It also freezes well, so if you spot a batch of reduced priced ripe bananas in the supermarket, grab them and make a few of these loaves. Keep one for now and freeze the rest. When you defrost them, the banana will be even sweeter and the cake even more delicious.

My daughter and I have an on-going debate about the benefit of adding walnuts to cakes. She's not a fan but I think it gives an extra dimension to the taste and texture. Feel free to omit or add as you desire. The cake tastes great either way.

Makes 8 slices

Ingredients

250g /1½ cups wholemeal or gluten-free self-raising flour
2 heaped teaspoons baking powder
1 tablespoon ground cinnamon
A pinch of salt
60g / just under ½ cup coconut sugar (or soft dark brown)
3 ripe medium bananas, mashed
75g / ½ cup olive oil
A dash of soya or rice milk, if needed
50g / ¼ cup chopped walnuts (optional)

Method

1. Pre-heat the oven to 180°C/350°F/Gas Mark 4. Grease and line a 900g / 2lb loaf tin.
2. Mix the flour, baking powder, salt and cinnamon together in a large bowl.
3. In a separate bowl, whisk the mashed banana together with the oil and sugar.
4. Pour the banana mix into the flour and stir well to form a thick batter. If it's too thick and dry, add a little soya or rice milk to loosen it up, but be careful not to add too much as you don't want a runny batter. Stir in the walnuts (if using) then tip into the prepared loaf tin.
5. Place in the oven and bake for 20 minutes until it has risen and is firm on top. Pierce the top with a cocktail stick or skewer – if it comes out clean, it's done. If not, pop the tin back in the oven for another 5 minutes or so.
6. Remove from the oven and leave to cool in the tin for 10 minutes, then turn out onto a cooling rack and leave to cool completely before cutting and eating.

Chocolate Cake with Sweet Potato Frosting

Chocolate cake deserves a mighty fine frosting. But although it's easy to adapt traditional recipes by using dairy-free spread instead of butter, that's still a highly refined fat and not suitable or desirable for everyone.

The Overcoming MS programme focuses on minimising saturated fat intake, which sadly means not eating chocolate because of the cocoa butter content. Fortunately, cocoa powder is allowed, so although it's easy to make a chocolate cake, it's not so easy to find a good replacement for the frosting. After a lot of thought and failed experiments, I realised that sweet potato was the answer.

With its own natural sweetness and creamy texture, it takes on the sweet chocolatey flavour from the cacao powder and maple syrup without dominating it. It also spreads well and stays where you put it, creating a fabulously covered cake. It is however not as sweet as a normal buttercream frosting but that's no bad thing.

I find that oat milk works particularly well in this cake, but rice or soya milk are both good alternatives.

Serves 8

Ingredients

225g / 1⅓ cups wholemeal or gluten free self-raising flour
½ teaspoon baking powder
75g / 1 cup cacao powder
A pinch of salt
180g / 1 cup coconut sugar (or soft dark brown if necessary)
90ml / just over ⅓ cup olive oil
370ml / 1½ cups dairy-free milk (see note above)
1 teaspoon vanilla extract
1 teaspoon cider vinegar or lemon juice

For the icing

1 medium sweet potato, baked, cooled and peeled
2–4 tablespoons maple syrup
4 tablespoons cocoa or raw cacao powder
Fresh or freeze-dried raspberries or strawberries, to decorate (optional)

Method

1. Pre-heat the oven to 180°C/350°F/Gas Mark 4. Grease and line the base of 2 round Victoria sponge cake tins.

2. Mix the flour, baking powder, salt and cocoa together in a large bowl.
3. In a separate bowl, add the sugar, vanilla extract, cider vinegar or lemon, olive oil and dairy-free milk together, whisking well to mix.
4. Pour the wet ingredients into the dry, stirring quickly to combine. Do not overmix or you'll lose the air bubbles needed for a good rise.
5. Pour the mix into the prepared tins, tap on the work-top and bake in the oven for 28–32 minutes until the cake is firm to the touch and a cocktail stick inserted into the middle comes out clean.
6. Remove from the oven, leave to cool in the tins for a few minutes then tip out onto a cooling rack. Carefully peel off the baking paper and leave to cool fully.
7. To make the icing, place the prepared sweet potato, maple syrup and cocoa/cacao powder into a small food processor. Whizz until the mix is well combined and smooth. Taste and add more maple syrup or cocoa for more flavour or a smoother texture.
8. Once the cake sponges are completely cold, transfer one to a plate and spread 2–3 spoons of frosting over the top. Position the other cake on top and use the remaining frosting to cover the top (and maybe the sides too, if there's enough). The amount of icing you have will depend on the size of the sweet potato. Decorate with fresh or freeze-dried raspberries or strawberries if you wish.

Apple and Date Squares

Flavoursome, full of amazing nutrients and satisfyingly filling, these squares are chock full of whole plant-based fats, sugars and goodness. Dried apple is used to keep down the moisture content and give a more intense apple flavour. If you don't have dried apples, fresh will work too, just be prepared for a softer, more collapsible square.

Makes 9 large squares or 12 medium rectangles

Ingredients

100g / ⅔ cup dates, chopped
50g / ½ cup dried apple, chopped
50g / ½ cup raisins
50g / ½ cup dried cranberries
100ml / just under ½ cup apple or cranberry juice
50g / ⅓ cup whole almonds
175g / 1 heaped cup ground almonds

100g / 1¼ cup mixed seeds (sunflower, pumpkin, flaxseed etc)
1 heaped teaspoon ground cinnamon
A pinch of salt
2 tablespoons maple syrup (optional)

Method

1. Mix together all the dried fruit in a large bowl then add the juice. Leave to soak for 5 minutes.
2. Grease and line a 22cm square baking tin. Pre-heat the oven to 180°C/350°F/Gas Mark 4.
3. Transfer the fruit mix to a food processor. Add the whole almonds and pulse the mix a few times to break down. Don't over-do this though, as you want some texture, not just pulp.
4. Transfer the fruit and nut mixture back to the soaking bowl and stir in all the remaining ingredients, except for the maple syrup.
5. Spoon the mix into the prepared tin taking care to spread it out evenly so it has a flat top and the mixture fills the corners.
6. Pop into the oven and bake for 18 minutes or until the top is lightly golden. Remove from the oven. If you want extra sweetness, brush the maple syrup over the top whilst hot.
7. Mark out 9 to 12 pieces (depending on how big you want them) with a knife and leave to cool in the tin. Once cold, turn out onto a board and finish cutting into pieces. Store in an airtight tin for up to 4 days.

Oat and Raisin Cookies

This is one of the first recipes I made when I switched to a plant-based diet. I started out using a dairy-free spread, when I had changed to a more whole-food way of eating, I needed to find an alternative. After many trials, I found that this recipe works well with all the options available: dairy-free spread, nut butter and tahini. Each gives the cookies a slightly different flavour, but every one of them is delicious. So, even if you're unable to eat certain ingredients, you won't have to miss out on these cookies. They are seriously moreish. You have been warned!

Makes 10-12 cookies

Ingredients

100g / 1 cup dairy-free spread/nut butter of choice/tahini
80g / ½ cup plus 1 tablespoon coconut sugar
2 tablespoons maple syrup
1 teaspoon vanilla extract
5 tablespoons dairy-free milk
95g / ½ cup plus 1 tablespoon plain wholemeal or gluten free flour
100g / 1 cup oats (gluten free if needed)
1 teaspoon baking powder
½ teaspoon salt
50g / ½ cup raisins

Method

1. Pre-heat the oven to 180°C/350°F/Gas Mark 4. Line a large baking sheet with a silicon mat or greaseproof baking paper.
2. Cream together the fat of your choice (dairy-free spread, nut butter or tahini), coconut sugar, maple syrup, vanilla extract and dairy-free milk in a large bowl with an electric whisk or wooden spoon until thick and well combined.
3. Weigh out the flour, oats, baking powder and salt into a separate bowl and mix together.
4. Add the dry mix to the butter mix and fold together with a metal spoon then fold in the raisins. The dough will be thick. Add a little extra dairy-free milk if it's too dry, but take care not to make it wet otherwise the next step with be a sticky nightmare.
5. Take a tablespoonful of mix and roll it into a rough ball. Place on the baking sheet and flatten slightly with your hand or the back of a spoon. Repeat until all the mix is used up.
6. Place the tray in the centre of the oven and bake for 8-10 minutes turning the tray after 4 minutes to make sure you get an even bake. Don't over-cook them as they will firm up as they cool.
7. Remove the cookies from the oven and leave to cool on the tray for 10 minutes. Transfer to a cooling rack until completely cool. Store in an airtight tin for up to 5 days.

Omega 3 Flapjack

I've had a bit of thing for flapjack since school. My best friend always had some in her lunch box and she often very kindly shared it with me. Her mum's recipe was amazing, packed full of butter and golden syrup – just too delicious to resist.

This flapjack recipe may not be packed full of butter and sugar, but it is still amazingly tasty and will hit all the right spots without giving you a sugar overload. It's also packed with healthy Omega 3 fats, so it's good for your body as well as your soul.

Makes 9-12 portions

Ingredients

3 tablespoons ground flaxseed
6 tablespoons water
200g / 2 cups whole oats (use gluten-free if necessary)
50g / ½ cup raisins or sultanas
50g / ½ cup dried cranberries
100g / 1 cup mixed seeds
A pinch of salt
90ml / ⅓ cup maple syrup
90ml / ⅓ cup hempseed or olive oil

Method

1. Mix 2 tablespoons of the flaxseed with the water in a small bowl to make 2 flax 'eggs'. Leave for 5 minutes to allow it to turn thick and gloopy.
2. Pre-heat the oven to 180ºC/350ºF/Gas Mark 4. Lightly grease a 22cm square baking tin and line with baking paper.
3. Mix the oats, dried fruit, mixed seeds, salt and the remaining tablespoon of ground flaxseed together in a large bowl.
4. Pour the maple syrup and oil into the flax 'eggs' and whisk together.
5. Pour the flax egg mix into the dry mix and stir well. If it seems too dry, add a little water to loosen. Spoon the oaty mix into the prepared tin.
6. Pop the tin in the oven and bake for 12–15 minutes or until the mix is firm and the top is lightly browned.
7. Remove from the oven and allow to cool for a couple of minutes then score lines into the top of the flapjack with a knife so you can cut it into pieces later.
8. Leave the flapjack to completely cool down in the tin, then tip it out onto a board and cut into pieces. It can be stored in an airtight tin for up to 4 days.

DELICIOUS DESSERTS

These recipes are my take on some classic – and not so classic – desserts using alternative plant-based ingredients. They're not your everyday puddings, so they do take some time to prepare. They may seem a bit complicated and fiddly to start with, but once you get used to them, you'll find they're worth the effort. Remember, I'm not a trained cook, so if I can make these, so can you.

Pecan Pie

I still remember the first time I ate pecan pie. It was at a Garfunkel's in Swiss Cottage, London, after a trip to the cinema with my student nurse friends.

The combination of crisp, rich pastry and the sumptuous dark gooey centre completely hit the spot. It was sweet, rich and just glorious. It's been a favourite ever since.

Pecan pie is usually a heavyweight dessert, packed with heaps of butter, eggs and refined sugar. In contrast, this little beauty is a light and body-friendly version. It packs a big punch on the satisfaction scale but is full of fabulously healthy nutrients and a huge dollop of fibre.

This was a dessert I mulled over in my head for a long time, so I was delighted when it came to fruition. The flavour is different to mainstream pecan pie because it's missing all the refined sugar, but it still carries a familiar satisfying flavour all of its own. And in the world of rainbow eating, brown is still good, so go ahead and spoil yourself.

Serves 8

Ingredients

100g / 1 cup oats
100g / 1 cup almonds
1 tablespoon ground flaxseed
A pinch of Himalayan salt
1 tablespoon hempseed or flaxseed oil
2 tablespoons coconut sugar
2 tablespoons water (use date soaking water if possible)

For the filling

300g / 2 cups dates
250ml / 1 cup dairy-free milk of choice
2 teaspoons vanilla extract
150g / 1½ cups pecan nuts

Method

1. Soak the dates in some hot water for a minimum of 10 minutes to soften them up, unless you're splashing out and using gorgeously soft Medjool dates which need no attention at all.
2. Make a flaxseed 'egg' by mixing the ground flaxseed with 3 tablespoons water. Stir well and leave to thicken for 5 minutes or so.
3. Pre-heat the oven to 180ºC/350ºF/Gas Mark 4. Take a loose-bottomed 20cm round flan tin and lightly grease with some olive oil.
4. Pop the oats into a high-powered blender or food processor and blitz until it resembles flour (it should only take a couple of seconds). Tip into a large bowl, then do the same with the almonds. You could use ground almonds, but I like to blitz my own as I use whole almonds not blanched ones to keep more of the nutritious goodies intact.
5. Add the almonds to the oats along with the salt and coconut sugar. Mix together well.
6. Pour in the flaxseed egg, oil and some water (or some of the date soaking water if you have it) then mix well, at first with a large spoon, then with your hands as it gets sticky. Form into a big sticky lump, then place it in the base of the prepared flan tin. This mix is too gloopy to roll out so you need to use your hands to gradually press it into the base and up the side of the tin. Try to keep the distribution as even as possible and make sure the edges are pressed in well or you can get too much crust and not enough filling.
7. Place the crust in the oven and bake for 7–10 minutes or until the base starts to firm up but the edges are not coloured. Remove from the oven.
8. While the crust is baking, drain the dates and place them in food processor with the dairy-free milk, vanilla extract and salt. Blend until thick and smooth. Add 1 cup of pecan nuts and blend again until smooth.
9. Pour the mix into the crust, spreading it out to smooth the surface then sprinkle the remaining pecan nuts over the top. Place the pie back into the oven and bake for a further 25–30 minutes or until the filling has set and the top is firm.
10. Serve hot or leave to cool and reheat later. I find the flavours develop over the next 24 hours, so if you have time, bake in advance and gently warm through before serving with some dairy-free cream or ice cream.

Rhubarb and Star Anise Upside-down Cake

This is a slight twist on the traditional pineapple upside-down cake. The tart rhubarb complements the sweetness of the coconut sugar and the star anise and ground mace infuse the cake with a hint of tropical delight.

Rhubarb has a high water-content which can be an issue when it comes to baking. By placing it on the bottom of the tin, the excess fluid doesn't weigh the sponge down, so you still get a good rise. Instead it gets absorbed into the layer just under the rhubarb, making it soft and gooey, making a delightful contrast with the fluffy sponge.

If you follow a special diet that excludes coconut (except coconut sugar), replace the desiccated coconut with ground almonds. This will make a denser sponge, but it will still taste lovely. When you're serving, don't forget to remove the whole star anise (or warn your guests to look out for them) as they're not supposed to be eaten whole.

Makes 9 squares

Ingredients

85g / ⅔ cup coconut sugar
250g / 9oz rhubarb, trimmed and cut into 5cm pieces
5 whole star anise
250g / 1 cup dairy-free milk (soya or rice milk is ideal)
A squeeze of lemon juice
250g / 1½ cups wholemeal or gluten free self-raising flour
100g / 1 cup desiccated coconut
1 teaspoon baking powder
½ teaspoon ground mace (or a pinch of nutmeg if you don't have mace)
2 teaspoons ground ginger
A pinch of Himalayan salt
75ml / ⅓ cup olive oil

Method

1. Pre-heat the oven to 180°C/350°F/Gas Mark 4. Grease and line the base of a 20cm round loose-bottomed cake tin. Scatter the base with a little of the coconut sugar. Arrange the rhubarb in a circular pattern then evenly distribute the star anise between the rhubarb pieces.
2. Make 'buttermilk' by mixing together the soya or oat milk and lemon juice in a small bowl. Leave for a few minutes to curdle.
3. Mix together the flour, desiccated coconut, baking powder, ground mace, ground ginger, salt and coconut sugar in a large bowl.

4. Pour the oil into the buttermilk and whisk to combine. Pour the wet mix into the dry and stir quickly to combine, then transfer to the cake tin, making sure the batter is equally spread out and all the rhubarb is well covered.
5. Tap the tin on the work top then place in the oven to bake for 30 minutes or until the top is golden brown and the sides start to come away from the tin. Pierce with a tooth pick – if it comes out clean, the cake is done. If not, pop it back in the oven for another few minutes.
6. Once you're happy the cake is cooked, remove from the oven and leave to cool in the tin for 10 minutes. Turn it out onto a cooling rack and carefully remove the tin. Be particularly careful with the base and baking paper – the rhubarb may stick to the paper and it will come away from the cake if you're too quick or rough. If it does, don't worry, just scrape it back on. It won't look so pretty, but it'll still taste gorgeous.
7. The cake can be eaten warm with some vanilla infused cream or cinnamon ice cream or left to cool completely and eaten cold.

Chocolate and Coconut Torte

This tart looks impressive and tastes amazing – it's rich, creamy and best of all, easy to make. You do need to plan ahead though as the torte needs time to set. Either make it the day before and leave it to set overnight or make it first thing in the morning. It can take up to eight hours to set properly depending on the quality of your chocolate and the viscosity of the coconut milk.

I prefer hazelnuts for the base because hazelnuts and chocolate are a heavenly combo. Feel free to use whatever nut you prefer – almond works particularly well. If you're nut intolerant, then opt for sunflower seeds instead.

Makes 8–10 slices

Ingredients

For the base

50g / 1 cup pitted dates
150g / 1 cup hazelnuts
50g / ½ cup cocoa powder

For the filling

400g / large tin of coconut milk
60ml / ¼ cup dairy-free milk of choice
30g / ¼ cup cornflour
A pinch of salt
100g / ⅔ cup dairy-free chocolate

Method

1. First make the pastry base. Soak the dates in warm water for 10 minutes then drain, reserving the soaking liquid. Place the dates in a food processor with the hazelnuts and cocoa powder and blitz until everything is broken down and well combined. You may need to add a little of the date water to help the pastry stick together.
2. Spoon the mix into a 20cm / 8inch round loose-bottomed cake tin and press it firmly into the base and edges, trying to make as flat and equal as possible. Place in the freezer to set while you make the filling.
3. Mix the cornflour and dairy-free milk together in a small bowl.
4. Pour the coconut milk into a small pan and heat gently. Do not let it boil. Once hot, remove from the heat and add the dairy-free chocolate and salt. Return to the stove but on a very low heat and stir continuously until everything has melted and is smooth. Finally, pour the cornflour mix into the chocolate and continue to stir until it thickens – this takes about 3 minutes. Remove from the heat and leave to cool for a couple of minutes.
5. Take the base from the freezer and pour in the chocolate filling. Place in the fridge to firm up. If you're not planning on eating it straight away, cover the tart with a layer of greaseproof paper and foil and store in the freezer until you want to use it. Remove at least 2–3 hours before serving so it has time to defrost, then simply dust with cocoa powder and serve.

Mango Panna Cotta

Traditionally made with gelatine, milk and cream, you may be surprised to see panna cotta in a selection of plant-based recipes. But with the magic of agar agar (*see* the Glossary of Unusual Ingredients on page 297), it's not only possible to make it fully plant-based, it's also surprisingly easy too.

Mango has a dual role in this deliciously light dessert. It provides sweetness, which means there's no need to add refined sugar, and it also provides a wide an array of wonderful phytonutrients. So, once again dessert becomes a health food!

Panna cotta needs to be made at least 2 hours in advance of eating, 4 to be on the safe side. You will need 4 pudding moulds but you can improvise by using with a muffin tin if you wish.

Makes 4–6

Ingredients

500ml / 2 cups almond milk
1 teaspoon agar agar powder
2 tablespoons maple syrup
1 teaspoon vanilla extract
1 ripe mango, puréed

To serve

2 passion fruit or a small punnet of raspberries

Method

1. Pour the almond milk into a small pan. Sprinkle over the agar agar, then slowly bring it to a gentle boil, lightly whisking to combine the agar agar into the milk, then simmer for 5 minutes.
2. Turn off the heat and leave to cool for 10 minutes (but no longer). Whisk in the maple syrup and vanilla then stir in the puréed mango. Mix well, then pour into moulds or a muffin tin. Leave to cool completely, then place in the fridge for a couple of hours to set.
3. To serve, use a knife to loosen the sides then tip the panna cotta out onto a plate. Serve with passion fruit or a mixture of lightly mashed and whole raspberries.

Pear Frangipane Tart

One of the most visited pages on my website is my recipe for vegan frangipane. It was one of my earlier posts, inspired by a dessert I had experienced at Terre à Terre, the award-winning vegetarian restaurant in Brighton. It seems I'm not the only one who enjoys a good pear and frangipane tart.

That early recipe used more refined ingredients than I like to use now. I've updated the original recipe with more whole ingredients so it not only still tastes delicious but it fits better with a whole-food way of eating.

I confess that tinned pears work much better than fresh, but if you have some lovely super-ripe pears to hand, then go for it, just give them a good dunking in lemon juice so they don't oxidise and end up looking jaded.

Serves 6–8

Ingredients

For the frangipane and pears

200g / 2 cups ground almonds
60g / ⅓ cup coconut sugar
A pinch of salt
2 tablespoons cornflour
½ teaspoon almond extract
½ teaspoon vanilla extract
6 tablespoons aquafaba
4 tablespoons almond milk
6 tinned pear halves or 3 pears, peeled, cored and halved

For the pastry

150g / 1 cup buckwheat flour (or flour of choice)
1 tablespoon ground flaxseed
2 tablespoons coconut sugar
5 tablespoons olive oil
120ml / ½ cup cold water

Method

1. Begin by making the frangipane. Mix the ground almonds, coconut sugar, salt and cornflour together in a large bowl. Add the wet ingredients and combine to form a thick paste. Put to one side while you make the pastry.
2. For the pastry, mix the flour, ground flaxseed, coconut sugar and salt together in a large bowl. Stir well to make sure everything is well combined.
3. Add the olive oil and cut into the flour mix with a spoon, then use your finger tips to form a breadcrumb texture. Add the water and bring the mix together to form a soft dough. Knead a little, then wrap in clingfilm and place in the fridge for 30 minutes. It will become firmer as the flaxseed absorbs the water.
4. Pre-heat the oven to 180°C/350°F/Gas Mark 4. Remove the dough from the fridge and place on a large silicon mat. Flatten slightly with the palm of your hand then cover with some greaseproof paper. Roll the pastry into a circle large enough to line a 20cm loose-bottomed tin.
5. Peel off the greaseproof paper, turn over the silicon mat and place the pastry over the tin. Carefully peel the silicon mat away from the pastry, allowing it to drop into the tin. If it splits, don't worry, just pinch it together to seal. Push the pastry into the edges of the tin and trim off any excess. Prick the base with a fork.
6. Blind bake in the oven for 10 minutes then remove from the oven and carefully fill the pastry with the frangipane mix, spreading it out evenly over the base of the

pastry case. Push the pears into the frangipane in a circular pattern then return it to the oven to bake for 20 minutes or until the frangipane has set.

7. Serve warm.

Baked Raspberry Custard Tart

I recently had a sudden craving for an egg custard tart. It was a bit of a surprise as I hadn't eaten one for years. We used to have them when I was a child – they were my dad's favourites. This craving got me wondering how I could create a whole-food, plant-based version of this sweet treat and this recipe is the result.

The raspberries are an added extra and give a wonderfully tart and juicy contrast to the thick, sweet custard. You don't have to use raspberries, though, as this tart works well with lots of different fruit, even apple pureé.

The cashew cream is another added extra. Again, it's not essential to the dessert as a whole but adds an extra texture and makes it look pretty too. Feel free to abstain if you haven't got time.

This tart keeps in an airtight tin for a couple of days. After that it becomes rather soggy and less appealing, which gives you the perfect excuse to finish it up the day you make it.

Makes 8 portions

Ingredients

For the pastry

1 tablespoon ground flaxseed
3 tablespoons water
100g / 1 cup oats, gluten-free if needed, ground into flour
100g / 1 cup ground almonds (or sunflower seeds if you can't tolerate nuts)
A pinch of salt
2 tablespoons coconut sugar (optional)
4 tablespoons of water

For the custard filling

750ml / 3 cups oat milk or dairy-free milk of choice
4 tablespoons maple syrup
2 tablespoons coconut sugar
1 tablespoon vanilla extract

85g / ⅔ cup cornflour
150g / 1 cup raspberries (or fruit of choice) fresh or frozen

For the topping

70g / ¾ cup cashew nuts, soaked overnight
1 teaspoon vanilla extract
1 teaspoon maple syrup
2–3 tablespoons oat milk

Method

1. Make a flax egg by combining the ground flaxseed and 3 tablespoons of water together in a small bowl. Put to one side for a couple of minutes to thicken.
2. MIx the oats, ground almonds, salt and coconut sugar together in a large bowl. Stir in the flaxseed egg and addition 4 tablespoons of water and bring together into a soft dough. Knead lightly with your fingertips then leave to settle in the fridge for 20 minutes.
3. Pre-heat the oven to 180ºC/350ºF/Gas Mark 4. Line a 27 x 18cm baking tin or dish with non-stick baking paper. Roll the pastry out on a silicon mat to form a rectangle slightly bigger than the tin, then flip the silicon mat upside down over the tin and peel it away, allowing the pastry to fall into the tin. It's a bit fiddly with the baking paper in place. Don't worry if it's not perfect, just patch up any missing bits with spare pastry trimmed off from the edges. Prick the base with a fork. Blind bake in the oven for 8 minutes or until the pastry starts to firm up.
4. While the pastry is in the oven, make the custard. Mix 3 tablespoons of the oat milk with the cornflour in a small bowl and set aside. Pour the remaining oat milk into a saucepan with the maple syrup, vanilla extract and coconut sugar. Gently bring to the boil over a low heat.
5. Pour the cornflour mix into the pan. Whisking constantly while it thickens to prevent lumps forming. Carry on whisking over a low heat until the mix is very thick and gloopy. Turn off the heat and leave to cool slightly, whisking from time to time so a skin doesn't form.
6. Scatter most of the raspberries over the pastry base, reserving a handful of fat juicy ones for decoration. Pour the custard over the top and spread out so all the edges of the pastry case are filled.
7. Bake in the oven for 35 minutes or until the top is very firm, then remove from the oven and leave to cool completely. Holding the edges of the baking paper, lift the tart out of the tin and carefully ease the paper away. Place the tart on a serving plate or board. If you aren't eating it straight away, pop it in the fridge until you're ready.
8. To decorate with the cashew cream, drain the soaked cashew nuts and place in a small blender. Blitz to a rough paste then add the vanilla extract, maple syrup and

30ml of oat milk. Blend again until smooth, adding extra milk if you need to. Try to use as little as possible to keep it thick and creamy.

9. Spoon the cream into a small piping bag and pipe swirls over the top to decorate, dotting the reserved raspberries in between. If you don't want to pipe, just dot small spoonsful over the top instead. Cut into slices and serve.

GLOSSARY OF UNUSUAL INGREDIENTS

You will find more information about many of these ingredients at www.thesensitivefoodiekitchen.com/book-links.

Agar agar

So good, they named it twice, it's a really useful ingredient to keep in your kitchen cupboard. Agar agar comes from seaweed, or at least a variety of red algae. When heated, it forms a thick gel which is dried, pressed then ground into a powder. When added to fluid and reheated, the gelling properties are reactivated and therefore make a wonderful replacement for gelatine. Agar agar comes as a powder or flakes; I prefer the powdered form as it dissolves more easily, although it can be trickier to find.

You can find agar agar in health food shops and sometimes larger supermarkets. Alternatively, buy online from specialist stores or Amazon. A small amount has a big effect, so a pot or packet lasts a long time.

Aquafaba

A revolutionary ingredient for plant-based cooking. Aquafaba, otherwise known as 'chickpea brine' is the water leftover from cooking beans, particularly chickpeas and white beans. Thick and gloopy, this viscosity is what makes it magical. The fluid mimics the molecular properties of egg white, meaning it can be used as a direct replacement in recipes. It's particularly great in baking meringues and roulades, creating light and fluffy mousses and can be used as a binding agent.

Asafoetida

A flavouring used in Indian cooking, often known as 'hing' (and much easier to say and spell!). Ground, dried gum from a bulbous plant called Ferula, it's mostly available in the UK in powder form. When you first open a jar, be warned – it stinks! Asafoetida has a highly pungent, sulphurous aroma that's so strong you may wonder why you'd add it to your food. But it's these sulphurous elements that provide a deep savoury flavour, enhancing the depth of a dish. It's also a great alternative for anyone who has to avoid onions or garlic, creating a similar flavour without the after effects.

Asafoetida can be found in the herb and spice section of larger supermarkets or specialist Asian stores. You only ever need to use a pinch of it, so a jar lasts a long time.

Buttermilk

Useful for creating lift in cakes and pancakes, dairy-free 'buttermilk' is easy to make. Soya milk is the best dairy-free milk to use. Adding a teaspoon of vinegar or lemon juice rapidly sours the milk, creating a thick yoghurt-like consistency that can be used as a direct replacement for dairy buttermilk in recipes.

Celery salt

This is an amazing flavouring to have in your herbs and spice collection. Made from ground celery seeds and salt (hence its name!), celery salt adds a lovely deep flavour to soups and stews.

Chickpea/gram flour

A staple ingredient for many traditional Asian and European dishes, chickpea flour is an amazingly versatile and nutrient-packed ingredient to have on hand. Known in India as gram flour or besan, it can be found in bigger supermarkets or specialist Asian stores. Chickpea flour is literally ground dried chickpeas, so you can also make your own if you have a high-powered blender.

Useful for gluten-free recipes, chickpea flour is a great ingredient to use for loads of plant-based recipes, whether as the star ingredient, or a thickening agent or egg replacement.

Chia seeds

These tiny black seeds taken from Salvia plants, a member of the mint family, have a long history going back to Aztec times. Packed full of fibre, omega 3 fatty acids and protein, they are also a great energy source. In plant-based cooking they can be the star ingredient or act as a thickening or binding agent due to the amount they swell when mixed with water. Chia seeds are widely available in supermarkets and health food shops but are more expensive than flaxseeds (*see below*).

Coconut amines

A sauce that provides that lovely umami flavour in savoury dishes. Made from coconut sap and salt, it's a good replacement for anyone who cannot tolerate soya sauce or tamari. Soya and gluten free, it's also naturally aged so should be more tolerable for anyone who also has to avoid fermented products. Found in specialist health food stores or online.

Coconut sugar

Otherwise known as coconut palm sugar, this refined sugar alternative is made from the sap of a coconut tree. Dark brown, heavy and with a strong caramel flavour, the sugar is formed by boiling the sap until the water has evaporated and crystals are formed. Often organic, it's a less processed sugar that retains some of the original nutrients. It is however still sugar and is used in limited amounts.

Curry leaves

These small, shiny green leaves add a delicious flavour to Indian dishes and are well worth hunting out. Native to India, curry leaves come from a small tree in the citrus family and are not generally grown in cooler climates. Dried curry leaves can be found in the herb and spice section of large supermarkets or specialist whole-food stores, but are far inferior to fresh leaves. Specialist Asian stores usually stock them but often only have a delivery once a week so when you find a local source, make sure you also find out their delivery day to avoid disappointment. Sprigs of curry leaves are usually sold in small bunches and last in the vegetable cooler section of the fridge for up to six weeks.

Flaxseeds

Cheap and versatile, flaxseed is a nutrient power house that also has useful binding properties for plant-based cooking. Packets can be found in supermarkets and health food shops; try to buy whole seeds rather than ground, as their nutritional properties and delicate omega 3 oils can be spoilt once the hard outer shell has been broken. Just grind small amounts at a time and keep in a jar in the fridge to use as you need.

Liquid smoke

A useful but not essential ingredient to have in the store cupboard, liquid smoke is literally smoke in liquid form! Wood is burned at high temperatures and the resulting smoke is captured in condensers, forming a liquid. This liquid is then reduced to concentrate the flavour and bottled. It provides the deep, smoky flavour associated with barbecue and TexMex food. As a flavouring, it's delicious but should only be used on occasion in small amounts due to the fact it is smoke, which may contain particles that could be harmful.

Nutritional yeast

Found in health food shops and online, nutritional yeast is a savoury flavouring that provides a 'cheesy' element to plant-based recipes. Grown on a type of sugar, it is then heated and deactivated so it won't ferment, making it safer for gut health and theoretically suitable for people with yeast intolerance. However, I have found I can only tolerate it in small amounts, so use with caution if you have a gut issue. As with brewer's yeast, it is a great source of B vitamins; some brands are additionally fortified with B12, the one nutrient that is potentially hard to come by in a plant-based diet.

Psyllium husk

This is a powder formed from the outer husk of the *Plantago ovata* plant. A particularly concentrated form of soluble fibre, psyllium husk is often used as a supplement for constipation. Sources of fibre are not a problem in a whole-food plant-based diet so it's main use here is as a natural bulking agent for bread and crackers. Found in larger health food shops or online you only need a small amount each time, so one bag will last a long time.

Smoked paprika

This is a staple in our store cupboard and give a big smoky flavour hit. Sweet paprika traditionally comes from Hungary, whereas smoked paprika is Spanish in origin – it's the smoky flavouring found in chorizo. Made from dried pimiento peppers that are then smoked and ground into a powder, it has a powerful flavour and adds depth to a whole range of plant-based dishes. Found in the spice section of most supermarkets, it can overpower a dish if used in large amounts. So if you're not familiar with it, start with smaller amounts and check the flavour, adding more if needed.

Tahini

Made from roasted sesame seeds ground into a thick paste, tahini is a key store cupboard ingredient for anyone eating a whole-food plant-based diet (unless you have a sesame allergy!). Known by most as the key ingredient for hummus, tahini has a wide range of uses from salad dressings, sauces and even a butter replacement for cookies. It can be found in most large supermarkets and health food shops but is also fairly easy to make at home if you have a powerful food processor. When you buy tahini, ensure it is 100 per cent sesame seed; some brands add some form of vegetable oil to make it cheaper. There is more information about tahini and a guide on how to make your own at www.thesensitivefoodiekitchen.com/book-links.

Tamari

This is the Japanese version of soya sauce. Still made from fermented soya beans, it has a gentle but deep flavour, providing a lovely savouriness to a range of plant-based dishes. Because it is less salty and intense compared to soya sauce, it has a wider range of uses in a range of plant-based dishes. It's also useful for the sensitive eater as it contains no wheat and is therefore gluten free. It is however still fermented, so may not be suitable for someone with a yeast intolerance. Coconut amines (see above) should be used instead. Found in larger supermarkets and health food shops, tamari can still be a bit hard to find; it can also be bought from online stores.

ONLINE RESOURCES AND ARTICLE REFERENCES

Chapter 1

WHO report on increasing worldwide malnutrition https://www.who.int/nutrition/double-burden-malnutrition/en/

Monteiro et al 2017. The UN Decade of Nutrition, the NOVA food classification and the trouble with ultra-processing. Public Health Nutrition 1 (1):5-17

https://www.ons.gov.uk/peoplepopulationandcommunity/birthsdeathsandmarriages/ageing/bulletins/estimatesoftheveryoldincludingcentenarians/2002to2017

https://www.independent.co.uk/news/health/womens-health-compared-men-poor-condition-life-new-report-public-health-england-a7840016.html

Abbasi et al, 2017. Body Mass Index and Incident Type 1 and Type 2 Diabetes in Children and Young Adults: A Retrospective Cohort Study. Journal of the Endocrine Society 1 (5): 524-537

https://digital.nhs.uk/data-and-information/publications/statistical/statistics-on-obesity-physical-activity-and-diet/statistics-on-obesity-physical-activity-and-diet-england-2018

Steel et al, 2018. Changes in health in the countries of the UK and 150 English local authorities areas 1990-2016: a systematic analysis for the Global Burden of Disease Study 2016. The Lancet 392:1647-61

https://www.telegraph.co.uk/news/2016/10/06/seven-in-ten-deaths-fuelled-by-diet-and-lifestyle-factors-study/

NHS expenditure on lifestyle conditions https://www.bbc.co.uk/news/health-37451773

https://www.independent.co.uk/news/health/uk-obesity-rate-rising-overweight-worst-country-western-europe-world-us-ranking-oecd-research-a8049451.html

Wild et al, 2006. Risk factors for diabetes and coronary heart disease. British Medical Journal. 333 (7576):1009-1011.

Chapter 2

The cost of diabetes https://www.diabetes.co.uk/cost-of-diabetes.html

https://www.drwf.org.uk/news-and-events/news/number-people-type-2-diabetes-uk-has-trebled-over-last-20-years

Diabetes statistics https://www.diabetes.org.uk/resources-s3/2017-11/diabetes-key-stats-guidelines-april2014.pdf

Heart disease statistics https://www.bhf.org.uk/-/media/.../heart-statistics/bhf-cvd-statistics---uk-factsheet.pdf

Urban and rural populations https://www.gov.uk/government/publications/rural-population-and-migration/rural-population-201415

Rise of ultra-processed foods https://www.theguardian.com/science/2018/feb/02/ultra-processed-products-now-half-of-all-uk-family-food-purchases

https://www.theguardian.com/environment/2016/jul/13/failure-teach-cooking-at-school-contributing-food-waste

https://www.telegraph.co.uk/news/2016/10/06/seven-in-ten-deaths-fuelled-by-diet-and-lifestyle-factors-study/

https://www.telegraph.co.uk/news/uknews/1566436/Half-of-adults-will-be-obese-by-2050.html

Obesity in USA https://stateofobesity.org/obesity-rates-trends-overview/

Obesity in Australia https://www.aihw.gov.au/reports/australias-health/australias-health-2018/contents/indicators-of-australias-health/proportion-of-people-obese-and-overweight

Neel, J. 1969. Diabetes Mellitus: a 'thrifty' genotype rendered detrimental by 'progress'? American Journal of Human Genetics. 14:353-362

JR Speakman, 2008. Thrifty genes for obesity, an attractive but flawed idea, and an alternative perspective: the 'drifty gene' hypothesis. *International Journal of Obesity, 32:1611-1617*

Southam et al, 2009. Is the thrifty gene hypothesis supported by evidence based on confirmed type 2 diabetes- and obesity-susceptibility variants? Diabetologia 59(9) 1846-1851.

Chapter 3

https://www.ncbi.nlm.nih.gov/pmc/articles/PMC4705836/

https://www.ewg.org/foodnews/dirty-dozen.php

http://food-studies.net/foodpolitics/agricultural-subsidies/jades-sample-page/

https://ec.europa.eu/info/food-farming-fisheries/key-policies/common-agricultural-policy/cap-glance_en

Sweis and Creasy, 2018. Potential role of the common food additive manufactured citric acid in eliciting significant inflammatory reactions contributing to serious disease states: A series of four case reports. *Toxicology Reports 5:808-812*

Pesticide residues on food http://www.pan-uk.org/our-food/

https://www.gov.uk/government/groups/expert-committee-on-pesticide-residues-in-food-prif

https://issuu.com/pan-uk/docs/pesticides_on_a_plate?e=28041656/44974894

Stefferl et al, 2000. Butyrophilin, a milk protein, modulates the encephalitogenic T cell response to myelin oligodendrocyte glycoprotein in experimental autoimmune encephalomyelitis. *Journal of Immunology 165:2859-2865.*

Jelinek, G. 2010. *Overcoming Multiple Sclerosis: An Evidence-Based Guide to Recovery.* Allen and Unwin, Australia.

Turner, 2009. Intestinal mucosa barrier function in health and disease. *Nature Reveiws Immunology 9:799-809.*

Chapter 4

http://www.inflammationresearchfoundation.org/inflammation-science/inflammation-details/time-cellular-inflammation-article/

Inflammatory markers https://www.bmj.com/content/344/bmj.e454

https://www.telegraph.co.uk/news/2017/03/30/just-one-four-adults-eating-five-day-nhs-reveals/

Shammas, M. 2011. Telomeres, lifestyle, cancer and ageing. *Current Opinion in Clinical Nutrition and Metabolic Care 14(1):28-34.*

Fritsche, K. 2015. The Science of Fatty Acids and Inflammation. *Advances in Nutrition 6(3):293S-301S.*

https://www.bmj.com/content/361/bmj.k2179 microbiota and health

https://www.allergyuk.org/information-and-advice/statistics

Bull, M. and Plummer, N. 2014. Part 1: The Human Gut Microbiome in Health and Disease. *Integrative Medicine 13(6):17-22.*

Inhamm, F. et al. 2016. Proton pump inhibitors affect the gut microbiome. *Gut 65:740-748,*

Campbell, T. 2014. 12 frightening facts about milk. Found online https://nutritionstudies.org/12-frightening-facts-milk/

https://www.viva.org.uk/white-lies/undesirable-components

https://www.takingcharge.csh.umn.edu/how-long-have-humans-used-botanicals

Anand, P. et al, 2008. Cancer is a preventable disease that requires major lifestyle changes. *Pharmaceutical Research 25(9):2097-2116*

https://www.acsh.org/news/2018/07/02/genetics-or-lifestyle-where-cause-disease-13139

Tilman, D. and Clark, M. 2014. Global diets link environmental sustainability and human health. *Nature 515:518-522*

Chapter 5

https://www.theguardian.com/environment/2018/may/31/avoiding-meat-and-dairy-is-single-biggest-way-to-reduce-your-impact-on-earth

https://www.peta.org/issues/animals-used-for-food/meat-environment/

https://pfaf.org/user/edibleuses.aspx

http://www.onegreenplanet.org/news/plant-based-milk-market-growth/

Chapter 6

https://sustainability.ucsf.edu/1.713

https://www.theguardian.com/food/2018/sep/05/ditch-the-almond-milk-why-everything-you-know-about-sustainable-eating-is-probably-wrong

https://anesthesiology.duke.edu/?p=846744

Xu, C. et al 2014. Light-harvesting chlorophyll pigments enable mammalian mitochondria to capture photonic energy and produce ATP. *Journal of Cell Science 127:388-399*

https://www.telegraph.co.uk/foodanddrink/10129729/Do-you-know-your-fruit-from-your-vegetables.html

Bao, Y. et al 2013. Association of Nut Consumption with Total and Cause-specific Mortality. *New England Journal of Medicine 369(21):2001–2011.*

Useful websites

https://www.carnism.org

https://nutritionfacts.org

https://nutritionstudies.org

https://overcomingms.org

https://www.pcrm.org

https://beachfood.co.uk

https://www.peta.org.uk

https://proveg.com

https://sharan-india.org

https://veganuary.com

https://www.viva.org.uk

Recommended Reading

Elizabeth Blackburn and Elissa Epel ,2017.*The Telomere Effect: A Revolutionary Approach to Living Younger, Healthier, Longer.* Orion Publishing Ltd, London.

Joanna Blythman, 2015. *Swallow This: Serving up the food industry's darkest secrets.* Fourth Estate, London.

Jonathan Brostoff and Linda Gamlin, 2008. *The Complete Guide to Food Allergy and Intolerance.* Quality Health Books.

T. Colin Campbell and Thomas M. Campbell, 2006. *The China Study.* BenBella Books Ltd.

T. Colin Campbell, 2014. *Whole: Rethinking the Science of Nutrition.* BenBella Books Ltd, Texas.

Sushana Castle and Amy-Lee Goodman, 2014. *Rethink Food: 100+ Doctors Can't be Wrong.* Two Skirts Production, USA.

Leon Chaitow and Natasha Trenev, 1990. *Probiotics.* Thorsons.

Garth Davis, 2016. *Proteinaholic: How our obsession with eat is killing us and what we can do about it.* Harper Collins.

Jared Diamond, 1998. *Guns, Germs and Steel.* Vintage, Random House.

Zsu Dever, 2016. *Aquafaba.* Vegan Heritage Press, USA.

Caldwell B Esselstyn Jr., *Prevent and Reverse Heart Disease: The Revolutionary, Scientifically Proven, Nutrition-Based Cure.* Penguin Group, USA.

Giulia Enders, 2017. *Gut: the inside story of our body's most under-rated organ.* Scribe.

Mike Harris, Carol Harris and CJ Jackson, *2016. The Ration Book Diet.* The History Press

Michael Gershon, 2003. *The Second Brain: Your Gut has a Mind of Its Own.* Quill.

Michael Gregor, 2016. *How Not to Die.* Macmillan, UK.

George Jelinek, 2016. *Overcoming Multiple Sclerosis: An Evidence-Based Guide to Recovery.* Allen and Unwin.

Lisette Kreishcher et al, 2015. *Ocean Greens: Explore the world of edible seaweed and sea vegetables.* The Experiment Publishing, USA.

Daniel Lieberman, 2013. *The Story of The Human Body.* Penguin Books.

Dr Michael T Murray. *The Magic of Food.* 2017. Atria Paperback, New York.

Michel *Pollen*, 2011 *The Omnivore's Dilemma.* Bloomsbury

Mark Schatzker, 2015. *The Dorito Effect: The Surprising New Truth About Food and Flavor.* Simon and Schuster.

Tim Spector, 2015. *The Diet Myth: The Real Science Behind What We Eat.* Weidenfeld and Nicholson, London.

World Health Organisation. The Double Burden of Malnutrition. Access at https://www.who.int/nutrition/double-burden-malnutrition/en/

GLOSSARY OF SCIENTIFIC TERMS

Amino acids

These are organic compounds that contain at least one amino group (made from nitrogen and hydrogen) and one carboxyl group (made from carbon and oxygen). Amino acids are the building blocks for protein and are therefore essential for life. There are 20 different ones that form chains to create proteins. 11 can be made by the body but 9 have to be obtained from food – these are described as 'essential amino acids'. When protein is eaten, it's broken down by the digestive system, releasing the amino acids, which are then used wherever they're needed in the body.

Blood brain barrier

An extra layer of protection for our brains that separates the circulating blood from the tissues and cells in the brain. The blood vessels in the brain have an extra-tight membrane that only allows small molecules, essential nutrients and oxygen in, and waste products of cell activity, like carbon dioxide out. It prevents any bacteria, viruses or harmful proteins and toxins that might be circulating in the blood from getting through into the brain, the most precious and complicated organ of the body.

Co-factors

These are organic and inorganic elements like iron or zinc that support enzyme activity. Sometimes called coenzymes.

Enzymes

These are essential protein molecules that act as catalysts for chemical reactions. Over 75,000 enzymes have been identified in the human body. These can be split into 3 main groups – metabolic (for cell activity), digestive (to break down the food we eat) and food (found in raw food that start the digestive process).

Fatty acids

These are the building blocks of fats made from different chains of carbon and hydrogen molecules. Most types of fatty acids chain combinations can be made by the body. Omega 3 and 6 has to be obtained from food, which are why they are called 'essential fatty acids'. Fatty acids play an important role in all parts of the body.

Macronutrients

Nutritional compounds humans need to consume in large amounts to sustain life (macro = large). Focus is generally on the protein, fat and carbohydrate parts of food, but could also include water, fibre and elements like potassium and phosphorus.

Microbiota

A term used for the populations of microbes that live in or on the body. The gut microbiota contains over 1000 different species with over 3 million genes and has co-evolved a mutually beneficial relationship over thousands of years. A happy and healthy microbiota is now thought to be key to human health.

Micronutrients

Elements or substances humans need to consume in small amounts (micro = small) essential for growth and health. These tend to be minerals like iron, magnesium or zinc, vitamins and tiny phytonutrients found in plants.

Pathogen

A bacteria, virus or other microorganism that can cause disease.

Peristalsis:
An involuntary muscular action in the wall of the gut that creates a wave-like motion. This enables the gut contents to be moved through the digestive system.

Prebiotic
Certain parts of indigestible plant-based foods that feed the microbiota, stimulating the growth and activity of friendly bacteria. Prebiotics are readily available in whole-foods and can also be taken as a supplement if deemed necessary.

Probiotic
Live bacteria or yeasts that support or re-establish the microbiota, found in food, particularly fermented foods, or taken as supplements.

Short-chain fatty acids (SCFA)
These a very short (a maximum chain length of 6 carbon atoms) fatty acid chains produced by the microbiota. End products from fermentation of indigestible fibre, these fatty acids play key roles in metabolism, inflammation and disease in the human body.

ACKNOWLEDGEMENTS

For as long as I can remember, I have wanted to write a book – and now I've finally done it! This could not have been achieved without the love, support and extreme patience of my wonderful husband, Steve, the man who helps my dreams come true.

And to my children Vicky and Ben, for playing a key role in developing many of my recipes, their forbearance with my many experiments and their (sometimes very) direct feedback – I thank you. They are by far my best creations and my inspiration to live well.

The courage to follow my dreams comes from deep within, and I would like to express my eternal gratitude for my mentor, Daisaku Ikeda as well as my fellow members of the Soka Gakkai International (SGI).

My sincere thanks go to Dr Nandita Shah whose fabulous courses inspired the beginning of my plant-based journey and The Sensitive Foodie. Her commitment to promoting the health of the Indian population and the message of using food as medicine was, and still is, a revelation and inspiration. I was delighted when Dr Shah received the Nari Shakti Award, the highest award for women in India, in 2016 for her pioneering work in health and nutrition – a well-deserved recognition for her contribution to helping other eat well and live well.

I would also like to thank everyone who has participated in my Eat Well Live Well course and various workshops for being part of The Sensitive Foodie community, for your enthusiasm and friendship. Your transformations and journeys are amazing and inspirational.

The world of publishing is hard to navigate as a novice with no idea where to start. So, I would like to thank Alison Jones of Practical Inspiration Publishing who provided the tools to get this book out of my head into a manuscript, and to Deborah Taylor of Book Launch your Business who has coached, coaxed, managed, edited and kicked my arse when needed. I've heard the book creation process is harder than giving birth; Deborah has been the calm and attentive midwife who now deserves to go home and have a stiff drink!

Finally, I would like to thank my wonderful mum, Betty, for your love, encouragement and support – and for just being my mum!

ABOUT THE SENSITIVE FOODIE KITCHEN

Karen Lee is a food blogger and owner of The Sensitive Foodie Kitchen, which offers courses, workshops, supper clubs and one-to-one sessions for people who are interested in eating a whole-food, plant-based diet or want to use food to manage a chronic health condition.

Karen is a qualified Registered General Nurse, with a BSc in Acute Clinical Care. She is an experienced intensive care nurse and a qualified nutritional therapist. She is married with two young adult offspring and splits her time between Sussex in the UK and the Silver Coast area of Portugal.

To find out more about Karen and The Sensitive Foodie Kitchen, go to www.thesensitivefoodiekitchen.com.

Printed in Dunstable, United Kingdom

73752542R00186